INTRODUCTION TO
MARKETING

Marketing in Action Series

Series Editor: Norman Hart

In producing this series, the advice and assistance has been sought of a prestigious editorial panel representing the principal professional bodies, trade associations and business schools.

The Series Editor for the Marketing in Action books is Norman Hart, who is a writer of some ten books himself. He currently runs his own marketing consultancy, and is also an international lecturer on marketing, public relations and advertising at conferences and seminars.

ALSO IN THIS SERIES

MARKETING IN ACTION SERIES

INTRODUCTION TO
MARKETING

A STEP-BY-STEP GUIDE TO ALL THE TOOLS OF MARKETING

GEOFF LANCASTER
& PAUL REYNOLDS

KOGAN
PAGE

First published in 1999

Apart from any fair dealing for the purposes of research or private study, or criticism or review, as permitted under the Copyright, Designs and Patents Act 1988, this publication may only be reproduced, stored or transmitted, in any form or by any means, with the prior permission in writing of the publishers, or in the case of reprographic reproduction in accordance with the terms and licences issued by the CLA. Enquiries concerning reproduction outside these terms should be sent to the publishers at the undermentioned addresses:

Kogan Page Limited
120 Pentonville Road
London
N1 9JN
UK

Kogan Page Limited
163 Central Avenue, Suite 4
Dover
NH 03820
USA

© Geoff Lancaster and Paul Reynolds, 1999

The right of Geoff Lancaster and Paul Reynolds to be identified as the authors of this work has been asserted by them in accordance with the Copyright, Designs and Patents Act 1988.

British Library Cataloguing in Publication Data

A CIP record for this book is available from the British Library.

ISBN 0 7494 2095 2

Typeset by Jean Cussons Typesetting, Diss, Norfolk
Printed and bound in Great Britain by Biddles Ltd, Guildford and King's Lynn

Contents

Marketing Defined

AN EARLY HISTORICAL OVERVIEW

The term marketing might be relatively new, but its philosophy has been practised since the beginnings of the exchange or trade system. Marketing now refers to the discipline that assures lasting customer satisfaction and is now very much an integral part of modern management literature and thinking. Exchange of goods has continued ever since communities or individuals produced a surplus. Traditionally this was agricultural produce that was traded for goods such as textiles or implements. Exchange was initially through local markets. These allowed for the specialisation of production by individuals of goods and produce, which could then be exchanged in markets for goods produced by other specialists.

A definition of modern marketing comes from the UK Chartered Institute of Marketing:

Marketing is the management process responsible for identifying, anticipating and satisfying customer requirements profitably.

Another definition is put forward by the American Marketing Association:

Marketing is the process of planning and executing the conception, pricing, promotion and distribution of ideas, goods and services to create exchanges that satisfy individual and organisational objectives.

Yet a further and perhaps a more maverick definition, is put forward by Albert W Emery:

> Marketing is a civilised form of warfare in which most battles are won with words, ideas and disciplined thinking.

MARKETING AND THE MICRO-ENVIRONMENT

The expression 'micro-environment' simply means those elements which the company can control or manage to its advantage for marketing purposes. Neil Borden termed these manipulable elements the marketing mix. The definition for marketing put forward by the American Marketing Association can now be extended to take in the idea of the four Ps which was first put forward by E Jerome McCarthy and consists of:

■ Product;
■ Place;
■ Price;
■ Promotion.

The term place simply means the medium through which goods (or services) reach their final destination. It has two implications – first, the physical distribution or transportation element that is now extended to include logistics and secondly, the outlets through which the goods are sold. These outlets mean different types of retailers, but in a broader sense it also means agents or even direct sales methods. More correctly, in marketing terms, these are called channels of distribution.

Promotion, too, has a wider implication than the term implies. In the four Ps context, it includes advertising (or what we call 'above the line' or A/L promotion), sales promotional activities such as consumer competitions or a free quantity for the regular price (or what we call 'below the line' or B/L promotion), public relations and selling. This is called the promotional mix or, more correctly nowadays, the communications mix.

In addition to the four Ps, which the company can directly manipulate, marketing has some direction over customers, but this control is more indirect and is carried out in a manipulative way. Later chapters go on to explain what we mean by this, but at this stage it is sufficient to say that customers will behave in different ways when making purchases. This is termed buyer behaviour. The process of aiming the efforts of marketing to more precisely suit the behavioural needs of the market-place is called target marketing and the act of breaking customers down into subsets that will respond to more precisely targeted marketing mixes is known as segmentation. Positioning is the final term that we examine and this means the characteristics of the product or service in terms of what it conveys to customers in relation to competitive products.

Also included in the organisation's micro-environment is information that comes from customers or the market-place, as a result of data collection and subsequent data analysis that are conducted by, or on behalf of, the company. This is termed marketing research. Sales forecasting is also included in this category of information that is collected from the market-place, which is then put into quantitative statements of future potential sales. This, arguably, is the starting point for all corporate planning activity, so its importance should not be underestimated.

What has been discussed so far can be regarded as the spectrum of activities that are included under marketing. Each of these is expanded throughout the text in order to give us a more detailed understanding of the activities that are included in the subject of marketing. In addition, marketing has an international dimension, but the tenets apply equally in the international arena, although there are a number of additional considerations. Social and green issues are also concerns of modern marketing. Strategic marketing planning is the set of techniques that brings marketing together in a cohesive actionable framework over the short (tactical) term and the long (strategic) term. These areas are also covered in later discussion throughout this text. Figure 1.1 puts the activities that we have described so far into a framework for better understanding the process of marketing.

As well as the elements discussed above and over which marketing has direct control, we also include other functions within the company as being part of this micro-environment. In a marketing orientated organisation, it is marketing that translates the views of customers into desires and wants and we shall see later how these needs are interpreted into tangible products and services.

The phrase part-time marketer was put forward by E Gummesson in 1991, who argued that everything a company does must be central to the needs of customers and indeed this has been

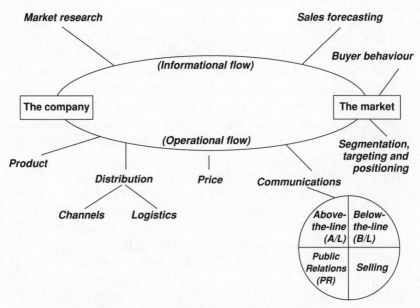

Figure 1.1 *The process of marketing*

Japanese business philosophy for many years. However, the notion that everybody in the company is a part-time marketer is interesting, for it suggests that the activities of other departments must always accord to the needs of customers and marketing is seen to be the integrator between customers and other operational parts of the organisation. This is not, of course, to say that marketing should be in charge of everything, but the notion of consumer sovereignty should pervade a company's thinking processes in all aspects of its operation, at both tactical and strategic levels. It just so happens that marketing is the interface between customers and the company.

The principal aspects of the company which impinge most on marketing and customers are: production; quality; finance and research and development. Human resource management and management services (or the information technology that manages a company's management information system) are other operational elements that more indirectly impinge on the organisation's customers. It is, therefore, important in a marketing orientated concern that general management marshals all of these resources together to serve the foremost requirements of customers and that the company is customer led. Indeed, the modern notion of marketing emphasises long term relationships with customers through relationship marketing. Here, direct liaison with customers is actively encouraged within all company departments and customer contact is not just through the marketing department. This is the notion of the part-time marketer being put into practice, for it is through such personal contacts and associations that long term relationships subsequently develop at different operational levels.

MARKETING AND THE MACRO-ENVIRONMENT

The macro-environment is all factors that are external to the company. This is split up into the proximate macro-environment and the wider macro-environment. The organisation's proximate macro-environment includes companies that supply components and raw materials as well as the various services that the company requires. It also includes the company's agents and distributors and its competitors.

The wider macro-environment is factors over which the company has very little control and when investigating these wider factors it is referred to as the company's external marketing audit. This process is also referred to as environmental scanning. The marketing audit is an integral part of the company's strategic marketing planning system which is referred to later in this text and also in detail in *Strategic Marketing, Planning and Evaluation* by Geoff Lancaster and Lester Massingham, in this *Marketing in Action* series. These wider macro-environmental factors are remembered by the acronym PEST, although some textbooks refer to it as STEP. (Extra dimensions have now been added to this and it is now sometimes referred to as PESTLE.) These acronyms have now entered the speak of marketing, so they tend to be shorthanded out in any of these formats. The full listing for PESTLE is: Political; Economic; Socio-cultural; Technological; Legal and Environmental. Each of these areas is now expanded in more detail:

■ **Political** factors relate to those political factors that might impinge on the operation of a business. Typical factors are: privatisation, international events, trading practices, monopolies and mergers legislation, levels of public spending and controls on advertising. Marketing has to be aware of these macro-environmental factors and although it has little control over them, such macro decisions can affect the success of an individual business enterprise.

▧ **Economic** factors include economic growth, income levels, interest rates, exchange rates, balance of payment levels, employment percentages, credit policies, income distribution, savings/debt, personal and corporate taxation and indirect taxation such as VAT. These economic factors must be monitored by a company at both domestic and international levels, so that it can be in a better position to capitalise upon any opportunities and be aware of any threats in sufficient time to take remedial action.

▧ **Socio-cultural** factors concern matters such as the changing age structure of the population, trends in the size of families, changes in the amount and nature of leisure time, changes in attitude towards health and lifestyles, improvement in education, changes in attitudes towards family roles, changing patterns of work and equal opportunities. In some countries, the religious environment might also be a source of opportunities or threats to companies doing business there.

▧ **Technological** factors concern such matters as automation, new methods of travel, computer assisted telephone interviewing, electronic point of sale, new materials and more powerful computing methods. All of these can have a direct influence on the marketing firm, particularly if its own methods of production, or the products/services that it produces, are directly affected by, or actually form, an integral part of the products that it offers to customers.

▧ **Legal** is normally inferred under political in a straight PEST analysis context. It is, however, separated out under PESTLE and in this context refers to such matters as monopolies legislation or European and other international legislation.

▧ **Environmental** is currently an issue for many companies because of the publicity it receives. Such issues include matters such as natural resource depletion, pollution, biodegradable materials and changes in world climate as a result of the depletion of the ozone layer. Many firms now emphasise green marketing to show how they place such issues on their strategic agenda and like to be seen to be putting such principles into practice.

SUMMARY

In this chapter we have traced the development of marketing from its early embryonic phases and looked at the concepts of production, sales and marketing orientation. We have explored various definitions of marketing and examined how the discipline should develop in the future. The notion of the marketing mix has been discussed plus the various elements that go to make up the subject of marketing. Marketing's macro-environment was then considered in terms of broader issues that impinge less directly on marketing operations.

In the next chapter we begin to discuss the various elements of what constitutes the subject of marketing when we explain segmentation, targeting and positioning.

2

Segmentation, Target Marketing and Positioning

SEGMENTATION AND TARGETING EXPLAINED

As was explained in the previous chapter, the needs of customers should be central to all business decision making. In particular, changing demand patterns, and the fact that companies must strive to make their product offerings different from their competitors have given rise to the idea of market segmentation. Different customers will need distinct products or modified versions of the same basic product. This is a result of a move towards individualism on the part of consumers, plus the fact that there is now greater competition in the market-place. This, coupled with greater spending power on the part of consumers, has meant that manufacturers must respond by producing products and services that suit the needs of specific sub-groups of customers.

This process is termed market segmentation, which amounts to a breaking down of the total market into distinct sub-groups or segments. Each segment has different tastes and requires a unique marketing mix in order to make the product or service more attractive to those customers who occupy that market segment. The process of manipulating the marketing mix in terms of differentiating products, methods of communication and other marketing variables is known as target marketing.

Target marketing can thus be said to be the process of identifying market segments that will be the most likely purchasers of a company's products, and devising inventive marketing approaches to suit these specifically distinguished needs. Marketers are looking to serve unfilled gaps in the market and this process is known as gap analysis. Gaps can be real (eg bitter, mild, gentle or moist) and in such cases products can be devised to meet these criteria. However, these gaps can also be illusory in terms of how customers want to perceive the product or service (eg convivial, reserved, sensible or lively) and in such cases these characteristics might have to be implanted in the understanding of customers through ingeniously prepared advertising messages.

The downside of not engaging in market segmentation is that a company can find itself attempting to satisfy all of the market with a mass marketing strategy, but in fact satisfying the needs of none of the market segments effectively, giving competitors the opportunity to exploit under-served segments and gaps in the market.

ADVANTAGES OF SEGMENTATION AND TARGETING

The advantages of segmentation and target marketing are:

1. It allows a company to identify specific customer groups with differing needs and wants.
2. Unfilled gaps in a market can be appraised and then satisfied through unique product or promotional offerings.
3. Through a manipulation of the marketing mix, the marketer can more easily target the needs of potential consumers, which should lead to increased customer satisfaction.
4. Company goals can be more easily achieved, be they goals of profit maximisation, long term growth in the market-place or other such goals.
5. The process of continually looking for new segments forces a constant appraisal of changing customer needs and wants and any potential opportunities and threats can be seen that might arise in the market-place.
6. This is known as market scanning.
7. It allows both large and small companies to compete more effectively.

SEGMENTATION CRITERIA

When considering appropriate bases for segmenting markets, a number of criteria are appropriate for assessing different bases:

1. **Measurability/identifiability.** Ideally, the base used should enable us to identify and measure the constituents and characteristics of a segment, ie how many people are in it and who they are.
2. **Accessibility.** Ideally, the bases used should enable the company to reach those segments through the chosen targeting strategies.
3. **Validity.** This important criterion means the extent to which the base is directly associated with the differences in needs and wants between the different segments. Given that segmentation is essentially concerned with identifying groups with different needs and wants, it is vital that the segmentation base is meaningful and that different preferences or needs show clear variations in market behaviour and response to individually designed marketing mixes.
4. **Substantial.** The base used should lead to sufficiently large segments to be economically and practically worthwhile serving with a distinctive marketing mix.

There are a number of logical sequential steps that should be observed when conducting a segmentation, targeting and positioning exercise:

1. Select the base or bases for segmentation and identify suitable market segments.
2. Assess the market segments identified from the first stage.
3. Choose an overall targeting strategy.
4. Decide which target segments will be your key customers.
5. Develop a positioning strategy for each segment to be targeted.
6. Devise a marketing mix for each preferred segment to support the product positioning strategy.

BASES FOR SEGMENTING CONSUMER PRODUCT MARKETS

Geographic segmentation

This is where a country is divided into regions for marketing purposes. This is normally seen as an industrial/organisational segmentation base and refers to sales territories. However, in large countries like the USA, companies frequently segment geographically because certain areas of the country have different tastes and buyer behaviour than other parts of the country, so a different marketing mix is devised for different geographical locations within the country.

Demographic segmentation

This consists of a wide variety of bases for subdividing markets, and each of these is now discussed:

Income is a valid segmentation base, but in the United Kingdom it is more common to use social class as a base (and income can be deduced from this) due to the fact that our culture tends to regard income disclosure as being a very private matter, so questions seeking to establish our level of income would be regarded as an intrusion of privacy.

Sex in terms of a male/female split is an obvious base and this prompts the target marketing of clothing products, deodorants and many personal items.

Age is a further variable for items like clothing where fashion plays an important part in marketing such products.

Social class is still the most highly regarded segmentation variable for marketing purposes in the United Kingdom. The National Readership Survey sub-divides the UK into a number of categories as can be seen in Figure 2.1.

A	Upper middle class (higher managerial, administrative or professional) which comprises about 3 per cent of the population
B	Middle class (intermediate managerial, administrative or professional) which comprises approximately 10 per cent of the population
C1	Lower middle class (supervisory, clerical, junior administrative or professional) containing around 25 per cent of the population
C2	Skilled working class (skilled manual workers) who comprise around 28 per cent of the population.
D	Working class (semi- and unskilled manual workers) or around 28 per cent of the population
E	Lowest levels of subsistence (state pensioners with no other income, widows, casual and lowest grade earners) who form the remaining 6 per cent, or thereabouts, of the population.

Figure 2.1 *Social grade structure (United Kingdom)*

Education is sometimes referred to as TEA which means terminal education age. Such a segmentation base is often linked to reading and media viewing/listening habits. The listening/readership profile of media is audited by the Audit Bureau of Circulation (ABC) and this lists the percentage of certain social grades and likely TEA profiles that form their respective audiences. This, in turn, is used by the media to induce advertising agencies to place their clients' advertising in more precisely defined and targeted media.

Ethnic background now makes up a discrete segment for segmentation and targeting purposes. Clothing, food items and hair fit into this category.

Family size will affect the amount and size of purchases, and this is a purposeful segmentation base.

Political leaning is a less used segmentation base in the United Kingdom, but in many countries it is very important, as is religion. This can relate to the type of media that is read or listened to or watched by such groups. This should, in turn, reflect the type of advertising that is carried by such media.

Family life cycle is based on the idea that consumers pass through a series of phases in their lives, each giving rise to different purchases and wants. Single people will have different needs to married couples with children. Wells and Gubar have put forward a system in relation to family life cycle stages that is shown in Figure 2.2.

Bachelor stage – young single people not living with parents (sometimes known as 'YUPPIES' or 'young, upwardly-mobile persons')

Newly marrieds – no children (often referred to as 'DINKIES' which means 'double income – no kids')

Full nest I – with the youngest child being under six years of age

Full nest II – is where the youngest child is six or over

Full nest III – is an older married couple with dependent children living at home

Empty nest I – with no children living at home, but family head in work (known as 'WOOPIES' or 'well off older persons')

Empty nest II – where the family head is retired

Solitary survivor in work

Solitary survivor retired

Figure 2.2 *Family life cycle segmentation base*

SAGACITY is a combination segmentation base which was devised by a company called Research Services Limited. The notion is that people have different behavioural patterns and aspirations as they proceed through life, depending where they fit in their particular social class grade. Stages of life cycle are described as:

- ■ *Dependent* (mainly under 24 living at home).
- ■ *Pre-family* (under 35s who have established their own household, but without children).
- ■ *Family* (couples under 65 with one or more child in the household).
- ■ *Late* (adults whose children have left home or who are over 35 and childless).

Occupation groups are defined as white (collar) – or the A,B and C1 social classes and blue (collar) – or the C2, D and E groups. Income groups are categorised as: better off and worse off. The grouping is illustrated in Figure 2.3.

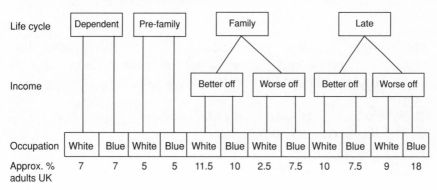

Source: Research Services Limited

Figure 2.3 *Sagacity life cycle classification system*

Type of neighbourhood and dwelling uses the fact that the type of dwelling and area a person lives in are potential predictors of likely purchasing habits. This system uses homes, rather than people, as a basis for segmentation. It is called the ACORN system (A Classification of Residential Neighbourhoods). Its source is the 10-yearly population census – the next full census being in 2001. It was developed by Richard Webber for Consolidated Analysis Centres Incorporated (CACI) and decomposes the census of population into various dwelling categories as shown in Figure 2.4.

Acorn Group	Type of dwelling	Approx % UK population
A	Agricultural areas	3
B	Modern family housing, higher incomes	18
C	Older housing of intermediate status	17
D	Poor quality older terraced housing	4
E	Better-off council estates	13
F	Less well-off council estates	9
G	Poorest council estates	7
H	Multi-racial areas	4
I	High status non-family areas	4
J	Affluent suburban housing	16
K	Bettter-off retirement areas	4
U	Unclassified	1

Source: CACI

Figure 2.4 *ACORN classification system*

These larger ACORN classifications are then sub-divided into smaller groupings and Group E, for instance, which refers to Better-off Council Estates, is broken down into:

■ E15 council estates, well-off older workers;
■ E16 recent council estates;
■ E17 council estates, well-off young workers;
■ E18 small council houses, often Scottish.

Mosaic system. This process was also developed by Richard Webber for CCN Marketing of which he is Managing Director. It is a sophistication of the ACORN system and bases its classification on individual postcodes, each of which comprises up to seven letters and figures. The term MOSAIC was coined because it categorises individuals into one of 12 groups and 52 total types. Therefore, each postcode is represented by one of these types. If a different colour was ascribed to each of these types on a map of the UK it would look like a mosaic pattern.

House occupier groups might be for instance: high income families, blue collar owners, Victorian low status or stylish singles. The system also has specialist geographical sectors like Scottish

MOSAIC which classifies postcodes into one of 10 groups and 47 types, including monied society, high-tech mortgagers, multi-let tenements and deprived schemes. London Tribes covers the 11 million people within the London TV region and includes affluent opinion formers, ethnic pride, time-serving commuters and bulldog estates. PSYCHE is a MOSAIC categorisation based on people's attitudes and values and includes conspicuous consumers, social resisters and self explorers. Financial MOSAIC uses direct measures of financial activity to identify 10 groups and 36 types including captains of industry, student innocence, over-committed owners and welfare dependency.

Direct segmentation

This system takes customer purchasing response as the segmentation criterion and this includes:

Brand loyalty which is where consumers are split into categories according to their loyalty in respect of repurchasing the brand. Such categories are:

■ hard core loyals or buyers of the same brand every time;
■ soft core loyals who might purchase two or more brands on a random basis;
■ shifting loyals purchase one brand and stay with it for a specific period, and then buy another brand and stay with it for a period and then perhaps return to the original brand;
■ brand switchers show no loyalty to any brand.

Usage status is where a distinction might be made between light, medium and heavy purchasers of a product.

Benefits sought is a base that seeks to establish customer expectations in relation to the product. An example that comes to mind relates to beauty product customers. Benefits sought might be to feel better, to look younger, to have an agreeable odour, to attract the opposite sex or to exhibit wealth if it is an expensive brand.

Occasions for purchase is another direct segmentation base and an illustration here is gift giving at Christmas, and this motivates much purchasing of socks, ties, underwear, chocolates and such products.

Psychographic segmentation

This presumes that lifestyle might be a more accurate reflection of brands purchased. Certain categories of lifestyle have been isolated for segmentation purposes:

Upwardly mobile – who are ambitious people seeking a better lifestyle through better paid and more interesting work. They are generally prepared to try new products.

Traditional and sociable – who seek conformity and compliance with group norms. They seek approval and make conformist purchases.

Security and status seeking – who purchase well known brands and whose purchases emphasise those products that confer status and make life more predictable.

Hedonistic preference – reflects those who believe in enjoying life for the present with little thought given to the future.

Psychographic segmentation is largely a function of the country in which consumers are based. Australia, for instance, offers different groups (Source: Reg Bryson, Campaign Palace Advertising):

Old bronzed Aussies (34 per cent) – conservative critics with strong traditional beliefs – tend to cling to the past.

Rosy optimists (30 per cent) – Australia has a secure future. Their main concern is for the environment.

Browned offs (21 per cent) – Disenchanted immigrants and offspring. Don't belong and don't identify.

True blues (15 per cent) – Strongly identified through TV images portraying Australians as macho/no-nonsense people.

Similarly, South Africa suggests cross-cultural comparisons (Source: AMPS):

Traditional non-earners – a quarter of the population, principally black rural dwellers with a subsistence agricultural lifestyle.

Self-centred non-earners – unemployed black people often in urban areas.

Hostel dwellers – who typically remit most of their incomes to families in the countryside.

Urbanised singles – eg maids, casual workers.

Young aspirers – mainly highly ambitious young people, often professional.

The emerging market – newly affluent people.

Established affluents – 'old money', landed gentry and typical professionals.

Progressive affluents – about 5 per cent of the population – almost exclusively white and containing highly sophisticated big-spending consumers.

The segmentation bases that have been described in this section relate principally, although not totally, to consumer goods. They are particularly useful to advertisers who can exploit variances in behaviour and demand in the form of differentiated and finely targeted communications appeals to smaller groups of consumers. This notion of targeting is more fully explained later in the chapter.

SEGMENTATION BASES IN ORGANISATIONAL MARKETS

Organisational markets defined

The term organisational markets refers principally to organisational buying behaviour, which is covered in the next chapter. At this stage it is sufficient to say that it covers the following sub-divisions:

Industrial markets – and here the major criterion is keeping production satisfied in order that materials and components are available for incorporation in production processes. The ultimate objective is to satisfy the needs of the company's customers, be they intermediate manufacturers further down the production chain or end customers.

Institutional markets – relates to purchasing for public institutions like the police force, the fire service, local and central government establishments and educational establishments. Here, the principal criterion is to keep spending within predetermined budget limits that have been set as part of previously agreed operational spending limits.

Resale markets – where the principal criterion is the mark-up percentage that can be added to goods that are purchased from manufacturers and wholesalers in bulk and then resold to individual customers.

Segmentation bases for organisational product and service markets

Many of the bases that are appropriate for consumer goods are equally applicable to organisational-type products and services. However, a number of additional bases are now suggested as being particularly appropriate:

Type of application/end use (sometimes referred to as product/technology segmentation) eg paint products for the domestic market and for industrial uses. Here the former might concentrate upon the latest fashions in colours and finishes, whereas for the latter, functional aspects like its protective ability might be more important.

Geographic segmentation is a countrywide split often based upon salespersons' territories, which are called regions or areas. For international operations, different parts of the world can comprise different market segments.

Benefits sought As with consumer market segmentation, benefits sought is potentially the most powerful direct form of segmentation.

Type of customer eg retail customers, which might be independent shops or part of a multiple group or light engineering customers versus heavy engineering customers.

Customer size and loyalty eg customers purchasing large amounts might merit a different sales approach to small purchasers. This is called key account selling whereby the sales manager deals directly with major accounts because of their importance to the company.

Usage rate eg heavy or frequent users versus light or infrequent users.

Purchasing procedures eg centralised or decentralised buying arrangements, the degree to which buyers are allowed any latitude in specification, the extent to which purchasing is by tender or closed bidding or by open negotiation.

Situational factors eg some purchasing situations call for a more personal approach whereas in others it is formal and businesslike.

The bases for organisational markets are similar to consumer markets in terms of them being indirect/associative (eg type of customer or geographic) or direct/behavioural (eg situational factors or benefits sought). Sub-segmentation or combination segmentation bases are also possible to obtain smaller sub-segments.

A suggestion of a nested approach by Shapiro and Bonoma in Harvard Business Review (May/June 1984) on the basis of a hierarchy ranging from the general to the particular is appropriate for organisational segmentation and this is shown in Figure 2.5:

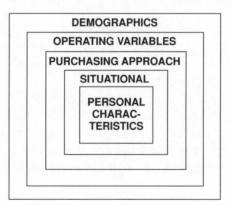

Figure 2.5   *A nested approach to segmentation in industrial markets*

The outer nest represents general demographic characteristics like the geographical location of customers and this goes down to specific issues at the centre which considers the individual personalities of buyers who actually make the purchasing decisions.

MARKET TARGETING

When the segmentation process has taken place, each identified segment must be assessed in order to decide whether or not it is worthwhile serving as a potentially profitable target market with its own distinctive marketing mix. If a company decides *not* to simply operate a blanket strategy (ie no segmentation) then it is engaging in what is called a concentrated or differentiated market targeting strategy. The company then has to decide which potential segments to serve based upon the criteria stated in section 2.3.

Favourable attributes of a target market will include segments where there is good sales and profit potential, where competition is not too intense and where the segment might have some previously unidentified requirements which the company is able to serve. It is this latter notion that we explore in the next section. The process of target marketing (NB the terms market targeting and target marketing are interchangeable) is the manipulation of the marketing mix such that a distinctive marketing mix is designed for each chosen market segment.

POSITIONING

This is the final stage in the segmentation, targeting and positioning continuum. The process of reaching target segments and ensuring the right perceptions about the product or service is referred to as positioning. A product or market positioning strategy has to be devised for each segment the company chooses to serve. Positioning forms the basis of developing detailed marketing mix plans. The idea of product and brand positioning is applicable to both organisational and consumer markets.

There are three sequential steps in the process of positioning:

1. Establish the relevant attributes which are used by customers in the segment when evaluating and choosing between brands in this market;
2. Using these attributes, assess the current perceived position of existing brands in the market;
3. Determine where the new brand is to be positioned against existing brands in the market and the brand attributes which will be emphasised in order to achieve this position.

Each of these steps is now explained in more detail.

Relevant attributes

At the first stage we are seeking to establish the key dimensions or attributes of the product or brand within the market segment. For instance, in the dishwasher detergent market the key attributes might be: grease/stain removal, value for money and kindness to hands, with attributes such as aroma and finish, colour of the liquid, type of cleaning agents contained in the liquid as less obvious attributes. The name of the product or brand is also an attribute and should logically be determined once the positioning strategy has been defined. But, in cases where an existing brand is being repositioned, it might not be easy to change the name because of the brand loyalty to the original name. Indeed, many manufacturers simply leave the old brand in its present position, and then introduce the new brand as competition to the existing brand as well as competitive brands. This is known as brand proliferation.

Some of these attributes are objective (eg colour of liquid and smell) and some are subjective (eg the product's name). Purchasers might also think about more than one of these attributes when making a purchase, so it is the key attribute(s) that must be emphasised most strongly. This is sometimes referred to as the unique sales proposition (USP). Positioning thus takes place in the mind of the customer, but it is how these ideas are implanted, through manipulating the marketing mix, that is the skill of the marketer.

Perceptual mapping

The second stage can be determined through the use of what is called perceptual mapping. An example of this in relation to the dishwasher detergent market is shown in Figure 2.6.

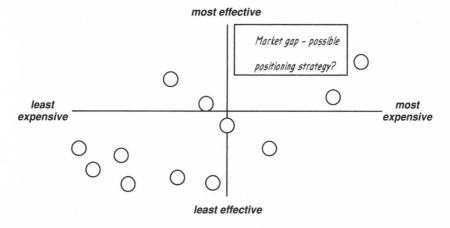

Figure 2.6 *Perceptual mapping (dishwasher detergent)*

Marketing research has established the positions of existing brands in the market along the criteria illustrated for dishwasher detergent, and each brand currently in the market is represented by a circle. The rectangle represents a market gap in which there is no occupant. A positioning strategy is suggested that means devising a new brand of dishwasher detergent that occupies this position. The illustration given in Figure 2.6 looks only at the criteria of effectiveness and economy, so other perceptual maps would need to be done in relation to other criteria like kindness to hands, colour and smell. The resultant position of the new brand would, therefore, be an amalgam of a number of perceptual (or brand) maps.

Marketing mix strategy

Once a positioning strategy has been devised, the final step is to develop a marketing mix strategy for the new brand that is appropriate to the position chosen. This sounds easy, but in the case of the dishwasher detergent example the reality is that for it to be successful the various elements of the marketing mix must integrate successfully to produce the right kind of product, supported by an appropriate communications mix at suitable price level. The launch of the new brand must be well thought through using above- and below-the-line media and supported with an appropriate publicity/public relations campaign. The message to distributors should be carefully co-ordinated and communicated to them through the field sales force in order to ensure that they are fully cognizant with the new brand before it is launched.

In explaining the concept of positioning we have used the example of developing and launching a new brand of dishwasher detergent. The concepts and techniques of positioning are also relevant to the development of existing brands. Continuous positioning research into existing brands is essential in order to track changes in customer choice determinants, changes in their perceptions of brands and new competitors to the market-place. Sometimes this research may suggest that brand positioning is still effective and that no changes are needed. However, marketing dynamics mean that for various reasons it may be necessary to consider repositioning strategies for existing brands. As with the initial positioning, repositioning may be achieved through a variety of strategies. The nature and effectiveness of these various strategies will depend on the reasons underpinning the needs to reposition including changes in competitive activity, changes in customer needs and tastes and changes in legislation.

STRATEGIES FOR TARGET MARKETING

Market coverage patterns

D F Abell put forward a summary of patterns of market coverage in the Harvard Business Review in 1980. This notion is illustrated in Figure 2.7.

The segmentation and targeting strategies suggested are single segments which might be appropriate for a niche manufacturer with limited capital, eg a manufacturer of adhesives for school, DIY, industrial and office users and here the product for each customer group has similar properties of adhesion. However, the communications approach to each category of customer will be different, probably utilising different selling and distribution channels for each.

Customer group coverage suggests a specialist industry manufacturer of, say, mining machinery. Here, all mining machinery products are covered including say, roof supports, coal cutting machinery, conveyors and materials-handling equipment. A specialist customer knowledge here is regarded as being more important than product specialisation. Selective coverage suggests a company that operates in a number of product or service areas without necessarily pursuing a deliberate policy of synergy between the organisation's different products. A financial holding group might be an example here which treats each product or company group as a separate strategic business unit (SBU) responsible for its own budgets and profits, but without necessarily looking for product or service synergy between each SBU. A suggestion here might be a holding company that owns companies that process food and manufacture machine tools, and has an insurance broking business. The final strategy is one of full coverage and here no attempt is made to segment the market so the communications message is universal and the product is undifferentiated. An example here might be washing powder.

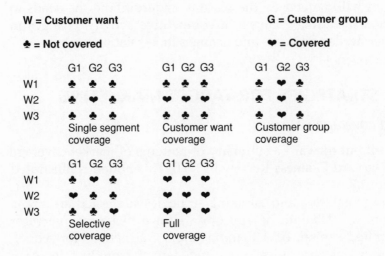

Figure 2.7 *Patterns of market coverage*

Options for target marketing

Following the ideas put forward in Figure 2.7, marketing literature suggests the following four strategies when considering target marketing:

1. **Differentiated** where there are multiple marketing mixes for different market segments.
2. **Undifferentiated** where there is a single marketing mix for all customers.
3. **Concentrated** which has one marketing mix for a segment of the entire market.
4. **Custom** which attempts to satisfy each customer's needs with an individual marketing mix.

SUMMARY

In this chapter we have considered segmentation variables for consumer and organisational markets and emphasised the importance of the validity of such segments. We have discussed targeting in terms of it being a strategic decision in relation to which segments to target, and we have looked finally at positioning in the context of providing an understanding of customer perceptions and the fact that positioning tends to take place in the minds of customers. We concluded by summarising that once positioning has been decided, an appropriate marketing mix should then be decided to reach the target market segments.

Market segmentation is based on the sentiment that customers have different needs and the starting point of target marketing is in identifying these different needs. Positioning them effectively informs customers what the brand stands for and how it differs from competitors' products. The next chapter takes the discussion further by looking at the motives of buyers and once these are understood, more meaningful targeting and positioning strategies might be possible.

3

Consumer and Organisational Buyer Behaviour

SIGNIFICANCE OF CONSUMER MOTIVES TO MARKETING

A basic requirement of marketing is to produce products that customers need. This demands both an investigation of the market-place through marketing research and also an understanding of why it is required. Marketing research is examined in the next chapter and the 'why' element is investigated here and explores individual and group behaviour in an attempt to determine why goods and services are required. An awareness of purchasing motives should be advantageous to the company in terms of being able to better target customers and to customers in terms of providing the products and levels of service required.

Consumer behaviour puts customers at the core of the decision making process, surrounded by an immediate micro- and a wider macro-environment that influences these purchasing objectives. These objectives are fulfilled as a result of the consumer passing through as a number of 'problem-solving stages' leading to the ultimate purchase. A study of consumer behaviour draws principally on psychology with additional inputs from sociology, anthropology and economics.

EXTERNAL INFLUENCES ON BUYING BEHAVIOUR

A civilisation rests on culture, which is evidenced through family, education and religious institutions. Culture is a powerful force that the company should understand in order to promote products and services that are appropriate for the market-place.

Culture is not permanent; it changes gradually, and such changes are progressively assimilated within society. During the past thirty years there has been an attitudinal move in relation to work which is no longer seen by the majority of people to be drudgery. The distinction between employers and employees has lessened and mutual co-operation is now more normal than the traditional 'master and servant' relationship. Work is increasingly regarded as being a means of earning enough to spend on goods and services that give enjoyment, rather than simply providing the means of subsistence. Working hours are shorter and holidays are longer and the period has witnessed a large addition of more effective home labour-saving devices. All of this has meant an increase in leisure time which has led to a growth in such industries as holidays (especially foreign holidays), short breaks, restaurants, convenience foods, food take-away outlets, hobbies and other leisure pursuits. The division between the traditional roles of men and women is now much more blurred than thirty years ago. For instance, it is now perfectly normal for men to share, or even perform, the food shopping task.

Subculture is also important and the UK has witnessed a significant growth of immigrant communities over the past forty years. Apart from forming specific market segments for certain products and services, immigrants have also had a great effect on traditional UK society. Nowhere is this more evident than in relation to our now diverse eating patterns, especially Indian, Chinese and Italian styles of cookery and eating out. Such changes, while providing a threat to traditional markets, can also be viewed as an opportunity for the establishment of new markets.

Social class is probably still the principal influence on consumer purchasing habits. Thirty years or so ago income was very much determined by this factor, but it is less marked now with C2 and D groups in particular moving more towards salary levels enjoyed by B and C1 groups. It is also a fact that we have moved more towards a 'white collar' society which now has a greater preponderance of A, B and C1 groups. However, it is still a fact that white collar groups are, for instance, more likely to drink wine with dinner than blue collar groups, but class distinctions are certainly more blurred than they were. As discussed in the previous chapter, lifestyle or psychographic segmentation is also becoming a more meaningful segmentation base. A combination of education, social mobility, geographical mobility and income levels has meant that people are now able to cross social barriers more easily than was the case with their parents. They then begin to assimilate new group influences and lifestyles that might be totally different to that of their parents. Occupation is thus a powerful determinant in consumer buyer behaviour.

A reference group is a group of people whose behaviour can shape an individual's dispositions and convictions. Reference groups range from the family, to social life to the workplace. Members of a reference group are unlikely to digress far from the norms of behaviour laid down by the members of the group – be this family, a sports club or a particular social set for fear of being ostracised or excluded.

'Opinion leaders' is the term given to individuals or small groups whose counsel is viewed as being knowledgeable. This can include members of a family group or individuals who might be outside the immediate group. These opinions are taken up by 'opinion followers' and the psychology behind advertisements showing sportswear endorsement by well-known sporting person-alities is an application of this principle in practice. Family is prob-ably the most potent reference group because of the familiarity between individuals, its continuance and the fact that members influence each other.

The notion of the family life cycle was put forward in the last chapter in Figure 2.2, which illustrated the idea put forward by Wells and Gubar. Clearly, the stage a person has reached, relative to this family life cycle, will be a function of the influence other members of the family group will have on individual purchasing. Where the person is at the Bachelor Stage (YUPPIES), then dispos-able income will be high relative to family commitments, which will mean more to spend on personal and leisure products. In many cases the person will be relatively free of family influences and will respond more to fashion influences. In relation to Full nest III, there will be less disposable income with most expenditure going towards purchasing everyday necessities. Here purchasing decisions might well be restricted by an implicit or explicit budget. For Empty nest I (WOOPIES) disposable income should be rela-tively high, but tastes are likely to be firmly implanted and regular procurement patterns will have emerged. So external influences on buyer behaviour will be minimal, except that many household durables and furniture might be replaced at this stage, or even a new house purchase might be contemplated.

PERSONAL BUYER BEHAVIOUR

People are individuals, so their own personalities, which have been shaped by the external environment, will play the most important part in the consumer decision making process. Marketers should know what shapes personality in order to use this knowledge when designing purchasing appeals. Human beings are distinct in terms of education, their personality and their physical and psychological makeup, which means that their likely responses to marketing endeavours will be different. Consumers assimilate information and then develop dispositions towards certain products or services. Marketers should attempt to distinguish patterns of behaviour, which are to be anticipated, and this will enhance the ability to fulfil customers' needs.

When endeavouring to comprehend the nature of buyer behaviour, there are a number of psychological concepts that should be considered.

Motivation

The marketing term for purchasers wishing to own goods or services is: 'goal-related behaviour'. Purchases to satisfy hunger, thirst, warmth and shelter needs are physiological, while motives such as the desire for approval, success and prestige are psychological. Staying alive is instinctive, while cleanliness, neatness and aptitude are motives that are learned during the course of life. It is also possible to distinguish between emotional and rational motives and many buying decisions are a composite of each of these. For instance a purchasing decision for an item of clothing might often be a composite of fashion (emotion) and price (rational). Many motives might be at play during the purchasing process and the final decision will probably be a compromise.

Abraham Maslow (1954), the psychologist, proposed a 'hierarchy of needs' model which is shown in Figure 3.1. This theory is now central to consumer buyer behaviour.

Figure 3.1 *Maslow's hierarchy of needs*

The base of the hierarchy shows the physiological needs that are concerned with self-preservation. Safety needs are next and once these more basic needs have been satisfied, more sophisticated needs can be fulfilled. The need at the apex of the triangle is 'self-actualisation'. At this stage, the need is one of acquiring products or services that allow for self expression which might be in the form of new purchases which have long been required, but have not been purchased until lower order needs have been fulfilled.

The importance of this theory to marketers is that it suggests that they should make appeals to the specific needs of consumers, having due regard to where they are in the purchasing hierarchy.

It does not follow that this hierarchy is universal, and it has been suggested by E C Nevin that a different interpretation of this original theory is needed for Chinese culture, which values basic family ties and bonds above all else. Here, the hierarchy places belonging as the base need, followed by physiological needs and then, safety. Self-actualisation is put at the top, but this is interpreted as 'self-actualisation in terms of service to society'.

McGregor has also advanced theories based on motivation and he contends that there are two rationales that motivate people – namely, Theory X and Theory Y. For Theory X the assumptions are:

■ people have an inherent dislike for work and will avoid it if possible;
■ they must consequently be coerced, controlled, directed and threatened with punishment in order to complete their work satisfactorily;
■ people like to be directed and do not seek responsibility. They have little ambition and need security.

For theory Y the assumptions are:

■ people are not naturally passive or resistant to organisational needs. They have become so as the result of experience in organisations;
■ motivation and the capacity to develop and assume responsibility are natural, and it is the task of management to develop these characteristics;
■ management should organise production towards economic ends and develop conditions and methods of operation so that people can achieve their personal goals best by directing their individual efforts towards organisational objectives;
■ if the right conditions prevail, individuals will not only accept responsibility, but they will actively seek it;
■ most of the population is capable of imagination, ingenuity and creativity in problem solving within an organisation;
■ industrialisation has meant that such capabilities are under-utilised.

McGregor argued that management by control (Theory X) was based on an inaccurate set of negative assumptions and that organisations would work more effectively if 'management by objectives' (MBO) or Theory Y, was applied. Insofar as applications to marketing are concerned the link is perhaps rather tenuous, but it does serve to illustrate that people, given the right work climate, will respond and be motivated by positive factors, rather than negative ones.

Frederick Herzberg developed the 'motivation-hygiene' theory. This states that performance is at a peak when people are satisfied with their jobs and requisite resources are granted to carry out this work. Work satisfaction and personal happiness are not always in complete harmony, but when they are there can be a feeling of 'self actualisation' (see Figure 3.1). This might be more apparent in domestic or leisure situations than at work. Herzberg states that self-actualisation depends on what he calls 'motivators' and these he distinguishes from another set of factors called 'hygiene factors'.

Motivators can positively contribute to satisfaction at work, whereas although hygiene factors cannot promote satisfaction, they can at least prevent dissatisfaction. He uses the medical parallel to describe hygiene factors and cites the case of unhygienic conditions as being a source of infection, which may make a person unhealthy. In a business, hygiene factors are financial reward, supervision, working conditions, company policy, status and relationships with colleagues. Similarly, motivators are recognition for achievement, opportunities for advancement, responsibility and the job itself.

Motivating factors are those that are part of the job, whereas hygiene factors are more concerned with the job environment. Again, the marketing parallel is rather tenuous, but a knowledge of these two sets of factors should make the marketer aware that they contribute to a person's make-up, in the motivational sense, and that this will be likely to affect purchasing behaviour.

Self-concept and personality

People need to create an image of themselves that is acceptable to their reference group, and this is expressed through their personality and behaviour. This is of interest to marketers in terms of how it relates to the purchase and consumption of goods and services. Self-image is asserted in a way that relates to a person's inner self and this promotes approval within the group. Advertising that promotes the concept of self-image is increasingly being made through psychographic segmentation campaigns. The idea is that consumers will make purchases that conform to their self-impression in order to safeguard and boost it. Personality strongly influences buyer behaviour and this should be taken into consideration when devising marketing appeals to satisfy inner needs.

Perception

Motivation needs a direct response to a stimulus, while perception refers to the meaning that is assigned to the stimulus. Marketers need to know how purchasers discern between products and services in details such as quality, taste and cognition and how these fulfil their need satisfaction. This image is only as good as the buyer's perception and it is affected by the actual product or service, the resources of the buyer and the buyer's state of readiness to make the purchase. Perception is selective and buyers have many stimuli competing for their attention, so the task facing marketers is to make their inducements as attractive as possible, since buyers only act on information they have registered. There is, however, no guarantee that this perception will be as the marketer anticipated, despite great attention being given to the appropriate components of the marketing mix.

Other considerations as well as those presented by the marketer affect consumers. Such perceptions might be favourable or unfavourable based on experience or information from peers or family, or indeed from other psychological considerations. A combination of all these factors can modify the decisive perception upon which the final purchasing decision is made.

Attitudes

Attitudes can be described as a set of perceptions that an individual possesses. Basic attitudes are learnt during the formative years from family and social interaction and more sophisticated attitudes develop later in life. These attitudes can be positive or negative, but this is not to say that they cannot be changed. Indeed, it is the task of the skilled marketer to alter a negative attitude, which might have been brought about as a result of a bad experience with the product or service in question. Attitudes can be considered to be a set of beliefs that a buyer might have in respect of a possible purchase. In order to make this favourable many retailers have now devised loyalty schemes in order to induce repeat purchasing.

Learned behaviour

Learned behaviour comes from experience. In the buyer behaviour context, this means that when a member of a reference group sees that particular products are more popular than others within the group then, if repeat purchases of this product are made, he or she will be more acceptable within this group. A repeat purchase pattern is called 'brand loyalty', and this is what successful marketers strive to achieve.

Such learned behaviour is a result of advertising or publicity as distilled through the reference group by various promotional means. Marketing effort should attempt to link the product with positive features and fortifying messages. This is especially the case with regular repeat purchases and it is often a function of such advertising to be repetitive in nature with a simple theme.

MODELS OF CONSUMER BUYER BEHAVIOUR

Having considered the background to what influences human

behaviour, we can now examine a number of models developed by marketing theorists in an attempt to explain how such influences translate into the actual purchase of goods and services. The employment of such models means that a more ordered commercial approach to marketing could be adopted when attempting to reduce the world of purchasing complexity to a number of easily discernible variables.

Buyer/decision models

The simplest model of the buying decision process concerns repeat purchase items which respond to immediate needs (eg thirst or hunger). The model here is simple and is shown in Figure 3.2.

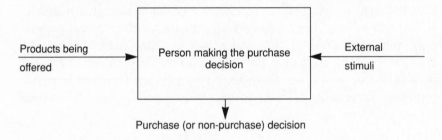

Figure 3.2 *Simple model of purchasing behaviour*

For example, the purchaser responds to thirst needs and considers the range of drinks on offer depending upon the situation (eg a social gathering, shopping in a supermarket or perhaps simply requiring a beverage to quench an immediate thirst). External stimuli will thus influence the purchase as will the products being offered. The outcome will be purchase or non-purchase.

Perhaps the most frequently cited buyer behavioural model is the 'AIDA' model, which is given in Figure 3.3. This model is also used for the stages to be considered when devising a promotional campaign and is dealt with later in the text. Figure 3.3 considers the stages leading to the purchase as a successive process in which the potential buyer passes through a number of stages starting from simple awareness and ending with action (ie the purchase). Some contemporary writers also refer to this as the AIDAS model, which takes account of the increasingly important phenomenon of post purchase behaviour, with the final 'S' meaning 'satisfaction'.

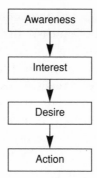

Figure 3.3 *The 'AIDA' model of consumer buyer behaviour (first proposed by E K Strong in 1925)*

The buyer/decision model is another more recent attempt to show the activities, rather than the stages, involved in the consumer purchasing process. This model, which is shown in Figure 3.4, shows the process of purchasing as a problem solving process.

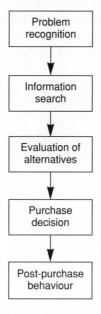

Figure 3.4 *The buyer/decision model (first proposed by Robinson, Faris and Wind in 1967)*

Once the need has been established (problem recognition) then purchase information will come from many sources including 'word of mouth' from family, friends and other purchasers; sales promotions; advertising; brochures and visits to stockists. The more sophisticated the merchandise, the more detailed this search for information will be. During this 'information search' period it is the role of marketing to promote the company's products to ensure that buyers will have a positive perception during the 'evaluation of alternatives' stage. The length of this stage can vary, depending upon the psychological makeup of the purchasers and the product or service being purchased. This automatically leads to the next stage of 'purchase decision' which is to purchase or not to purchase, depending upon the process that has taken place beforehand.

The final stage is 'post-purchase behaviour' and this is where reassurance is important, for if a customer is not completely satisfied with a major purchase then any subsequent statements of dissatisfaction by that buyer might then feed back through negative 'word of mouth' statements and affect the decisions of future purchasers. There is also a phenomenon of what is termed 'cognitive dissonance', where customers begin to doubt whether a major purchase was indeed the correct purchase. It is the reassurance that marketing gives during the purchase decision phase that is beneficial here, and a good selling tactic is to give the impression that the purchase was the customer's own choice and that they were not 'sold' the product. Encouraging phrases such as: 'That is a good choice you have made' are part of the professional salesperson's vocabulary.

Another confidence building approach is a method used by major car manufacturers who deliberately follow up each new car sale with a telephone call and/or questionnaire enquiring about the standard of service they received at point-of-sale and delivery. This confidence building approach is seen to be very important in encouraging repeat business, for repeat purchasers are easier to find and to sell to than new customers. From this has developed the notion of 'customer care', which is dealt with on page 124.

Engel, Blackwell and Miniard originally put forward the idea of the buying centre for consumer purchasing in 1990. This is an adaptation of the notion of the buying centre, or decision making unit model originally proposed by Webster and Wind in 1972 as a model for organisational purchasing and is dealt with later in this chapter (see Figure 3.11). It is argued that the following consumer purchasing roles can be witnessed for members of the family including children, parents, other family members, peer groups, etc as inputs to the buying centre:

- *initiator* – the person who begins the purchasing procedure (eg a partner might feel that a bedroom needs redecoration, so decorating materials will have to be purchased);
- *influencer* – persons who might persuade other members of the buying centre on the outcome of the purchasing decision (eg advice on colour or design);
- *decider* – the person(s) with the final say, which might be largely controlled by costs;
- *buyer* – the one who implements the actual purchase;
- *user* – the final consumer of the product or service.

The adoption process

The models we have considered so far (Figures 3.2, 3.3 and 3.4) have been associated with regular purchasing situations and not to products or services that have never been purchased before. The model illustrated in Figure 3.5 relates to new purchasing situations.

Figure 3.5 *The adoption process*

The product adoption process appears later in our discussion in Chapter 10, which relates to the diffusion of innovations in relation to product categories. In this context, it can be seen that marketers must first create an 'awareness' of their new product or service and then assist buyers through the remainder of the process. This awareness can come from the promotional actions of the company or by 'word of mouth' or by other means.

The 'interest' phase is supplemented with adequate 'information' from the company in the form of demonstrations, advertising and other promotional appeals that are presented in an informative vein.

The next stage is 'evaluation' and here the new product or service can be evaluated against existing products. If the new product is entirely innovative to the market (eg compact disc players in the early 1990s) then certain innovator categories are more likely to purchase than others and this is discussed in Chapter 10.

'Trial' will probably precede 'adoption' in the case of a major purchase. This might involve goods on approval, free samples in the case of say, a new beverage, or perhaps a demonstration in the case of a durable product.

The 'adoption' stage follows and this is the purchase phase. Continued adoption might also feature in the case of a repeat purchase fast-moving consumer good (FMCG).

'Post adoption confirmation' is similar to the 'post purchase behaviour' phase of the 'buyer/decision' model described in Figure 3.4 and this is especially relevant in the case of a major purchase when customers will be seeking to allay cognitive dissonance. For FMCG products, post adoption confirmation will depend upon whether or not repeat purchases are made. This concerns brand loyalty issues which are discussed in Chapter 8.

Figure 3.6 develops the new product adoption process further by describing inputs to the knowledge base which come from family reference groups and self (perception, attitudes, motivation and learning). This is supplemented by cultural, social and marketing inputs. The degree of persuasion controls ultimate adoption, and this is influenced by:

■ the relative advantage the product has over other offerings;
■ its compatibility with the needs of the buyer;
■ its relative complexity (on the basis that the less complex the product, the more easy will be the opportunity to bring about persuasion);
■ the opportunity to conduct some kind of pre-trial (eg taste test or test drive) before purchase;
■ its observability or its ability to be scrutinised during the persuasion period.

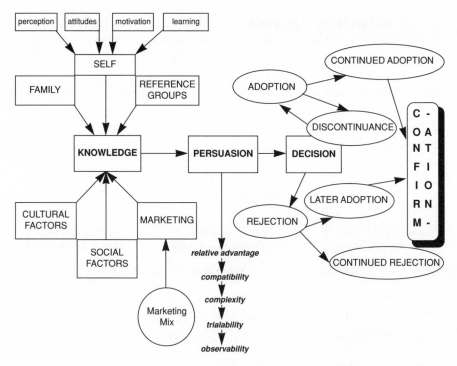

Figure 3.6 *New product purchasing decision process*

The model then permits re-examination after the decision stage which can result in adoption (purchase) and then continued adoption (brand loyalty) or discontinuance or, alternatively, rejection with the possibility of later adoption or continued rejection.

There are many more models of consumer buying behaviour and indeed entire textbooks are devoted to the subject. The purpose of describing the most fundamental models here has been to explore the topic in the overall context of marketing and to show its relative importance which will be appreciated when we examine personal selling in Chapter 7. As a logical follow on, we now examine the more prudent subject of organisational buying behaviour, where it is contended that purchasing decisions are based upon more rational motives than is the case in consumer purchasing, because organisational buying is a full-time professional vocation.

ORGANISATIONAL BUYING BEHAVIOUR

'Industrial buying' is the term often used to describe what should be more correctly described as 'organisational buying'. Figure 3.7 shows that industrial buying is a sub-set of 'organisational buying' which is the correct term to describe the overall process, with the other two sub-elements being 'institutional buying' and 'buying for resale'.

Figure 3.7 *Components of organisational buying*

The three sub-components of organisational buying are now explained:

1. *Institutional buying* refers to purchasing for organisations such as local government, the police service, hospitals and the military. Here, the principal purchasing criteria are specification and budget.
2. *Buying for resale* refers to purchasing for wholesale and retail establishments, with the principal purchasing criterion being potential mark-up and its likely appeal to ultimate consumer buyers.
3. *Industrial buying* is the largest sector of organisational buying, as it takes place right down the supply chain from raw materials to components to finished products. Demand for industrial products is termed 'derived demand', for it is the demands of the end customers for the finished products that trigger off the purchasing sequence. This demand tends to be inelastic, as goods are not usually purchased speculatively or on impulse, (unlike consumer goods), but are purchased with a specific end in mind. The entire process represents many purchasing sequences of the same product at progressive stages during the manufacturing cycle. Industrial purchases are placed into a number of categories, each of which requires a different approach to the purchasing routine.

These are:

■ materials for production;
■ components which are incorporated into the finished product;
■ capital plant and equipment and materials and services required for maintenance, repair and operation (MRO) of the manufacturing plant.

Price has traditionally been cited as the principal criterion for purchasing, but with the modern notion of supply chain management, which is dealt with specifically in Chapter 13. Logistics, delivery and quality are becoming increasingly important.

Organisational buying models

Figure 3.8 is an adaptation of what was first proposed in 1967 by Robinson, Faris and Wind as a model of organisational buying decision making. It is more practical in its descriptors than consumer purchasing models and indeed this model is still applicable as an organisational purchasing routine.

For purchases to fulfil the demands of production, as a result of an order or demand for goods that the sales department has received from customers, the first phase is automatic. This will simply be a purchase requisition or a works order. A works order is the breaking down into its various component parts of an item that is manufactured by the company. For example, if the sales department requires 10,000 photocopiers to sell and which the company manufactures, then 10,000 component parts for the photocopiers must be purchased. Some will be single component items or parts and others will have multiple applications, and these will be requested on a scheduled basis to meet the production programme. However, not all purchases are for a specific production programme and their needs can be triggered perhaps as a replacement item, or the need to purchase additional plant or machinery, or even replacements for consumable items such as office stationery.

The second phase is the specification phase. For works order items, this will be automatic, as the specification will have been decided at the design stage of the product. If, however, the item is 'one off' for incorporation into a bespoke item for a client (termed 'jobbing manufacture') then the specification might be made by the designer in consultation with the client. However, for capital plant or equipment, the 'decision making unit' might decide these specifications, which is explained later in this chapter.

The next stage qualifies potential suppliers who may be 'in' suppliers who have supplied goods in the past, or 'out' suppliers who have never supplied. 'Out' suppliers are often vetted prior to an order being placed, especially if the intention is to use such suppliers on a regular basis. Purchasing and quality personnel often visit the potential supplier beforehand to see whether or not they fulfil quality and reliability criteria to become an 'approved' supplier. This stage is called the 'enquiry' phase. Quotations are then received from potential suppliers and the purchasing department will analyse these in terms of price, quality and delivery times. Once quotations have been analysed an order will be placed to the supplier and the purchase routine will specify delivery

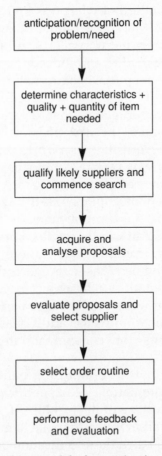

Figure 3.8 *The buy phase model of organisational purchasing*

instructions and confirm specification and price details. The final phase is feedback on how the supplier performed in terms of quality and delivery and this will be an indicator of whether or not they will be used for future purchase transactions.

Figure 3.9 was put forward by Hill and Hillier in 1977 and performs a similar function to that proposed in Figure 3.8, except that this takes each of the stages as a problem in the decision process. The first stage is **precipitation** and commences the process with the recognition of a need which a purchase will solve. This might be routine (eg materials for the production line) or 'one off' (eg a new computer). This might also be triggered by external factors through talking to sales representatives or the fact that the competition have invested in new manufacturing equipment.

The second stage is **product specification** and here information will be required on, for instance, quantity, delivery, quality, design, levels of after sales support and price. This will require inputs from those who determine the specification, which might be all or a combination of designers, accountants, buyers or customers whose views might be represented by marketing. This is termed the 'decision making unit' (DMU) which is dealt with later in this chapter.

The third stage is **supplier selection** and this considers whether existing or new suppliers are needed and how these might be chosen to participate in the 'enquiry' process. This will largely depend upon the buying situation, which can be:

■ a repeat purchase (termed a *'straight rebuy'*) which requires little purchasing effort as it is a continuing item where suppliers are already tried and tested. Here, it will be difficult for 'out' suppliers to be considered:

■ a *'modified rebuy'* where the specification might be slightly altered or the need continues at an increased or decreased level, or where the buyer might wish to seek better service or quality from a new supplier, which will give an opportunity to previously 'out' suppliers. Indeed, a marketing technique that is sometimes used by 'out' suppliers is to attempt to convert what might be a 'straight rebuy' into a 'modified rebuy', perhaps through a meeting with one of the design team, in order to be given an opportunity to quote;

■ a *'new task'* purchase is where buyers might be unfamiliar with the requirement (eg in the case of a new model that the company is about to manufacture) and have to engage in an extensive search for a supplier. This is a challenging task that occurs infrequently, but it might set the pattern for more routine straight rebuy tasks in the future. Creative sales representatives, of both 'in' and 'out' suppliers, will recognise and anticipate this through marketing intelligence they have gathered and will attempt to ensure that they are afforded the opportunity to quote.

The final stage is **commitment**, which means that price, delivery, quality and other criteria have been agreed and the order is placed. It also includes evaluation procedures in relation to the supplier to see whether or not performance while executing the order was as expected.

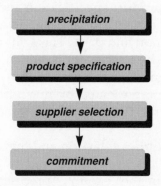

Figure 3.9   *The buyer/decision process*

Wind developed a sophisticated model in 1978, which was based on the idea that, when large contracts are at stake, sellers should attempt to locate powerful buyers with more direct inputs into purchasing decisions at the earlier stages of the specification. He said that it was important to recognise personal traits within buyers in this respect and to this end put forward a number of personality traits that such buyers might possess. This is not to say that buyers without these traits should be discounted, because lower status buyers can also affect purchasing decisions. Five power bases have been recognised:

1. *Reward:* providing monetary, social, political, or psychological rewards to others for compliance;
2. *Coercive:* an ability to withhold monetary payments or other sanctions for non-compliance;

3. *Attraction:* the ability to obtain compliance from others because they like you;
4. *Expert:* a capacity to elicit compliance because of actual or reputed technical expertise;
5. *Status:* power from the capability attained from a legitimate position of power in a company.

With these purchasing characteristics in mind, Wind developed the model that is shown in Figure 3.10.

The decision making unit (DMU) or buying centre

Organisational purchasing often involves group decision making and this trend is growing as manufacturers in flow production line situations increasingly move towards holding fewer stocks of components and raw materials. This is termed 'just-in-time' management, or 'lean manufacturing' and it demands that deliveries of components should be made exactly when needed, with zero defects. In 1972 Webster and Wind advanced the idea that there were a number of different roles in the purchasing process that could be held by different people, or the same people having a combination of roles. They termed this the 'decision making unit' (DMU) or the 'buying centre'. This is illustrated in Figure 3.11.

The role of selling is to reach appropriate members of the DMU, depending upon the position that has been reached in the purchasing cycle or transaction. Earlier stages might mean targeting users or influencers while later stages will involve deciders and buyers.

ADVANCES IN ORGANISATIONAL BUYING

'Lean manufacturing' is a cost reducing method of production where savings can be made as a result of holding minimum amounts of stock (often for only a few hours). This means that storage of components and raw materials is eliminated and raw materials and component parts can be marshalled direct from the delivery point to the production line. Storage and stock control costs can be virtually eliminated, with transactions being concerned with logging in materials as they arrive and then despatching them to production. It is vital that goods are delivered exactly as specified, so the onus for quality control is on the supplier and not at the point of delivery.

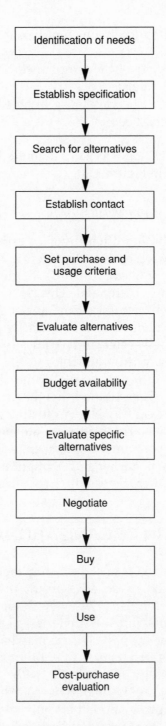

Figure 3.10 *Wind's organisational purchasing model*

Users	are those working with, or using the product including supervisors. In some purchasing circumstances they help to mould the product specification and in others their input is minimal.
Influencers	are those who might influence the product specification or who can affect the buying decision in other ways (eg accountants might influence purchasing budgets).
Deciders	are people with authority to make the purchasing decision. In most cases this will be the buyer, but for high value items it might be a team decision.
Gatekeepers	are personnel who control the flow of information to and from buyers (eg technical staff, secretarial staff who may arrange appointments for buyers, other purchasing personnel with whom potential suppliers might have to liaise prior to contacting other members of the DMU).
Buyers	are people with responsibility for signing orders and administering and progressing the order through to its final delivery. They sometimes assist in shaping the specification, but their main role is in supplier liaison and selection.

Figure 3.11 *The decision making usnit (DMU) or buying centre*

This situation has resulted in the establishment of long-term relationships between buying and selling organisations. In some cases buying organisations have taken a stake-holding in supplying companies to underline this long term commitment. This has led to the notion of 'relationship marketing' which views long-term relationships as being the norm where customer retention is as important as winning new customers.

In such situations, it is quite common for members of the purchasing team to visit their suppliers and these visits can involve design, financial, production and quality control personnel as well as purchasing staff. The traditionally held view is that sellers generally take the commercial initiative and visit buyers to conduct transactions. The new notion is that buyers take the initiative in sourcing new suppliers, who must measure up to their commercial and quality criteria. They also visit their long-term suppliers on a regular basis and contracts tend to be open-ended (ie for no specified amount, but with a 'wind-down' clause in case of termination). This is termed 'reverse marketing' and is illustrated in Figure 3.12.

Figure 3.12 *Reverse marketing*

It is acknowledged that just as consumer purchasers are amenable to marketing actions, organisational purchasers are also individuals. They are subject to marketing actions, but because purchasing is their profession, their judgement is more likely to be qualified and based upon more rational criteria than for consumer goods purchasers. However, organisational buyers are also susceptible to personal emotions, so the impression that the salesperson creates and the image that the sales company conveys are important in terms of generating a feeling of dependability and trustworthiness in the mind of the buyer.

The human element also extends to personal relationships, which the seller might have with people in the purchasing organisation. As we move towards 'relationship marketing', with its longer-term implications, it is important that a positive interface continues to develop. This has brought about a whole new concept of 'customer care', with its intricate attention to tactical detail, which is marketing's practical response to the notion of reverse marketing.

SUMMARY

This chapter has established that consumer and organisational purchasing are different in that each buying situation has dissimilar buying motives, although some common strands are evident. The main differences are in terms of purchasing motives, purchasing influences, authority to purchase, purchasing power and negotiation.

For consumer markets the principal form of communication is one of encouragement through the mass media and ensuring that the right channels of distribution are available for consumers to make purchases. For organisational markets the commercial transaction is accomplished at a more 'informed' level and is a routine task performed by professional buyers and sellers, although non-routine methods of approach are always being sought by marketers to gain a competitive advantage. The objective of organisational buying is to satisfy commercial needs, whereas for consumer purchasing psychological needs are very important.

Now that we have investigated the motives for purchasing, an important question concerns marketing planning to predict the needs of customers and being geared up to supply such needs. Marketing research and forecasting are the methods whereby such demand is estimated, and these are the subject topics of the next two chapters.

4

Marketing Information Systems

INTRODUCTION

Marketing is fundamentally about understanding customers. In a for profit situation, marketing is the range of commercial activities that identify the needs and wants of specific target markets and then produce goods and services that satisfy these more efficiently and effectively than the competition. It is sometimes said that information is the very life blood of successful marketing. It is of tremendous strategic value to marketers, as well as having importance in tactical and more routine operational decision making. An appreciation of what sort of information to amass and how to make best use of it is the key competence of strategic marketing.

Such material gives the firm a chance to gain competitive advantage over competitors. Armies win wars not always because they have superior armed force, but because of more effective intelligence gathering methods. Likewise marketing firms are carrying out commercial war in a free market competitive economy. They too will have an increased probability of winning if they have superior intelligence to their enemies. The military saying, know your opponent or know the mind of your enemy, can be used just as well in a commercial context. How can a firm expect to achieve a competitive advantage over its rivals if it knows little or nothing about what they are doing in the present and what they might be planning for the future? Knowledge is power and marketing is concerned with creating superior competitive power through the superior use of information.

THE NEED TO MANAGE INFORMATION

All aspects of information including its collection, storage, processing, retrieval and use must be managed. The marketing-oriented firm needs a system devoted to the management of the entire information needs of the organisation. Such a system is called a Marketing Information System (MkIS) of which research is a component part. This management process anticipates and delivers customer value more effectively and efficiently than the competition and, in a profit making organisation, does so at an acceptable level of profit. Note the word anticipate.

Many markets are dynamic rather than static and the only thing really certain about the future is that it will be different from today and marketing management needs to anticipate and stay ahead of these changes. Decision making at the strategic level requires some form of prediction or forecast of likely future conditions across a wide variety of areas. MkIS can be used to provide information for use in a wide range of decision areas although not all of these involve forecasting. However, it would be true to say of any information system or decision support system, that the end product is usually a decision about the future made in the present, often based largely on information about the past. This process by its very nature involves forecasting.

MARKETING INFORMATION SYSTEMS

The term system often summons up thoughts of computers in the minds of many people. They incorrectly feel it must be too complicated for their firm and requires a lot of technical skill to design, implement and manage. This is not the case at all, as we shall see later in this chapter. Such a system can be purely manual and the level of technical knowledge required to get a basic system up and running can be acquired by virtually everybody. Firms of all sizes and types are carrying out information audits in an attempt to design systems that will meet their information needs and give them a competitive advantage over the competition. Philip Kotler defines an MkIS as:

> ... consisting of people, equipment and procedures to gather, sort, analyse, evaluate and distribute needed, timely and accurate information to marketing decision makers.

A formal MkIS can be of great benefit to any organisation whether profit making or non profit making, no matter what its size or the level of managerial finesse. It is true today that in many organisations an MkIS is integrated as part of a computerised system. If no computing capability is available, the design and implementation of an MkIS is still possible and can be based entirely on a manual system of reference cards and files. It will lack the ease of storage and retrieval of a computer system, but some form of manual system is better than having nothing and leaving the management of information to destiny.

To manage a business well is to manage its future and this means the management of information in the form of a company wide Management Information System (MIS), of which the MkIS is an integral part. It is an indispensable resource to be carefully managed just like any other resource that the organisation may have, eg human resources, production, transport and finance. Marketing information is vital to the marketing effort and is far too important to be left to chance. Unfortunately in many organisations, particularly in small and medium sized enterprises (SMEs) information is not managed as well as it should be and many firms do not attach the same importance to the management of information as they do to the management of other areas of the firm, such as finance. Many firms see information handling, processing and storage as a cost, which can always be reduced as a first economy in times of economic downturn, rather than a investment in their future competitive position.

COMPONENT PARTS OF THE SYSTEM

When most lay people hear the term MkIS they tend to think of marketing research. Of course, formally produced marketing research information is valuable to all firms, but it is not the only form or source of marketing information and not necessarily always the most important. The information requirements of the modern firm go way beyond what can be gained by the application of formal marketing research. It needs to make competent use of this information in storing it, disseminating it, processing it and in its utilisation. The MkIS is a system that will assist marketing management conduct all of their necessary information duties in a systematic and planned way.

The concept of an integrated marketing information system is shown in Figure 4.1 with a brief explanation. Three of these four component parts or sub systems collect and produce information. The fourth sub system takes the information provided from the other three parts and processes it, models it and carries out other procedures on the data that adds and enhances its value to marketing decision makers.

Marketing Intelligence System

Marketing Research System

Decision Support System

MkIS

Internal Accounting System

Analytical Marketing System

Figure 4.1 *Marketing Information System (MkIS)*

The Internal Accounting System

All organisations produce information as part of the general process of conducting their business. Business forms and documentation are fairly standard within a particular country and reasonably similar throughout the world. In the UK ready made business forms and other commercial documentation can be purchased from any business stationers. For a small charge they will print the company's name, address, telephone, fax, e-mail and VAT registration number on the forms to customise them. The generation, recording, storage and retrieval of such data is referred to as the internal accounting system of the firm. The term refers to all information received and generated by the firm and not just financial information. Maybe a more accurate name for this system would be the internal documentary system as it reflects where the information is generated much more accurately.

Marketing firms need to fully realise that such information is obtainable and can be reaped from within the internal documentary system or internal accounting system of the firm with a little imagination and at limited cost. To be of value as a planning, monitoring and control tool, management needs to understand how to use this internally generated information in a commercially effective manner. The information comes in many different forms, for example, purchase orders are received by the marketing firm from customers and delivery notes are generated by the firm to be signed by the customer on delivery. The time between the dates on the two documents gives the total order processing time and can be continuously reviewed to ensure predetermined service delivery levels are being met by the firm.

When faulty products are returned to the marketing firm for whatever reason, a goods return slip is usually generated by the staff operating the warehouse. Again, this document can be used to monitor and measure quality performance of either internally manufactured goods or goods bought in from other suppliers. It is basically a tracking and control device and if used in an imaginative way can provide management with extremely valuable quality control information. The total number of goods returned or total number of complaints as a percentage of goods sold supplies marketing management with a measurable standard of performance.

Sales force expenses as a percentage of sales, the number of telephone enquiries converted into sales, orders for a given product or range of products and which might attest to seasonal or cyclical demand, are indicative of the uses to which internally produced and internally received information can be put for marketing planning, monitoring and control purposes. Unfortunately many firms, especially small and medium sized enterprises do not capitalise on the information that the business processes and procedures generate. A wealth of potentially valuable information lies literally and metaphorically under their nose. More imaginative use of this information could very well improve their competitive position, especially as small firms, in particular, need greater monitoring and control and access to cheap marketing information.

The Marketing Intelligence System

As we have seen from the previous section, firms produce a treasure of information internally through the very action of managing and administering their business. Apart from the official purpose for which such information was produced eg sending out invoices, auditing etc, it often remains a neglected marketing resource. There are other data sources that are under-utilised by marketing management. The type of information we are talking about here is not rigorously collected marketing research information, but that which is less formally collected, often in a very ad hoc fashion as and when it presents itself. The system that attempts to collect, collate and manage this source of loosely collected information is referred to as the Marketing Intelligence System. Professor Philip Kotler, an expert in the field, defines the marketing intelligence system in the following way:

> A Marketing Intelligence System is a set of procedures and sources used by managers to obtain their everyday information about pertinent developments in the marketing environment.

In the process of carrying out their management or general business functions for the firm, members of staff may come across potentially useful and commercially interesting information. Most of the time staff do nothing with it because there is no process within the firm for handling it. Some firms have suggestion boxes but that is about as far as it gets. The type of information we are referring to here has not been generated or collected in any special way. On the contrary it is the sort of information that many employees generate or come across every day as part of their regular job. In many firms such information is thought to be of little or no consequence and hence no one bothers to report it and it simply becomes a wasted resource. Often the people who might have access to such information may be of a lower working status within the firm and management may not think that what they have to say would be of use to the running of their company. However, they would be quite wrong. For example, lorry drivers, van delivery drivers, receptionists, engineering technicians, telephone switchboard staff and others all come in touch with suppliers and/or customers during the conduct of their job and all have the inherent capability to contribute to the marketing intelligence gathering function of the firm's MkIS.

A further example of an often under-utilised source of potentially valuable marketing intelligence data is the sales team. The use of sales personnel to collect and supply marketing intelligence is but one example of the type of information that can make up the firm's marketing intelligence system but it is indicative of the richness of marketing intelligence information that can be generated by staff. Sales professionals often possess a treasure of marketing intelligence assembled during the course of their sales activities, but only a relatively small number of firms make full commercial use of this potentially valuable, readily available, relatively inexpensive and important source of commercial marketing intelligence. Salespeople make it their business to network effectively with other salespeople within the industry; it is part of the salesperson's function. These networking interactions can often produce very valuable information. Obviously if information is given in confidence by a colleague or friend, no one would expect or desire the salesperson to betray a confidence. But general information obtained during attendance at conventions, exhibitions, training programmes and such like should be reported by sales staff if they think it has commercial strategic value to management.

Members of the sales team are active in the market-place every day as a matter of routine, after all that is basically what their job is all about. Their main occupation is to keep themselves well-versed in what is going on in terms of developments in the market, competitors' products, prices and concessions, in terms of customers and future customers and their future buying intentions. Salespeople attend conferences, conventions, courses, stands at trade shows and exhibitions, sponsored events and assist with hospitality. All of these expanded roles of the modern professional salesperson give rise to marketing intelligence gathering opportunities.

The Marketing Research System

This is the final input to the marketing information system and makes use of both primary data (data collected for a specific piece of research for the first time) and secondary data (data that are already in existence). Marketing research is the scientific method modern marketing firms use in order to build value in the minds of their target market. The primary objective of marketing research is to find, in a systematic way, reliable, unbiased answers to questions about the market for goods or services and to look at ideas and meaning on many issues. Marketing research is often concerned with the action of collecting, analysing and interpreting the material to try and establish what it is that people actually want and why they actually want it. The people themselves may not always be aware of their motives for desiring or purchasing particular goods and/or services. Many of the motivations for purchase are subconscious and take the skill of the trained consumer behaviourist working with the marketing researcher to establish. Marketing is the business process used by firms in order to create bundles of values or satisfactions in the form of products and services which their customers will purchase.

In the value creation process marketing firms try to at least meet, but preferably exceed, customer expectations for their products or services. To stay competitive marketing firms have to create consumer value more effectively and efficiently than other firms in the market. Firms that are customer focused and market driven in this way are considered to be marketing oriented firms. However value is somewhat subjective. What one person considers valuable in terms of the benefits possession of a particular product might yield, another might consider of no value at all. Value lies in the minds of individuals and groups of people. Value systems alter over time within people's minds. For example what is regarded as fashionable in terms of clothing or popular music might not be next year. What might have been regarded as unimportant say ten years ago may become more important a decade later. For example, green and climate issues were not something that moved the bulk of people twenty years ago, whereas in the late 1990s most people express some concern about such environmental issues. This concern is manifested in a wide range of products that claim to be safe for the environment, ethical or healthy.

Marketing research operations can be classified by their purpose or general objective. Some marketing research exercises are meant to produce results that are purely exploratory in character. Such research is quite often conducted at the start of the overall research project. Other research may produce data that are descriptive, predictive or conclusive in nature. Whatever the exact nature of the data, it is employed by marketing management in the planning, appraisal and control of marketing tactics and strategy. Research must be thoughtfully planned with a professional and systematic approach and a series of steps should be taken in the development, planning and execution of research.

In order to stay abreast of the changing tastes and changing value systems of consumers, the performance of the competition and important changes in the external business environment, the marketing orientated firm requires information. Long term marketing strategy and marketing plans at the more tactical and operational levels need information. Such information is the life blood of the marketing orientated firm. Without the right kind of information, effective marketing is impossible. Marketing research provides the firm with a wide range of useful information, but marketing research in isolation is insufficient at a strategic level; it must form an intrinsic part of the extended marketing information system.

The Analytical Marketing System

This sub system of the overall MkIS does not and is not intended to, produce any new data. Rather, it takes the data from the other three component parts of the system in the form of input data and enhances its value. Users of the system are able to do this by applying what might be termed management science techniques to the data, thereby transforming it into a form that makes it more easily understood and more valuable to the marketing decision maker. The techniques applied to the data by the marketing management scientist are usually statistical in nature and many computer packages such as the Statistical Package for the Social Sciences (SPSS) are commercially available and can conduct very sophisticated analysis.

For example, information collected from formal marketing research, marketing intelligence and the gathering of internally generated information can be used as input data in a wide range of sales forecasting models. Data collected over a period of time can be extrapolated on to the future by the use of time series techniques. The use of such techniques also allows the manager to model seasonality and cyclicality effects. Trend fitting, using the mathematical functions of known curves can also be used to forecast sales and model likely future product life cycles. Linear and multiple regression are more sophisticated forecasting techniques which make use of econometric procedures. This is but one such example. Analytical techniques such as Chi Square, Analysis of Variance, Conjoint Analysis are available as well as a range of descriptive statistics and graphical presentation methods.

COST–BENEFIT ASPECTS OF MkIS

Marketing information systems and sales forecasting have been discussed in the last section and it has been shown that in a practical, pro-active marketing firm the acquisition and management of information cannot be left to chance. What is required is a type of formal system devoted to the entire information needs of the organisation. Ideally an MkIS will have been thoughtfully designed to yield information which is relevant, pertinent and useful to the users of the system in terms of assisting them in improving their marketing decision making. In fact the entire rationale for a firm adopting a rigorously designed MkIS is that the system assists members of the marketing team to make improved decisions, or enables them to make decisions faster and more efficiently. Management do not want to go to the time, expense and trouble involved in designing and implementing an MkIS just to make the firm look as if it is up to date in adopting the latest marketing ideas. They want the system to generate a financial return. Like any other resource, information has to pay its way. If it does not yield any commercial benefits then it is not worth the cost involved.

Information, just like any other product has a marginal cost and a marginal value. Theoretically the marketing firm should continue to collect and store information up to the point where the marginal cost of information equals the marginal value. This is similar to the economists' concept of profit maximisation. The firm continues to collect additional information as long as it yields a positive return, that is the benefits are greater than the costs of collection. Marginal analysis is difficult to carry out in practice with something like information because the cost and revenue functions of information are difficult if not impossible to calculate. However, there are advanced techniques available based on Bayesian decision making models utilising subjective probabilities. A full treatment of such techniques is beyond the scope of this text, but readers should at least be aware of their existence. A diagrammatic illustration to the marginal approach to determining the amount of information to collect is given below in Figure 4.2.

MARKETING RESEARCH

Introduction

Without the information that marketing research supplies, management cannot hope to employ the marketing concept as a principal business philosophy. It is not the intent to give a comprehensive account of marketing research in this section and indeed it would take an entire textbook to do so. The objective of this material is frankly to give you a feel for the subject and describe how it fits into contemporary marketing practice. The object is to give an

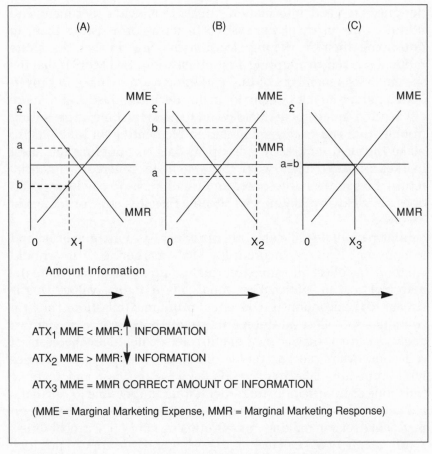

Figure 4.2 *A marginal approach to determining the amount of information*

adequate, but general view of a number of topics without going into detailed methodological technicalities. On an understandable definitions point, there is sometimes puzzlement about the term marketing research which is the overall descriptor, and market research which is a sub-set of marketing research. The term market research is often used to describe research into a particular market, the market for machine tools for example. Marketing research on the other hand describes all forms of research relating to marketing.

The marketing concept states that the character of the marketing orientated organisation, whether product or service based, profit or non profit based, is the identification and true delivery of consumers' needs and wants, more effectively and efficiently than the competition. The marketing concept has been determined as the key to achieving organisational goals and the marketing concept is based on market focus, customer orientation, co-ordinated marketing and profitability. In a profit making business the firm of course has to endeavour to carry through this level of customer satisfaction as a process of staying ahead of the competition and creating a profit. In a not for profit organisation, management substitutes profit for some other criterion such as highest social benefits; a political party would be inclined to substitute maximising votes for financial profit. A university on the other hand may substitute research excellence for purely financial profit. In order for organisations to be able to organise their assets and resources in such a manner that they are able to deliver bundles of satisfactions that satisfy the authentic desires of specifically determined target markets better than the commercial opposition, they are required to appreciate what the market considers as valuable. The concept of value is subjective and lies in the mind of the particular prospective customer. Hence, in a broad sense, marketing management needs to understand the minds of their target markets, their attitudes, feelings, beliefs and value systems. They require a formalised, managerial approach to this most important job. This is the basic role and purpose of formal marketing research.

Definition of marketing research

The American Marketing Association (AMA, 1961) defines marketing research as the systematic gathering, recording and analysing of data relating to the marketing of goods and services. Professor Philip Kotler (1994), a world renowned expert on marketing issues, defines marketing research as systematic problem analysis, model-building and fact-finding for the purpose of improved decision making and control in the marketing of goods and services. The stress is precisely on the improvement in marketing decision making. Marketing research is the scientific approach to building value in the eyes of the organisation's target market. The aim of research is to find, in a systematic way, reliable, impartial answers to the firm's inquiry about the market for goods or services and to look at consumers' ideas and intentions on many issues. Marketing research is often concerned with the process of collecting, analysing and deciphering the facts to establish what it is that people want and why they want it, ie what the market considers to be valuable and hence worth paying money for. Marketing research is employed by marketing management in the planning , evaluation and control of marketing tactics and strategy, but it is also of use in helping to make policy decisions in the non-commercial public sector. The present Labour Party in the UK makes full use of focus groups and many other forms of what might be called marketing research techniques. Whatever the end use research must be carefully planned, with a disciplined and systematic approach and a series of steps need to be taken in the development, planning and execution of research.

TYPES OF MARKETING RESEARCH

Marketing research activities can be classified by their general objective. Remember, the term marketing research, unlike the term market research, refers to all research activities related to marketing. Different types of marketing research are used for obtaining different types of data or helping to solve different types of problems. Certain marketing research activities are designed to produce results that are altogether exploratory in character. Such research is generally carried out at the start of the overall research scheme. Other research can produce data that are descriptive, predictive or conclusive in nature. These general classifications are now considered in more detail.

Exploratory research

Exploratory research lays down the foundations enabling the rest of the research exercise to be built soundly. When a builder builds a house he or she spends a great deal of time getting the foundations right first. If this is not done properly the building is likely to suffer from many problems such as subsidence or similar defects. To get the finished job right a lot of preparation work has to be done first. The same principle of building good foundations applies to marketing research and it is exploratory research that is used to do this. This type of research is most often conducted in the initial stages of the overall research process. Unless researchers have knowledge of a specific industry or research area within a particular industry, they will have to accustom themselves with the general characteristics of that industry or research area in order for them to make a competent job of conducting the main body of the research. Exploratory research is fundamentally a 'what is it all about' type of operation. It is not designed to provide the means to the researcher to draw solid conclusions about the research situation, rather to empower him or her to form the general characteristics and limits of the research situation.

The use of secondary data, ie those data that are already in being, usually in printed form or on some kind of computerised data retrieval system, is a significant part of the exploratory process. In terms of primary data collection, ie those data that are collected for the first time specifically for a particular research exercise, qualitative research methods are more often used than quantitative methods. Depth interviews and group discussions permit the researcher to explore respondents' feelings and attitudes on a wide variety of topics. Both of these interviewing techniques use small samples and hence by their very nature can only hope to supply general exploratory data. Nevertheless, information resulting from qualitative exploratory research helps the market researcher to design a more effective research schedule than would be the case if the exploratory stage were not used. Returning to the building analogy, any job requires a certain amount of planning and preparation if it is to be done well, whether it is painting and decorating, building a house or indeed, marketing research. One should always be suspicious of any research work produced without the aid of any exploratory work whatsoever.

Descriptive research

When the researcher has carried out the exploratory stage of the research process and determined the current parameters in terms of market size, main segments, main competitors, etc, they may then progress to types of research of a more predictive and/or conclusive type. All kinds of research data needs describing in a way that users can understand. This is true of exploratory, predictive and conclusive research. As the name suggests descriptive research carries out this role. Descriptive research often utilises descriptive statistics to help the user comprehend the structure of the data and any significant patterns that may be found in the data. All measures of central tendency such as the mean, median and mode are often used along with measures of dispersion such as the variance and standard deviation. Descriptive research results are often presented using pictorial methods such as graphs, pie charts, histograms, etc as these formats are easier for the non-research specialist to understand. Such pictorial or graphical techniques are very similar to the ones that you may have seen on television during a general election. The television presenter tries to communicate often complex data, usually statistics, in a way ordinary viewers can grasp. Pictures, charts and graphs are often used to try and achieve this with varying degrees of success. This type of research is intended to describe certain factors that marketing management is possibly interested in such as market conditions, customers' feelings or opinions toward a particular company, purchasing behaviour and so forth. Such research is not intended to allow the researcher to establish causal relationships between marketing variables and sales or consumer behaviour, or to enable the researcher to predict likely future conditions. Descriptive research merely examines what is. Such research, just like exploratory research, usually forms part of an on-going research programme.

Predictive research

The role of predictive research, as the name suggests, is to enable the marketing researcher to predict something about future market conditions such as market growth or decline, increased competition, greater import penetration in a particular market, future price levels or changes in consumer taste, to name but a few examples. Many marketing research techniques can be used to produce information that might be useful to the researcher in predicting such conditions. When using qualitative research such as depth interviews or group discussions, the researcher can interview individual salespeople or experts in the industry. Group interviews can be conducted in order to produce a consensus as to what might occur within a particular market in the future. Opinions can be elicited from respondents for different time periods, for example the next few months, next year, next five years. Similarly, questionnaire surveys can be used to elicit responses. For example, the sales force could be surveyed and asked for their opinion concerning future sales or market conditions. Results are aggregated to produce nationwide forecasts and disaggregated to provide forecasts for individual sales territories. Results can also be disaggregated by product, size, colour, market segment and even individual customers. Such a method is known as the sales force composite technique. A survey of buyers' intentions is a useful method of securing sales forecasting data. Formal statistical and mathematical techniques specifically developed for forecasting exercises can also be used to process the data from interviews and surveys. Secondary data acquired from existing sources can also provide the researcher with useful input data for forecasting.

Conclusive research

Conclusive research goes further than merely describing a situation or predicting future conditions, although conclusive research does have a predictive element as well. It is used in order to establish causality of a particular phenomenon which in a marketing context is usually sales or some form of buyer behaviour. When using conclusive research techniques the researcher is striving to establish causal relationships between marketing variables such as price, advertising or packaging to some other variable such as sales or patterns of consumption. In order to accomplish this kind of test it is essential to employ a formal experimental design in order to be able to test a specific hypothesis.

For example, presume the area sales manager desired to verify which set of merchandising materials, price promotion and shelf configuration would be most effective in delivering sales within a multiple grocery store chain. Assume that there were four different configurations of each of the marketing variables, eg four merchandising sets, four price promotions that could be applied in store and four different shelf configurations. The researcher needs to establish which permutation of these three marketing variables is the best and designs an experiment in which each permutation of experimental treatments is randomly allocated to retail stores. Differences between stores will be accounted for in the experiment using statistical techniques such as weighting. The experiment will be permitted to run until adequate data has been produced. The results are then analysed using statistical techniques and used to see if the hypothesis that one set of experimental treatments has been more effective in generating sales than the others was in fact true or false. Statistically designed experimental methods such as Analysis of Variance (ANOVA) or Chi Square might be utilised in such an experiment. These techniques are available on a number of computer data analysis packages such as the Statistical Package for the Social Sciences (SPSS), discussed previously.

All experimental treatments which allow the researcher to establish causation in tests have a number of factors in common. The researcher starts with the marketing variables which are to be tested; these are known as the independent variables. These variables are then applied to a given situation and certain effects are monitored. These effects are usually sales, but might be something else such as behavioural changes of some kind, eg store loyalty, and are regarded as dependent variables because they are dependent on the marketing variables discussed earlier. Experiments are used to establish scientifically, using statistical tests, whether the effects witnessed in the dependent variables are in fact the result of changes in the independent variables (ie the marketing variables) and if so what the characteristics and magnitude of these effects are. The marketing researcher wishes to establish whether the experimental effects caused by the independent variables acting upon the dependent variables are in any way commercially important and if so how the firm can make use of the results to improve its competitive position.

STAGES IN THE RESEARCH PROCESS

Marketing research is an organised formal approach to the collection of marketing information and the overall marketing research process has a number of distinct stages. These are briefly discussed below.

1. Problem definition

Problem definition, which leads on to an initial proclamation of research goals to provide information of a certain type and in a certain amount, making this stage an identification of information requirements which may include:

▣ market size, structure and performance;
▣ market segments, growth, market potential;
▣ competitive forces and competitive behaviour;
▣ international aspects and future opportunities, imports, exports;
▣ demographic, socio-economic etc;
▣ knowledge, facts, behaviour, actions;
▣ attitudes, opinions and values;
▣ evaluations, attitudes, intentions;
▣ satisfaction levels, service requirements;

▓ sales impact and effects;
▓ communication effects and efficiency.

The above list is not exhaustive but does illustrate the diverse types of information that might be required in a marketing research exercise. The problem definition stage, as the name suggests, tries to establish what the research goals should be. They are usually fairly tentative because further exploratory research might highlight previously unknown requirements. It is not uncommon for details to be altered in the light of exploratory research. However, the broad research direction and objectives can usually be established at this stage. This is done by consultation between the researcher and the person or people commissioning the research, who might be from within the organisation, as a sort of internal customer, or from outside. Those commissioning the research will provide a research brief after initial consultation and this is used to make a detailed research proposal. When this is agreed upon the researcher has a mandate to carry out the research as per the agreed proposal. If the research provider is from an outside agency agreement of the research proposal usually results in a legally binding commercial contract being signed by both parties.

2. Review of secondary data sources

Secondary data sources are legion, the following list gives some examples:

▓ company records, reports, previous research;
▓ trade associations, government agencies, research organisations;
▓ advertising/market research agencies;
▓ books, periodicals, theses, statistics, conference proceedings, etc;
▓ quality financial press and business journals;
▓ competitors' product brochures and price lists, advertisements etc.

General speaking secondary data is cheaper to collect than generating primary original data specifically for your particular research exercise. The general rule is to exhaust all sources of secondary data that might be useful before embarking on a programme of primary data collection, otherwise you might be wasting both time and money duplicating material that is already available and in the public domain.

The problem with secondary data is that it is rarely exactly what is wanted and some adjustment to the data usually has to be made to make it fit specific research requirements. It is often out of date and so some indexing or extrapolation of figures may be necessary. However, it is generally available in university and other public libraries and provides a cost efficient source of marketing research information.

3. Select the research approach for collection of new/primary information

The collection of primary data is usually carried out using one or a combination of the following methods:

■ experimentation, laboratory based experiments or field studies such as a test market;
■ observational studies including the use of consumer panels and retail audits;
■ surveys – mail, telephone, personal, e-mail, fax, post;
■ motivational research techniques – depth interviewing, group interviewing, projective techniques.

Which methods are used obviously depends on the research situation at hand and the specific type of data required. The majority of research exercises use more than one technique. If you approach a problem from more than one angle and end up with similar results you can expect to have more confidence in the validity of the results, because whichever way you have examined the problem you see more or less the same pattern or phenomenon. Taking a multi-method approach to conducting research is sometimes referred to as triangulation, which means looking at the research problem using three different approaches or vantage points. Even if more than three approaches are used the term triangulation still seems to be used.

4. Determine details of research design

This is concerned with who is going to be contacted, how many people or firms are going to be contacted and how they are to be selected. The selection of households, firms or individual respondents falls under the heading of sampling. There are many sampling designs available to the researcher and they basically fall into two categories:

1. *Probability sampling* involves selection using some form of random selection device such as computer-generated random numbers. This type of sampling is regarded as scientific and adheres to the general principles of probability. It allows the application of a wide range of statistical tests which themselves require the data to have been collected using probability or random selection methods.
2. *Non probability sampling* is subjective and pragmatic. It does not use random selection right the way through the sampling procedure and in parts uses subjective human judgement. Statistical purists criticise this kind of sampling as unscientific, but in fact researchers like it because it is cheap and administratively convenient and many also claim that it gives an acceptable approximation to a random sample. This stage is not only concerned with sampling, although this is a major consideration here. All aspects of research design including the selection and training of interviewers, timing of the field work, the setting up of depth interview schedules, the type of analysis to be carried out on the data all have to be considered and planned for here.

5. Data collection

The data collection stage is, as the name suggests, everything to do with the process of going out into the field and obtaining marketing research data. It will involve conducting in-depth interviews to obtain qualitative data, including recruiting people to attend group discussions as well as organising the venue. Instructing, transporting, monitoring and controlling the interviewing field force is also an important job and also necessitates the hiring and training of field supervisors, usually freelance researchers with many years' experience of working in the field.

▓ If observational research is used it might mean the commissioning of retail audit and consumer panel services or the organising and transportation of cameras, tape recorders or other mechanical devices.

▓ If marketing experimentation is employed to obtain data then laboratory facilities may be required. Town halls may have to be hired in order to conduct hall tests in the testing and evaluation of product prototypes.

▓ A full text market may be needed and will take an incredible amount of work, from commissioning of advertising to setting up control areas and monitoring the results of the test.

Whatever method or combination of methods are used in the collection of primary data you can see by the examples given here that they all require a lot of administration, time and effort. Nothing must be left to chance. Once the data has been collected it has to be sent to the researchers' headquarters for the next stage in the marketing research process, the data analysis stage.

6. Analysis and interpretation of data

Raw data in itself is not useful to the practical marketing manager who is expected to make plans and draw up effective marketing strategies. As we have stated earlier in the chapter, information is the very life blood of successful marketing. As true as this statement might be the information is no good unless it is in a form that management can understand so it can be used profitably.

Analysis of data starts with the examination of secondary data and the extraction of salient facts and figures. This part of data analysis is usually carried out prior to the collection of primary data, after all there is little point collecting primary data on an area where you already have adequate secondary data.

Primary data will fall into two broad general categories, qualitative data and quantitative data:

▓ Qualitative data will be derived from qualitative research such as depth interviews and group discussions. A transcript or at least a tape recording is produced so the researcher can carry out a content analysis of the interviews. Computer programmes are available which claim to be able to analyse qualitative interviews as long as the interview transcript is scanned into a computer data file for reading.

▓ Observational data can be examined by looking at films, photographs or examining figures resulting from retail audits or consumer panels, both a type of observational research. Data from questionnaires is again usually fed into a data analysis package via an acceptable data file. The Statistical Package for the Social Sciences (SPSS for Windows) is widely used in universities. Most business and social science students doing their PhDs analyse their data using SPSS. Other more commercially orientated packages go under the names of SNAP and Marquis. The Marketing Research Society in London can supply details of such packages.

7. Evaluation of results and recommendations

Once the data, both qualitative and quantitative, has been analysed and interpreted for its statistical meaning and significance, the marketing implications of the findings will have to be established and firm recommendations for future marketing actions formulated. As we said earlier, data in itself is of little use. It only becomes valuable to the marketing manager if it can be translated into firm guidelines for action and long term strategy. Whether the data is used for strategic or tactical and operational decision making will depend on the time frame used in the data collection, for example were questions relating to the long term, medium term or short term?

TOOLS OF MARKETING RESEARCH

Motivational research techniques

The aim here is to uncover underlying motives, desires and emotions of consumers that influence behaviour. These techniques often penetrate below the level of the conscious mind and there are two approaches: the psycho-sociological approach which relies on the group behaviour of consumers and the impact of culture and environment on their opinions and reactions and the psychoanalytical approach which relies on information drawn from individual respondents in depth interviews and projective tests.

Techniques used include:

1. Depth interviewing and observational methods. Topics for discussion are chosen by the interviewer and indirect questioning leads the respondent to free expression of motives, attitudes, opinions, experiences and habits in relation to adverts, products, brands, services, etc. Depth interviewing is based on the psychoanalytical principle of free association interviewing.

The interview is not intended to be a formal question and answer session using a structured questionnaire, which would merely be the administering of a questionnaire by personal interview. A depth interview is intended to be something far more subtle and sophisticated and falls under the heading of qualitative research. It is concerned with collecting information on beliefs, attitudes and opinions rather than quantitative information that might more readily lend itself to statistical analysis. Depth interviews usually involve small samples. They are expensive and time consuming. Although the interview may only take an hour or so to actually conduct, the researcher will take much longer than this in preparation, making the appointment, listening to tapes and making transcripts and analysing the information.

2. Focus groups or group discussions are where the interviewer stimulates and moderates group discussion. In this method freedom of expression and interaction between individuals are encouraged.

3. Sensitivity panels are a form of group discussion or focus group where respondents are trained to take part in such groups and the members of the group are used again and again for different research subjects such as different products or packages, advertisements etc.

Surveys (using questionnaires)

This is the most commonly used method of data collection which can be conducted by mail, telephone or personal interview. Questionnaires can be self-administered or used in an interview situation, depending on:

■ cost;
■ timing;
■ type of information needed;
■ amount of information needed;
■ ease of questioning;
■ accuracy required.

The practicability of any survey by questionnaire is best checked by a pilot study. To check the questionnaire:

1. Use a non-probability purposive sample as it is not intended to

use the results in the final data set. At this stage we are only testing the design of the questionnaire, whether it is of a suitable length, ordering of questions, whether the questions are easily understood, etc.

2. Pilot testing should involve the best trained and most experienced staff because it is important to get the questionnaire right as the success of the entire survey depends on it. It is possible that a number of versions of the questionnaire will need to be tested first. The last pre-test should use the final approved questionnaire.

QUESTIONNAIRE DESIGN

The information collected must be accurate, so the design of a questionnaire is of great importance. It should consist of questions that have the same meaning, a single meaning and the intended meaning to everyone. Questions should be numbered and have instructions to the investigator concerning the conduct of the interview in bold face, capital letters and underlined. Answer codes should be as near to the right-hand side as possible and lines drawn at suitable intervals can bring clarity to the design.

The types of questions most commonly used are as follows:

1. **Open-ended questions** give the informant a hint of what answer might be expected. A question which begins 'What do you think of...?' will bring forth large amounts of data which cannot always be satisfactorily summarised, but this type of question is useful in the pilot stage to show the range of likely answers.
2. **Unaided recall questions** do not mention the nature of the answer material and avoid asking leading questions, eg 'How did you travel to the station to catch this train?'.
3. **Dichotomous questions** offer two choices of answer, usually yes and no.
4. **Multiple-choice questions (cafeteria questions)** offer a graduated range of possible answers, listed in order from one extreme to the other.
5. **Thermometer questions** ask informants to rate their feelings on a numerical scale, eg 0–10. This type of question seeks to minimise the disadvantage of discrete classification in the multiple-choice type question.

6. **Checklists** are a standard way of prompting the memory of a respondent without being biased by the interviewer. However, brand leaders may be selected more frequently because of the weight of advertising.

There are a number of basic questions which should be asked about any questionnaire:

▧ Will the answers be in a format that will allow checking against established data?
▧ Is each question unambiguous – will both the researcher and the informant have the same understanding of the question?
▧ Are the questions ones which will elicit the answers required to help solve the research problem?
▧ Is each question clearly worded?
▧ Will the answers to each question be in a form in which they can be cross-tabulated against other data on the same or other questionnaires?
▧ Does it contravene any of the principles of question design?
▧ Is each question concerned with one factor only so as not to be confusing?
▧ Are all the possible answers catered for in the coding?
▧ Are the recording procedures foolproof?

Questionnaire design is a skill that comes with many years of practice. Even the professionals make mistakes and produce questionnaires that do not work properly. The first draft of a questionnaire usually results from the researcher studying the secondary data available and after exploratory depth interviews and/or group discussions have been conducted.

One aspect of questionnaire that is absolutely vital is pilot testing. A good questionnaire has usually evolved and may in fact be the fourth or fifth version. Pilot testing massively reduces the probability that a poorly designed questionnaire will be allowed through to the actual field work exercise. The following are some of the main points a researcher should consider when designing a questionnaire:

▧ Avoid questions or words with an emotional bias.
▧ Use understandable words that are customary to everyone (ie shop not outlet, shopkeeper not retailer).
▧ Keep questions short and to the point.

■ Do not ask double-barrelled questions (eg 'Have you a refriger-
ator and/or freezer?').
■ Do not ask leading questions (eg 'Do you buy frozen meals
because it is the fastest way to prepare food in the evening?').
■ Do not mention brand names (eg 'Do you consider Nescafe to
be the best coffee?').
■ Do not ask questions which may offend (eg 'Are you employed
or on the dole?').
■ Avoid using catch phrases or colloquialisms.
■ Avoid words which are confusing in their meanings (eg 'Do you
read a newspaper regularly?').

The above list is not intended to be exhaustive but is merely indicative of some of the major pitfalls in questionnaire design. Good
design still requires a lot of practice and of course extensive pilot
testing of the questionnaire is still necessary.

MARKETING EXPERIMENTS

Marketing experiments are one of the four main groupings of
research methods that marketing researchers use in the collection
of primary information for a specific research programme. The
other three classes of techniques as we have seen are:

1. interviews, such as depth interviews and group discussions;
2. observation, such as retail audits and consumer panels;
3. surveys, such as a postal questionnaire or telephone surveys.

Marketing experiments are in principle the same as any other
experiment in the sciences and the social sciences. They are based
on the general principles of scientific method and use the statistical
technique of hypothesis testing. A hypothesis is put forward and
tested by collecting information and rigorously analysing it,
usually using standard statistical techniques, to see whether the
hypothesis can be statistically supported or whether it should be
rejected.

An experiment is a way of collecting primary data in which the
researcher is able to establish cause and effect amongst the
variables being experimentally tested. It can be conducted in an
artificial laboratory type setting or as a field experiment, the best
example of which is the test market where researchers choose a

representative geographical area or one where they can statistically adjust data to make them representative of a wider market area. The test market is a model of the total market.

Test markets can be very costly, but being a field experiment they have the advantage of the test being close to real world conditions or true to life (external validity) over laboratory experiments. Another experimental technique involves surveying a small sample of consumers and showing them pictures or samples of products and ascertaining their preference as if they were really shopping. Such a test simulates as closely as possible real world conditions. Other techniques include extended user tests, blind and simple placement tests. In addition, there are certain techniques used in the pre- and post-testing of advertising themes and copy.

OBSERVATIONAL TECHNIQUES

The consumer panel is a domestic home audit in which an extensive range of households are continuously monitored as to their buying behaviour. Respondents are from a range of different socio-economic groups reflecting the socio-economic structure of the country as a whole. Family size and stage in the family life cycle are also matched with the national profile. Respondents are chosen using subjective interlocking quota sampling, for example if 12 per cent of the population are married, have no children, are under 30 years of age and live in a mortgaged semi-detached house in a rural area, then 12 per cent of the quota sample will do likewise. Respondents record their purchases using a mini computer supplied by the consumer panel company, for example, Audits of Great Britain Ltd, or Neilson Ltd, which has a special bar code reader similar to those used in modern supermarket checkouts and they then send the data to the research company's headquarters using a telephone coupler or modem.

At times it is only possible to collect the type of information required by observational techniques. This could take the form of humans observing humans, humans observing objects (eg the type of house people live in), electro-mechanical devices such as video cameras or tape recorders observing inanimate objects or people. Retail audits and consumer panels in which stock checks or audits are carried out by researchers in retail stores or people's houses, are also categorised as observational techniques. Retail audit firms such as Neilson Ltd, carry out store audits in an extensive range of retail outlets every month.

Product managers and other interested parties such as the marketing manager, can purchase the retail sales information and other related data on a continuous or on-going basis month by month. Other related data on competitors' products and marketing activities in-store, such as merchandising, pricing, promotional activity, shelf space etc is also made available at extra cost. Staff from the retail audit firm visit the client firm every month and personally present the data, explain its significance and submit an illustrated report for future reference. In the retail audit most stores use electronic point of sale (EPOS) and again can transmit retail sales data down the telephone line to the auditing company. Smaller stores that do not have the technology still have to be audited manually.

Observational techniques are an important source of primary data and this method is often used in conjunction with other research methods. It provides the marketing firm with an on-going source of continuous data that enables them to construct a time series of data. It is analogous to a moving picture of conditions, whereas an on–off ad hoc survey is more like a still picture.

MAIN RESEARCH AREAS

Product research

This area of marketing research encompasses all aspects of design, development and testing of new products, as well as the improvement and modification of existing products. New product development is a minefield of potential problems and the fact is that the majority of new product ideas are unsuccessful. They do not arrive in the shops because they have been screened out of the system earlier on in their development. Occasionally a new product hits the market and fails, costing the manufacturer a great deal of money and loss of commercial prestige. Hence product research is vital not only in the development of new product concepts and ideas but also to reduce the risk of bad product ideas reaching the market only to become an embarrassment and an expensive failure.

Product research, as the name suggests, is concerned with all aspects of the product and/or service. The specific range of activities falling into this category of research is legion and includes the following (this list is not intended to be exhaustive but indicative of the type of research areas included under this heading):

▓ comparative testing against competitive products;
▓ test marketing under real market conditions;
▓ concept testing and development;
▓ idea generation and screening of ideas;
▓ product elimination/simplification;
▓ brand positioning and re-positioning;
▓ product enhancement and improvement.

Brand positioning is particularly important when one considers modern day competitive pressures. It is one of the most crucial areas because no matter how technically good a product may be, it is likely to be unsuccessful if it is badly positioned.

Pricing research

Price is an intrinsic part of the product or service concept and not something that should be worked out by management as an after-thought. Getting the price right, especially in the case of new prod-ucts, can mean the difference between success and failure. Price has a strong psychological dimension to it and should not be arrived at using some simplistic cost plus pricing formula.

The right price for the product or service needs to be established before it is developed, as part of the research going on in the new product development process. If the business analysis discovers that no adequate level of profit can be secured from the market at the price that marketing research has established that the market is prepared to pay, then the development of the product should be stopped. After all, anyone can give a product or service away, it is producing them and marketing them at a profit that is the key to business success.

Hence pricing research is absolutely paramount to the marketing oriented firm. The philosophy of marketing states that firms are driven by customers and what they want. This includes the price. It is little use producing good products set at a price few will buy at. However, it is not simply a case that the product or service might be priced too high. Price can also be set too low for market expectations. There is a strong correlation between the price of many products and services and consumers' perception of quality, this is known as the price/quality relationship. Put in a simple way, for some products it might be a case of if it is so good, then why is it so cheap? Price conveys meaning, it says something about the product or service whether we are talking about an airline, a hotel or a bottle of wine. In a sense, price can be viewed as part of the product itself and a strong communication tool. Price contributes extensively to the brand image of a product or service.

Most of the general marketing research techniques discussed earlier in this chapter can be used in pricing research including qualitative depth interviews and group discussions and questionnaire based surveys. Marketing experimentation, both in a laboratory and test market setting can be used to test the commercial acceptance of a given level of price. Some marketing research techniques have been developed especially for pricing studies by university researchers for academic research and have been modified or adapted for commercial use. One method is termed the buy-response model and uses statistical techniques based around the plotting of acceptable price levels on a graph. The information is obtained from respondents who are shown products or pictures of products and then questioned. Pricing research can be used to undertake investigations into the following areas. Once again the list is not exhaustive but serves as an example as to the type of research areas falling within the remit of pricing research:

■ find out what kind of price consumers associate with different product variations (eg packaging);
■ establish market segments in relation to price;
■ establish price elasticity of demand;
■ identify the extent of price/quality relationship;
■ investigate the promotional aspects of price;
■ establish appropriate price discounts for bulk purchases;
■ assist in establishing a more market-orientated pricing strategy;
■ establish competitive response to alterations in price.

As you can see from the above, price has an impact on many facets of marketing including promotion, quality, competitive response, market segmentation, demand stimulation as well as other aspects.

Distribution research

Distribution research is concerned with two separate but interrelated facets of the subject – logistics (physical distribution) and channels of distribution. New developments in the area of logistics can be continually observed and to a certain extent forecast using marketing research techniques. For example, the idea of just in time delivery systems, used by an increasing number of firms, originated in Japan. This is a new business method that could have been predicted long before it became established outside Japan, by continuous monitoring of the external business environment using established marketing research methods. Transport technology and materials handling is ceaselessly undergoing change, with effects on the logistics industry particularly transport. Computer technology has now made tracking systems accessible so that clientele can exactly locate where their order or delivery is in the order processing system.

In terms of channels of distribution, marketers are constantly trying to secure a competitive advantage by using innovative, creative and more effective methods. Channels of distribution are changing and evolving over time and new channel formats are being developed. For example, the Internet now holds out a lot of promise as a shopping medium particularly for financial services like insurance, mortgages and personal banking. The commercial use of the Internet is growing at a phenomenal rate, something approaching 40 per cent per month worldwide.

Other types of no shop shopping are also growing in popularity, such as the use of mail order tied in with the large growth in direct mail. Television shopping is very prevalent in the United States and is increasing in use elsewhere in the world, especially in the developed economies. Other retail formats have grown to become increasingly salient, such as out of town shopping complexes. Marketing research has a valuable part to play in evaluating the efficiency of existing channels and predicting probable future retail innovations in terms of the distribution formats likely to be used in the years ahead and the technology used within them.

Techniques such as the retail audit can monitor the efficiency of different types of distribution channels and detect any regional variation. They can establish which channels are in comparative decline in terms of their efficiency in retailing certain products. They can also establish which channels are most likely to go through significant development in the future and a growth in acceptance and use. For example, the shopping areas within petrol service stations or garages have increased significantly in the last 20 years in terms of the amount of business carried out, the range of products available and particularly in terms of the growth of products and services coming on stream. Qualitative research such as depth interviews and group discussions, as well as larger scale sample surveys using questionnaires can be employed in the appraisal of existing channel efficiency and in predicting likely future directions and advances.

Marketing communications research

Marketing communications research is concerned with the analysis and evaluation of each aspect of the integrated marketing communications mix. This includes:

▓ telephone marketing;
▓ trade journals;
▓ evaluation of below the line sales promotions;
▓ sponsorship appraisal;
▓ evaluation of direct mail;
▓ exhibitions;
▓ personal selling;
▓ corporate communications;
▓ communication on the Internet;
▓ advertising research and many other facets of marketing communications including the use of marketing communications within the firm eg internal public relations and internal marketing in general.

To begin with a firm will need to research the attributes of customers or potential customers for their product or service. These customers may form distinct sectors or market segments. In terms of marketing communications planning these represent the target audiences for any future campaigns. Once the target audiences have been established it is necessary to define the most effective medium or media to use to send a marketing message to these audiences. What television programmes are the target audiences most likely to watch? What newspapers, magazines, journals or commercial radio programmes will have the most impact in communicating the desired message? Marketing communications involves business to business communication as well as communicating with domestic consumers. Many consumer goods are marketed using middlemen such as wholesalers or other marketing intermediaries and the people in these independent firms also need communicating to effectively.

In business to business communications, personal selling is very important and is the main marketing communication tool. In many industrial firms up to 95 per cent of the overall marketing budget is used in support of the personal selling function. This includes things such as sales support, cost of salespersons' vehicles, training and other expenses. Sponsorship, telephone marketing, trade exhibitions, direct mail, transport livery, corporate workwear and trade journals are all significant business to business marketing communication tools.

Marketing research thus has a very important role at every stage of the communications process; establishing target audiences, choosing the most effective communication media, designing the message and appraising how efficiently the message has been received by the target audience and with what impact.

SUMMARY

Marketing is the commercial process in which organisations strive to create bundles of values or satisfactions in the form of products and services which their customers willingly buy. In the value generation process marketing firms attempt to at least meet, but preferably exceed, customer expectations in terms of value perception. To remain competitive marketing firms have to create customer value more effectively and efficiently than their competitors, otherwise customers will switch their loyalty and buy from the competition.

Firms that are market driven and customer focused in this manner are said to be marketing oriented firms. However, value is somewhat subjective rather than objective and really rests within the minds of individuals and groups of people. Values change all the time within people's minds. For example, what is considered to be in vogue in terms of car design or hair styles might not be so next year. In fact firms operating in industries such as fashion often build in a certain amount of obsolescence to allow them to bring out a new product to tempt consumers to spend more money. For example, the computer hardware and software industries are continually upgrading their products which soon make existing machines and software programs out of date. It seems to many people that no sooner have they purchased a new computer system from somewhere like Computer World than the manufacturer has produced something better, making their machine redundant. Football clubs are continually changing their strip to encourage further purchase, usually by young fans, although also some older ones. What might have been considered as unimportant say 20 years ago may become more important two decades further on. For example, environmental issues were not something that concerned the majority of people 20 years ago, whereas in the late 1990s many people express some concern about the environment in general. This concern has been reflected by marketing firms in a wide range of products that claim to be environmentally friendly, ethical, not tested on animals, etc.

In order to keep up with the ever-changing tastes and changing value systems of customers, the activities of the competition and important dynamics in the external business environment, the marketing orientated firm needs information. In fact it would be true to say that it could not hope to operate effectively without it. Long term strategy and subsidiary plans at the tactical and operational levels also require data of the right type and for the right time frame. Such data is the very foundation of the marketing orientated firm. Without the right kind of information, proper marketing is very difficult if not impossible.

Marketing research supplies the enterprise with a wide selection of potentially valuable information, but in isolation it is simply not enough for the types of decision making being made at the strategic level; marketing research has to form an intrinsic part of the wider marketing information system (MkIS). The information requirements of the modern firm should be professionally managed in a positive way, using a formal system that will assist in the collection, storage, retrieval and analysis of various forms of marketing information, not simply consisting of information collected using formal marketing research. As discussed in this chapter, MkIS is made up of four component parts. Three of these components collect or produce information of various sorts in its raw form. These are the Internal Data, Intelligence Data and Marketing Research Data parts of the system. The information from these three component parts of the system are fed as input data to the fourth component part, which can be described as Models and Statistics. This part of the system adds value to the data produced from the other three component parts by altering it or modelling it in some way. Basically the Models and Statistics part of the system employs management science techniques to the data derived from the other three component parts and in so doing makes the information more salient and valuable for strategic marketing planning purposes.

Formal marketing research may well provide an enormous percentage of the information requirements of a firm, but it is highly unlikely that marketing research on its own will be able to supply the firm's total needs. As we have seen there are other valuable sources of marketing information besides formal marketing research.

5

Sales Forecasting

INTRODUCTION

The creation of sound sales forecasts are fundamental to any purposeful marketing organisation. Marketing management needs sales forecasting data in order to plan and make appropriate and effective decisions about future conditions. Much of a manager's time is utilised making decisions to do with the future in the present with little to help except past experience. Hence in most of our decision making we are compelled to 'take a position' on likely future events. We use forecasts every day in our personal lives, but whether we actually call them forecasts is another matter. When we decide to take an umbrella with us to work we are taking a position on the weather. When we decide the time is right to buy our US dollars to take on our holidays we are taking a position on the future direction of foreign exchange trends. Even the decision to study for a particular academic course, as many of you are doing now, is done in a purposeful manner and with certain future expectations about employment prospects.

The marketing or sales manager, out of practical need, will also have to predict future conditions especially regarding future sales. The level of future sales forms the basis for many other resource allocation decisions that managers are called upon to make. They will need accurate sales forecasts to make a wide variety of decisions for different points in time. If the 'master' sales forecast they are working on is in itself inaccurate then other important decisions will be based on the wrong premise; it is a case of 'rubbish in–rubbish out'. For example, for the marketing function short term sales forecasts are needed for products and services in order to plan the total promotional effort, distribution arrangements, storage facilities and sales planning.

These forecasts outline the principal targets that the selling function must meet and act as the propelling force behind the managerial process of objective setting, planning, organising and co-ordinating. The overall sales forecast can be seen as the 'bedrock' from which nearly every other budget related decision stems. The sales budget and individual salespeople's quotas are based on the short term forecast, which acts as a planning device in the setting of short term objectives and the allocation of resources within the marketing function.

PREDICTING FUTURE CONDITIONS

In many texts the term 'forecast' refers to objective, quantitative techniques and the term 'predict' denotes subjective estimates. In this chapter the terms subjective and objective forecast will be used.

The development of a forecasting system requires a considerable amount of data to be collected and analysed for usefulness and validity. The company's ability to acquire relevant data influences which of the wide choice of forecasting techniques should be used, and a forecast will only be as good as the data used in its compilation. Short term sales forecasting has been used here by way of illustration. Management also requires forecasting information to make medium and long-term decisions. The longer into the future people are asked to look the more tentative their predictions. If you ask me what is going to happen at work tomorrow I could make an educated guess and probably turn out to be reasonably accurate, although unexpected events occur even in the short term. However, if you were to ask me what conditions at work would be like a year or five years from now it is likely my predictions would be less accurate. The further into the future we are asked to travel the more difficult it is to estimate what those future conditions will be.

Managerial decision making involves forecasting future conditions and these decisions often tend to be longer term and strategic in nature rather than operational. Basically the higher up the management scale a person is, the more strategic and longer term the decisions he or she is called upon to make. Forecasting data also assists management in making the operational decisions that take up a lot of time day to day.

It is often said that forecasting is the key to success, and that poor forecasting can lead to high inventories and associated costs which eat into working capital, or under-production and unrealised market potential. A major research exercise carried out in the USA by Ledbetter and Cox in 1977 showed that forecasting techniques were used by 88 per cent of the 500 largest industrial companies in the USA, and that forecasting was more widely used than any other planning technique. Most planning decisions make use of some form of forecasting information. Forecasting is important in almost all areas of the firm, but sales forecasting is especially salient, since this is the base upon which all company plans are structured. There are several methods available to the manager or researcher and these fall into two basic categories: subjective or objective methods or a combination of the two.

COLLECTING INPUT DATA FOR FORECASTING

Following the decision about how much time, expense and effort is to be expended on the data collection stage of the forecasting process, it has to be located. All forecasting techniques, no matter how simple or sophisticated, are in themselves, only procedures. They all need input data to use as raw material if they are to be of any functional use. The old adage 'rubbish in–rubbish out' certainly applies here. A forecasting technique if based on mathematical or statistical procedures will process any form of data whether good or bad. You can feed data into a computer program and a forecast may result but the forecast will be worthless if the input data is itself faulty. A forecast is only as good as the data used to produce it.

There are two main categories of existing data:

Internal data sources

These are sources of data generated within the company, eg previous company plans, sales statistics and other internal records. Many firms fail to capitalise on the wealth of data available to them which has been generated internally as part of the ordinary day to day administrative procedure of doing business. Many firms keep business records going back many years; in fact publicly limited companies are compelled to do so by law. This information provides very valuable forecasting input data as long as management knows how to make use of it effectively. Also small and medium sized enterprises rarely make full use of this treasure of information available to them without further cost. Internal documentation and records are a valuable source of potentially useful information, especially in the case of immediate and short-term forecasting.

There are questions that can only be answered by a detailed examination of the company's own data, which should be collected, recorded and stored as a routine administrative procedure. The most valuable and cost effective source of internal data is desk research, which should form the beginning for information collection in any forecasting programme. The accuracy of such data can easily be established by the departmental manager concerned, but on the other hand it may be problematic. This may be due to inflexibility of the system or lack of co-operation from departments who seem to regard the information that they produce as their own, rather than it being part of the data generation process of the firm as a whole. To succeed in getting the right kind of internal information the forecaster must be familiar with the firm and its procedures and must have authority from senior management.

External secondary data sources

Examples of these are government and trade statistics and published marketing research surveys. You only have to enter the library of a major business school or a big commercial public library to see the vast amount of secondary commercial data generated every year, particularly the wealth of government sponsored research.

Much of this is available at little or even no cost to the potential forecaster, who only needs to know where to look, what to ask for and how to make effective use of what is available. The British Library holds most of the published work generated within the UK and there are similar institutions in other countries. If a particular report or journal is not available in your local commercial or university library, a request can be made to the British Library for a copy at a very modest charge. Most forecasting situations use both sources. Data can also be generated expressly for the forecasting task using marketing research, eg a sample survey. As this is an expensive way of collecting data, existing data should be examined first as it can give sufficient information.

INTERNAL INFORMATION SOURCES

The forecaster would be advised to take a 'systems analysis' approach to securing the right kind of internal data for forecasting purposes, examining what records are stored and how data is obtained, altered, processed and circulated within the organisation. This means recording every document in detail, as well as listing the type of document, its purpose, origin and destination. Most company systems start with an inquiry from a customer and end with a customer's invoice, but much paperwork is generated in between these two extremes.

The forecaster builds up a picture of the overall system, from individual members of departmental staff and ultimately the company as a whole. This is a 'systems analysis' approach. Unless you are familiar with how the administrative documentary procedure of the firm works you cannot hope to be able to make full use of the information that it generates. 'Unofficial' records kept by members of staff for their own purposes are often very valuable to the forecaster, but they may only come to light after a careful search. They are not part of the 'official' administrative system and the person who keeps such unofficial records may have to be persuaded to contribute them.

PLANS FROM FUNCTIONAL DEPARTMENTS

Changes in company plans or methods of operation already planned could have an impact on a forecast. For example, plans to expand the sales department or increase advertising activity will affect a sales forecast because of the likely impact on sales. In addition to this source of information, other departments such as personnel and research and development also provide useful information and the choice of sources will depend on the type of forecast required. Most functional departments make plans at the beginning of the calendar or financial year, but invariably these alter as outside influences change. Obviously if forecasts were produced based on a particular set of commercial assumptions any changes will also have to be 'factored' into the forecast to bring it into line with the new reality.

SALES DEPARTMENT INFORMATION

It stands to reason that a great deal of historical and present sales related information is likely to be situated within the sales department itself. This is where the marketing firm and its customers interact and therefore it should be able to provide a great deal of highly valuable information, including the following:

Enquiries received and quotations supplied

Written and verbal enquiries from customers may lead to a detailed quotation being submitted. This will provide information that is useful to the forecaster, especially if patterns can be established in the percentage of enquiries that are followed by orders and the time that elapses between quotation and order. The number of quotations converted into orders indicates the firm's market share.

Sales volume by product and by product group

These combine to give total sales volume, but also show each product or product group in the overall mix in terms of the contribution to total volume.

Sales volume by area

Either salespersons' territories, standard media areas as used by the Joint Industry Committee for Television Advertising Research (JICTAR) or other geographical areas.

Sales volume by type of channel of distribution

In a firm that has a multi-channel distribution policy, the effectiveness and profitability of each channel can be calculated. It also allows for trends in the pattern of distribution to be identified and used when forecasting future channel requirements. Channel information by geographical area may show a difference in the profitability between various types of channel in different parts of the country, allowing for profitable geographical channel differentiations. A more realistic forecast can be developed from information gathered by type of retail outlet, agents, wholesalers, distributors and factors, revealing promising channel opportunities and resulting in more effective channel management.

Sales volume over time

This reveals actual sales and units sold and allows for seasonal variations, inflation and price adjustments to be taken into consideration.

Pricing information

The effects of price increases and decreases can be established through historical information, giving an opportunity to forecast the effects of future changes.

Sales representatives' records and reports

The customer file kept by professional sales representatives contains detailed information on live customers such as company information, likely future requirements etc and the reports that they make to the sales office contain much information that is useful to the forecaster.

Communication mix information

The effects of previous advertising campaigns, sponsorship, direct-mail programmes or exhibitions can be evaluated, as can the effects of various levels of expenditure in marketing communications, giving a guide to future effectiveness.

Sales promotional data

This allows assessment of past promotional campaigns in terms of their individual effects on sales.

Sales volumes by market segment

Segmentation may be regional or, in industrial markets, by type of industry. It will show which segments are likely to remain static, which are declining and which show growth possibilities. Where the company deals with a small number of large companies, segmentation may be by customer, and any change in demand from any of these may be highly important when forecasting sales and material requirements.

SALES BUDGETS

Many different departmental budgets such as the sales budget, marketing budget, production budget and administrative budget are derived from the master sales forecast. A budget is different from a forecast in the sense that it is a representation or 'model' of what the firm expects or plans to happen. The sales forecast on the other hand is far more uncertain. It is affected by factors, many of them extraneous to the organisation and beyond the control of the individual firm.

The budget is under the control of management, who use the master sales forecast as a guide to what the appropriate budgetary figures and expectations should in fact be. The relationship between the sales forecast and the creation of budgets for managerial planning and control purposes is shown below in the form of a schematic diagram in Figure 5.1.

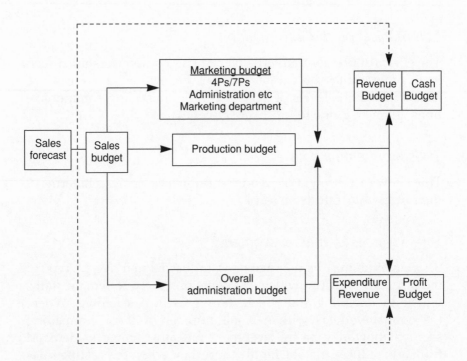

Figure 5.1   *The relationship of the sales forecast to the firm's budgetary procedure*

The reader can see from the above figure that budgets are derived from the sales forecast and the business budgetary procedure cannot begin until the forecasting has taken place and the figures agreed by management. These figures are then passed on to the people responsible for formulating budget, usually cost and management accountants as well as marketing and sales planning staff. They interpret the figures and factor them into the necessary budgets, eg sales budget, advertising budget and so forth.

Budgeting requires very precise planning of all the activities that are to be undertaken during the period that the budget refers to, usually one year ahead of current time. The total sales budget is split amongst all the products and services in the firm's portfolio, in terms of apportioning expenditure on advertising, personal selling, merchandising, packaging, Internet, trade exhibitions, sales promotions, etc. The precise manner in which this budgetary 'split' is decided is a management decision and differs from firm to firm. It is important to make sure that the sales budget is linked and co-ordinated with other budgets within the organisation. For example the sales budget should not set plans to sell more product than the production capacity of the firm can cope with, unless there is a contingency plan to contract out some of the additional production work. Budgets must also allow for some flexibility and many firms use a flexible budgetary system, where figures are fed into the budgetary process each month and budget figures are adjusted to take into account any new unforeseen factors that would render the original budget figures obsolete.

INFORMATION FROM ELSEWHERE IN THE FIRM

Dispatch department

Here the forecaster will find chronological information on what goods were dispatched and how, including copies of advice notes and other delivery documents.

Production department

Works orders, material lists, design information, order completion dates and much other useful information can be easily obtained from this source.

Purchasing department

Useful information includes old purchase orders, material lists, requisitions, material status schedule reports, information on suppliers and stock control data relating to reorder levels, buffer and safety stock levels, economic order quantities and stockturn by inventory item.

Accounts department

Accurate cost data is available from the management accountant and previous management reports are also a useful source of information on such matters as:

- number of new customers in a given period;
- number of withdrawals;
- number of items sold by product in volume and monetary terms;
- total sales by salesperson, area, division, etc.

Production capacity can be forecast using the information on staff that is given in management accounting reports, including absenteeism. Historical information can be obtained from past budgets with variance analysis showing budgeted figures against actual figures. Information such as orders received, dispatched and on hand will be most accessible in the accounts department.

SALES FORECASTING: SUBJECTIVE METHODS

These are qualitative techniques relying on human judgement rather than on numerical calculations. They are sometimes known as intuitive techniques using experience and judgement. There are a number of subjective techniques.

Customer-use projections

Survey techniques such as market research surveys or simply conversations between the sales representative and existing and potential customers can make clear the purchase intentions of customers and/or users. Test marketing, in a small representative area, is also used to produce forecasts and in many ways is similar to surveys.

Advantages
■ Information is elicited with the use of proven marketing research methodology such as sample surveys, projective techniques and questionnaires.
■ Prospective purchasers provide information on what and how much they are likely to buy in the future.
■ Production of sales forecasts can be subcontracted to professional market research agencies, particularly useful when time is short.

Disadvantages
■ There may be variance between what respondents say they are going to purchase and their actual purchases.
■ There is a limit to how often the same people (ie a company's purchasing manager) can be approached.
■ Sample surveys are expensive and very time-consuming, and not suited to producing forecasts on a regular basis.

It does appear from evidence that the jury of executive opinion and sales force composite methods, discussed in detail below, have greater application than customer-use projections, particularly in industrial markets where a close relationship exists between supplier and customer. What are the main drawbacks in using a survey of buyers' intentions to produce medium term sales forecasts? Contacting a selection of your customers or potential customers and asking them what their purchasing plans are regarding your type of products, seems eminently sensible. The information comes directly from the 'horse's mouth' so to speak. One of the main problems is that people don't always do what they say they intend to do. Business people live in hope and are generally enthusiastic about their business and look forward to future growth. They very often tend to be on the over optimistic side. When asked about their medium term investment and other purchasing plans their reply can often be based on 'too rosy' a picture of future business conditions. Consequently what they say they are going to do concerning their future purchasing intentions and what actually happens is very often quite different.

Executive opinion (or jury) method

The sales or marketing manager makes an informed subjective forecast that is discussed with other executives from production, finance and other departments, who deliver a 'verdict' on the forecast. Thus the forecast is based on the collective experience of the group.

Advantages
■ Because of the status of the contributing panel, the people who use the information see the figures as having a high level of source credibility.
■ The final forecast is based on the collective experience of a group, rather than on the opinion of a single executive.
■ The sales forecast is put together by people with many years' experience in a particular industry.
■ Because the final forecast is based on a consensus of opinion, variations in individual subjective estimates are eliminated.

Disadvantages
Forecasts based on guesswork because of salespeople not having enough time to devote to producing them. The salesperson's expanded role leaves little time for forecasting activity, especially when a large number of product forecasts are required on a regular basis.

Production of a pessimistic forecast by a salesperson whose sales quotas or targets are linked to payments of bonus or commission in order to boost earnings.

Sales force composite technique

As the name suggests this subjective technique is based on the views of the sales force. In many ways it is very similar to the 'jury' of executive opinion technique discussed earlier. In fact as you can probably see by the few examples given here, all subjective methods of sales forecasting are similar and are in fact variations on the same type of theme.

The method involves asking each person in the sales team to produce a detailed, disaggregated sales forecast for his or her particular sales territory. The forecast is disaggregated in the sense that it is produced by breaking it down into individual products, colours, sizes, segments, etc to whatever level would be most useful for forecasting information. Sales staff are asked to do this on a regular basis, usually once every month and these are then put together to create a detailed forecast for the whole of the firm's area of sales operations.

Advantages
▓ Those people closest to the actual customer produce forecasts.
▓ Only individual sales personnel could have such an intimate knowledge of their own sales territory.
▓ Does not involve mathematics or statistics in terms of composing the forecasts.
▓ Can be produced at any level of disaggregation.
▓ Can be produced on a regular basis.
▓ Means that sales staff are actively involved in planning activities.

Disadvantages
▓ Sales people already far too busy – this is yet another additional task.
▓ Sales people tend to be over optimistic.
▓ If sales staff think forecasts will be used to fix bonus payment levels they may be deliberately pessimistic.
▓ Involves a lot of staff time if carried out on a regular basis.

BAYESIAN DECISION THEORY

The methods of subjective forecasting described so far do not form an exhaustive list but the main methods have been covered, albeit briefly. Most of the other subjective methods are variations on the three techniques examined here. The main exception to this is what has come to be known as 'Bayesian' forecasting.

Bayesian forecasting is based on a statistical technique known as decision theory. The Bayesian approach to producing forecasts is really a mixture of qualitative and quantitative techniques. The method is named after the Reverend Thomas Bayes (1702–61), a statistician and generally an all-round polymath, so common amongst the intellectuals of the period. Despite the fact that the technique was developed in the 18th century, it has only recently begun to be widely used especially in the business and operational research fields. The method incorporates expert management 'guesses', or subjective probabilistic evaluations, at data inputs for the statistical calculation of sales forecasts.

Up until the time of Bayes probability was thought of as something that had to be objectively calculable. For example, the chance of obtaining a head or tail when tossing a fair coin or the probability of winning the National Lottery are examples of events which lend themselves to objective calculation based on the scientific laws of probability. Unless a person had an objective prior probability of an event occurring, such as the result of tossing a coin, you could not start the 'ball rolling' in terms of using probability to calculate the likelihood of future conditions.

Bayes said that it was quite acceptable to arrive at the initial or 'prior' probability subjectively using experience or human judgement to put a numerical figure to the subjective estimation. The researcher or, in our case, forecaster, could then use this subjective estimate in statistical processes. Bayes found an acceptable way of arriving at the initial probability for a whole range of situations for which the calculation of initial prior probabilities was virtually impossible. This then opened up the use of Bayesian techniques, including the use of decision tree analysis, to a much wider range of problems including the kind of ill-structured problems commonly found in business scenarios.

Bayesian decision tree analysis makes use of network diagrams exhibiting the probable outcome of each decision alternative considered in the model. These are shown together with expected values and associated probabilities, initially derived on a subjective basis, the revolutionary mark of the Bayesian approach as discussed in the last paragraph. As explained, one of the problems of using probabilities in any statistical model is in ascertaining initial probabilities to commence the forecasting process. Bayesian statisticians differ from 'purist' statisticians in one respect: purists view the concept of probability as the relative frequency with which an event might occur, whereas the Bayesian view is that probability is a subjective measure of our belief and that we can always express our degree of belief in terms of probability ie we can express it numerically in terms of a percentage or proportion, such as the probability of this event occurring is 0.3 with total certainty being equal to 1 (unity). Although the initial probabilities are derived subjectively (ie the figures are based on judgmental opinion, rather than on objective calculation), proponents of Bayesian theory believe that such probabilities are perfectly valid and hence perfectly acceptable as initial starting points in an extensive quantitative forecasting process.

It is the subjective nature of arriving at the initial probabilities that makes the Bayesian approach so useful in solving business problems for which initial probabilities are often unknown and are either very difficult or impossible to calculate using objective methods. Many marketing problems are of this type and lend themselves well to the Bayesian approach.

To use the Bayesian approach, the decision maker must be able to assign a probability to each specific event. The sum of the probabilities of all the events considered must be unity (one). These probabilities represent the magnitude of the decision maker's belief that a particular event will take place. In practical business situations, such decisions should be delegated to staff who have the expertise and experience to assign valid initial subjective probabilities to the occurrences of various business events. These initial probabilities are all based on previous experience of information (such as published secondary data for example) obtained prior to the decision making process. For this reason, the initial subjective probabilities are called prior probabilities.

When making business decisions, the financial implications of actions must be considered. For example, when a manager is thinking about investing a firm's surplus cash in a new product acquisition, he or she must consider the probability of making an acceptable return on the investment greater than the profit that could be achieved in a safe investment such as bank interest. Applying Bayesian decision theory involves selecting a specific option and having an idea of the economic impact of selecting a given course of action. Once the future events have been specified, the decision maker gives prior subjective probabilities to them in numeric form, usually in the form of a percentage or proportion. The expected pay-off for each act is then calculated and the act with the most attractive pay-off is selected. If pay-offs represent income or profit, the decision maker would normally select the act with the best, normally the highest, expected financial pay-off.

SALES FORECASTING: OBJECTIVE METHODS

Objective methods of forecasting are statistical or mathematical in nature. Historical data are analysed to identify a pattern or relationship between variables and this pattern is then extended or extrapolated into the future to make a forecast. Objective methods of forecasting can be classified by considering the underlying models involved. They fall into two categories: causal models and time series models.

CAUSAL MODELS

Causal models exploit the relationship between the time series of the variable being examined and one or more other time series. If other variables are found to correlate with the variable of interest, a causal model can be constructed incorporating coefficients that give the relative strengths of the various causal factors.

The sales of a product may be related to the price of the product, advertising expenditure and the price of competitors' products. If the forecaster can estimate the relationship between sales and the independent variables, then the forecast values of the independent variables can be used to predict future values of the dependent variable (in this case, sales).

For example, the demand in the UK for building bricks is based on the demand for houses and other commercial buildings built from brick. This is called derived demand, that is, in this case the demand for bricks is derived from the demand for houses. There are many factors influencing the demand for houses and other brick-built buildings. These include the following:

▨ number of newly married couples;
▨ interest rate levels;
▨ income lending ratios used by banks and building societies;
▨ fashion;
▨ levels of unemployment;
▨ inclement weather (stops building);
▨ local authority housing policies.

All of the above factors have a 'causal' effect on the demand for brick. These variables would have to be included in a forecasting equation and their relevant strengths and effects assessed before the demand for brick could be estimated for future periods. This is an example of what is meant by 'causal techniques'.

Regression

One of the most widely used causal techniques is what is known as regression analysis. This technique tries to calculate the statistical relationship between at least two variables. These variables take the form of one or more independent variables and one dependent variable. For example advertising and merchandising expenditure may constitute the two independent variables whereas the resulting level of sales of a certain product in a certain store may constitute the dependent variable. This method starts from the assumption that a basic relationship exists between two variables eg diet and health. The method most commonly used is the method known as 'ordinary least square linear regression'. This method produces a line of best fit in a scatter diagram using mathematical equations called 'normal equations'. The concepts of a scatter diagram and a line of best fit produced mathematically using the ordinary least squared method are shown below in Figures 5.2 and 5.3.

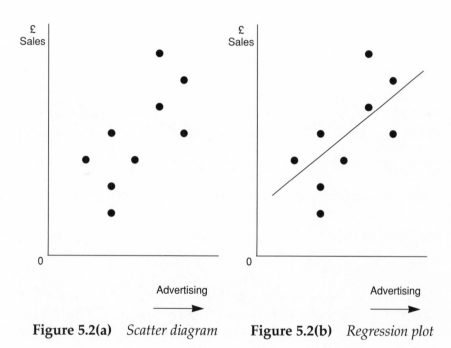

Figure 5.2(a)　*Scatter diagram*　　**Figure 5.2(b)**　*Regression plot*

In Figure 5.2 you can see that the values of X are plotted on the horizontal axis for any given value of the variable Y. This produces a number of points scattered on the graph. To estimate the relationship, if any, and the type of relationship we can plot a line of best fit through the scatter points by eye. Ordinary least square linear regression takes a more scientific approach and plots the line mathematically by using equations to minimise the cumulative value of the squared differences from the line.

If we consider the individual points on the graph in Figure 5.3 some of the differences from the line are negative and some positive. We square the differences and minimise their total to calculate the line of best fit or 'regression line'. Various forms of regression are available. Ordinary least square linear regression assumes a

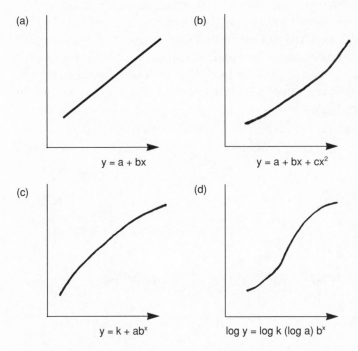

(a)

$y = a + bx$

(b)

$y = a + bx + cx^2$

(c)

$y = k + ab^x$

(d)

$\log y = \log k \,(\log a)\, b^x$

Figure 5.3 *The mathematical functions and graph plots of well known curves*

linear relationship between variables, which basically means that the line of best fit will be a straight line. Multiple regression can handle non-linear relationships and is used extensively in economic calculations or 'econometrics'.

TREND PROJECTION TECHNIQUES

Lines of various shapes can be described by mathematics. We say that a particular line or curve has a 'mathematical function'. For example most of you will probably remember from your school days that the mathematical equation for a straight line can be shown as $y = a+bx$, where y represents the vertical axis of a graph, a the intercept of the y axis, b the gradient of the curve and x the units of time plotted on the horizontal axis. So a five period ahead forecast can be calculated from the intercept (a) plus the gradient component (b) multiplied by five ($x=5$) or $y = a+bx5$. Basically if the forecaster has some data and has some idea of the likely mathematical function of the plot of the data he or she can use the appropriate mathematical equation to extrapolate the plot of the curve into future time periods and use this extrapolation as a basis of a forecast, in the context of our discussion, a sales forecast. Below are the plots and mathematical equations that describe the plot of some of the better known curves.

Trend projections are perhaps more suitable to long term forecasting rather than to short term. They provide the forecaster with evidence of the shape and extent of the underlying trend exhibited in the data. For example a 10-year plot of the FTSE100 index shows an underlying upward trend imbedded in quite erratic random fluctuations from the trend line. Many stock analysts, often known as 'chartists' because they plot share price movements on charts to assist them in their investment decisions, use this approach.

TIME SERIES MODELS

As their name suggests, time series methods operate on the assumption that the past is a good indicator of the future and that future demand is simply a function of time. This time dependence includes such factors as seasonality and cyclicality. For example, shops tend to sell more ice cream in the summer and more warm clothes in the winter. Their whole purpose is to identify patterns in historical data, model these, and extrapolate them into the future.

Such methods are unlikely to be successful in forecasting future demand when the historical time series is very erratic. In addition, because it is assumed that future demand is a function of time only, causal factors cannot be taken into consideration. For example, such models would not be able to incorporate the impact of changes in management policy. Such techniques are epitomised by two of the simpler models, moving averages and exponential smoothing which will be looked at here. Other, more sophisticated, time series models include decomposition models and auto-regressive moving averages (Box-Jenkins) techniques.

Time series analysis uses the historical series of only one variable to develop a model for predicting future values. The forecasting situation is treated rather like a 'black box', with no attempt made to discover the other factors that might affect its behaviour. Because time series models treat the variable to be forecast as a function of time only, they are most useful when other conditions are expected to remain relatively constant, most likely true of the short term rather than the long term future. Hence such methods are particularly suited to short term, operational, routine forecasting – usually up to six months or one year ahead of current time. Time series methods are not very useful when there is no discernible pattern of demand.

MOVING AVERAGES (TIME SERIES)

Simple moving average

The simple moving or rolling average is a useful and uncomplicated method of forecasting the average expected value of a time series. The process uses the average individual forecasts (F) and demand values (X) over the past n time periods. A suffix notation is used, which may seem complicated at first, but it is really quite simple: the present is referred to as time t and one period into the future by $t + 1$, one period into the past by $t – 1$, two periods by $t + 2$, and so on. This is perhaps best appreciated with reference to a time diagram:

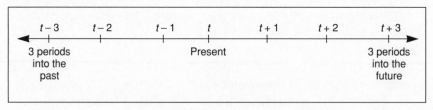

Figure 5.4 *Time diagram showing notation for present, past and future*

The simple moving average process is defined by the equation:

$$F_{t+1} = F_t + \frac{1}{n}(X_t X_{t-n})$$

where F_{t+1} = forecast for 1 period ahead
F_t = forecast made last time period for present period
n = number of time periods
X_t = actual demand in present time
X_{t-n} = actual demand in period $_{t-n}$

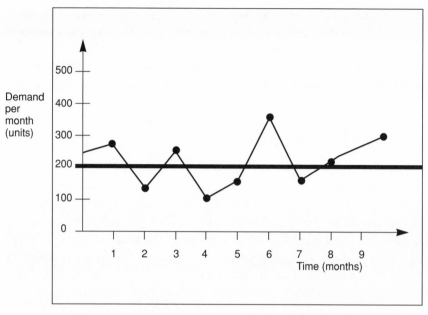

Figure 5.5 *Example of a stationary time series*

Weighted average

The simple moving average has the disadvantage that all data in the average are given equal weighting, ie:

$$\frac{1}{n}$$

More recent data may be more important than older data, particularly if the underlying pattern of the data has been changing, and, therefore, should be given a greater weight. To overcome this problem and increase the sensitivity of the moving average, it is possible to use weighted averages, with the sum of the weights equal to unity, in order to produce a true average. In decimal form, a weighted moving average can be expressed as:

$$F_{t+1} = 0.4\,X_t + 0.3\,X_{t-1} + 0.2\,X_{t-2} + 0.1\,X_{t-1}$$

(Notation as defined for the simple moving average).

Problems common to all moving average procedures still remain, the major ones being:

1. No forecast can be made until n time periods have passed, because it is necessary to have values available for the previous $n - 1$ periods.
2. The sensitivity or speed of response of moving average procedures is inversely proportional to the number of periods n included in the average. To change the sensitivity, it is necessary to change the value of n. That creates problems of continuity and much additional work.

The methods of simple and weighted moving averages discussed so far are only suitable for reasonably constant (stationary) data – they are unable to deal with a significant trend. An example of a stationary time series is shown in Figure 5.5. It can be seen from the graph that over a period of nine months the time series fluctuates randomly about a mean value of 200 units, which is not increasing or decreasing significantly over time.

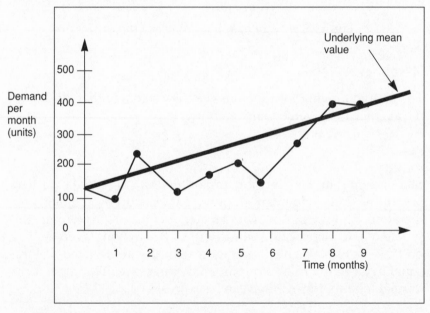

Figure 5.6　*Example of a time series with a linear underlying trend*

In the time series shown in Figure 5.6 the underlying mean value of the series is not stationary. If a line of best fit is drawn through all the points, you can see that while the actual values are fluctuating randomly, the underlying mean value is following a rising linear trend. A method of moving averages designed for a reasonably stationary time series cannot accommodate a series with a linear trend. In such situations, the forecasts tend to lag behind the actual time series, resulting in systematic errors.

To counter such error factors, the method of double (sometimes called linear) moving averages has been developed. This method calculates a second (or double) moving average which is a moving average of the first one. The basic principle is very similar to linear exponential smoothing methods, which are themselves a kind of double moving average but which utilise a more sophisticated weighting system. This form of time series method is shown next by way of illustration.

Exponential smoothing (time series)

The use of exponentially weighted moving averages was first developed from a number of unpublished reports by C Holt of the Carnegie Institute of Technology. Such techniques overcome many of the shortcomings and limitations of the moving average method. Exponential smoothing is very simple and is really just a more elaborate form of the moving average. The updating equations for exponential smoothing can easily be stored in a computer in the form of a program.

Exponential smoothing is useful in the production of a large number of routine short term sales forecasts which are required on a regular basis. Apart from the need to input the most recent information in order to update the present values, much of the calculations can be carried out by computer making the system as a whole a semi-automatic system.

Double exponential smoothing

Simple exponential smoothing is only really appropriate for a relatively stationary time series. In particular, the method will do rather badly if the series contains a long term trend. Like the simple moving average, if simple exponential smoothing is applied inappropriately to a time series with a trend, the forecast will continually lag behind the actual value of series X_t.

The method of double exponential smoothing is technically known as Brown's one parameter linear exponential smoothing. This method introduces additional equations to those of the simple exponential smoothing to estimate a trend. The method uses the same principle as the double or linear moving average discussed earlier, that is, if simple exponential smoothing is applied to a time series with a significant trend it will lag behind. If single exponential smoothing is applied again to the first smoothed series, the second smoothed series S_t^2 will lag behind the first S_t^1 by approximately the same amount as the first smoothed series S_t^1 lagged behind the original time series X_t. This is illustrated in Figure 5.7.

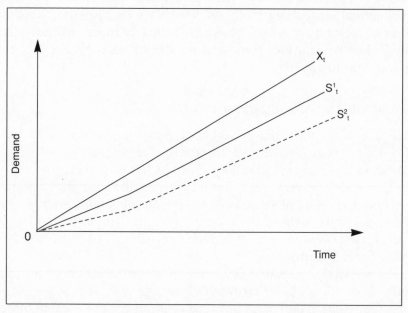

Figure 5.7 *The lagged response of a sample exponential smoothing model, applied to a series with a linear additive trend*

Brown's method accepts that after initial transients have died down, S_t^1 will lag behind X_t by amount A. A second single exponentially weighted average S_t^2 will lag behind the first S_t^1 by the same amount, A. At time t, the difference between S_t^1 and S_t^2 is added to the S_t^1 to give the level component a_t. A proportion of the difference between S_t^1 and S_t^2 is then used to provide a trend component, b_t, which is multiplied by the number of periods ahead to be forecast, m, and the product added to the level a_t to produce a forecast for m steps ahead. Brown's model of double exponential smoothing is made up of two components: a level component (or intercept) (a) and a trend component (b). These components are combined to provide a forecast, as illustrated in Figure 5.8.

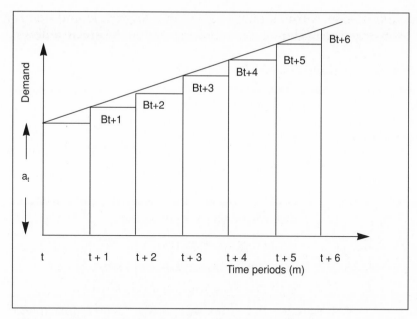

Figure 5.8 *The level (a_t) and trend ($B_t m$) components of Brown's Double Exponential Smoothing*

The updating equations for Brown's model are as follows:

Single smoothing $S'_t = \alpha X_t + (1-\alpha) S'_{t-1}$

Double smoothing $S''_t = \alpha S'_t + (1-\alpha) S''_{t-1}$

Level component $a_t = S'_t + (S'_t - S''_t) = 2S'_t - S''_t$

Trend component $B_t = \dfrac{\alpha}{1-\alpha} (S'_t - S''_t)$

Forecast $F_{t+m} = a_t + B_t m$

where m is a multiplier of the trend component.

Winter's trend and seasonal model

The exponential smoothing models discussed so far cannot deal with seasonal data. When seasonality does exist, these methods may perform poorly, because the seasonality will produce a systematic error pattern. Such a data series requires the use of a seasonal method to eliminate the systematic pattern in the errors. Winter's trend and seasonal model is based on three smoothing equations – one for stationary series, one for trends and one for seasonality. The updating equations for this model are as follows:

Overall smoothing $S_t = \alpha\, \dfrac{X_t}{I_{t-L}} + (1-\alpha)\, I_{t-L}$

Trend $\qquad\qquad\quad Z_t = \gamma\, (S_t - S_{t-1}) + (1-\gamma)\, (Z_{t-1})$

Seasonality $\qquad\quad I_t = \beta\, \dfrac{X_t}{S_t} + (1-\beta)\, I_{t-L}$

Forecast $\qquad\qquad F_{t+m} = (S_t + mZ_t)\, I_{(t-L+m)}$

where: L is the length of seasonality (eg the number of months or quarters in a year)

$\qquad\ Z_t$ is the trend component

$\qquad\ I_t$ is the seasonal adjustment factor

$\qquad\ F_{t+m}$ is the forecast for m periods ahead

$\qquad X, Y$ and β are the smoothing coefficients for overall smoothing, trend and seasonal components, respectively.

This section on sales forecasting does not give an exhaustive treatment of the subject, but it does give you, the reader, a general understanding of the main methods and techniques. Some of the more advanced techniques such as multiple regression and other 'econometric' techniques are unfortunately beyond the scope of an introductory text such as this and a more robust treatment is given in the specialist texts available on forecasting.

A more comprehensive range of moving average and exponential smoothing applications are also given in the dedicated forecasting textbooks. The examples given here are by way of illustration and provide readers with the general idea of the methods discussed rather than claiming to make them an expert in the subject. Most of the other forecasting techniques available are variations of the methods discussed in this chapter.

Certainly the examples given here will furnish the reader with a good basic grounding in the subject and at least give a good idea of how sales forecasts can be produced by marketing management or the specialists working for them. Also, just as importantly how management can go about obtaining the data necessary to produce forecasts and finally how the forecasts can be used by management once they have been produced.

SUMMARY

The creation of sound sales forecasts is fundamental to any purposeful marketing organisation. Marketing management needs sales forecasting data in order to plan and generally make appropriate and effective decisions about future conditions. Much of a manager's time is utilised in making decisions to do with the future in the present, with little to help him or her except what has happened in the past. Hence in most of our decision making we are compelled to 'take a position' on likely future events. It is not a question of whether or not marketing management will make sales forecasts in order to make decisions, merely how they will be produced.

Managers have to make decisions about the future. This is true of marketing and sales management just as much as any other form of management. Marketing and sales management are concerned with future demand for their products and/or services and this means also being concerned with sales at the end of the day.

Marketing and sales managements are forced to take a position on the level and nature of future sales if they are to function as managers effectively. Whether they choose to produce such forecasts formally or informally, whether they choose to use qualitative or quantitative techniques is a matter of choice. What is certain is that sales forecasts form the very heart of decision making in sales and marketing.

In many texts the term 'forecast' refers to objective, quantitative techniques and 'predict' denotes subjective estimates. In this chapter the terms subjective and objective forecast are used. The development of a forecasting system requires a considerable amount of data to be collected and analysed for usefulness and validity. The company's ability to acquire relevant data influences which of the wide choice of forecasting techniques should be used, and a forecast will only be as good as the data used in its compilation.

Many different departmental budgets such as the sales budget, marketing budget, production budget and administrative budget are derived from the master sales forecast. A budget is different from a forecast in the sense that it is a representation or 'model' of what the firm expects or plans to happen. The sales forecast on the other hand is far more uncertain. It is affected by factors, many of them extraneous to the organisation and by and large beyond the control of the individual firm. The budget is under the control of management who use the master sales forecast as a guide as to what the appropriate budgetary figures and expectations should in fact be.

Information collected from formal marketing research and marketing intelligence gathering of internally generated information can be used as input data in a wide variety of forecasting models. Data collected over a period of time can be extrapolated in to the future by the use of time series techniques. The use of such techniques also allows the manager to model seasonality and cyclicality effects. Trend fitting, using the mathematical functions of known 'curves', can also be used to forecast sales and model likely future product life cycles. Linear and multiple regression are more sophisticated forecasting techniques that make use of 'econometric' procedures.

It is important to remember that forecasting is the logical starting point for all business planning, so if the forecast is incorrect then all strategic and tactical plans will be affected. It follows that the most important link is with planning and control. Forecasting does, of course, impinge on other areas like marketing research. Indeed, marketing research provides marketing management with a wide range of important forecasting techniques such as qualitative depth interviews and group discussions, the Delphi technique used for technological forecasting and the survey of buyers' intentions, to name but a few. The subject of sales forecasting is linked to the topic of marketing information systems. It would be true to say of any information system or decision support system, that the end product usually contributes to a decision about the future usually made in the present and often based, at least in part, on information collected about the past. Hence sales forecasting is itself a very important function of a firm's integrated marketing information system.

6

The Tools of Marketing

THE MARKETING MIX

As the term mix infers, marketing can be compared to a recipe, with the constituents being the elements over which marketing has control. As recipes differ according to different dishes being prepared, so the marketing mix will differ according to the circumstances that prevail at the time. Such circumstances will include the state of the market, competitive activity, the company's own resources and company policy. It is, therefore, important that the recipe is changed according to the circumstances prevailing. Manipulation of this recipe is the task of marketing management and the success of the company in the market-place rests upon the skill of this manipulation. Even a minor recipe miscalculation can lead to an unsuccessful outcome.

The marketing mix describes the functional aspects of marketing over which the company has control. This includes what E Jerome McCarthy dubbed the 'four Ps' in 1960, namely, Product, Price, Promotion and Place (distribution). In addition to these four Ps, is sometimes added a fifth P– People, which includes the people who carry out the function of marketing and who interface with customers. These have been described as the key elements of the marketing function. There are two further Ps that relate particularly to the service industry because of its intangible nature. These are: Process and Physical evidence. These are called the 'seven Ps' of service marketing. Process is particularly relevant in transactions where customer interaction is high (eg a restaurant) and here an attempt must be made to involve the customer as much as possible so that they depart with a good feeling towards the service provider and give repeat business. Physical evidence refers to the relative intangibility of services and here attempts must be made to highlight the service through such things as house style, logotype and even the wearing of uniform by service providers. However, the notion of the four Ps still prevails in marketing literature and each of the mix elements is shown in more detail in Figure 6.1. The importance placed on each of these varies according to market circumstances.

PRODUCT	PLACE
Design	Warehousing
Packaging	Transportation
Display	Service level
Function	Stockholding
PRICE	**PROMOTION**
Level	Advertising
Discrimination	Sales promotion
Discount	Personal selling
Policy	Branding

Figure 6.1 *The four Ps expanded*

The elements of the marketing mix are all related in terms of how they combine in the marketing planning process. It is the skill of marketing management to ensure that the combination chosen is a successful one. We shall now examine each of these elements in greater detail in order to be clear about their different functions and to provide a greater understanding and a perspective, because markets are dynamic and are affected by a range of environmental, uncontrollable variables. Marketing must devise strategies to counteract these variables by using the tools at its disposal. These marketing mix tools are the controllable elements that good marketing should attempt to apply imaginatively within given financial constraints.

THE PRODUCT (OR SERVICE)

The product, along with advertising, is the most visible element of marketing. Its tangibility is an important asset in the minds of customers and marketers should seek to exploit this fact. This is why less tangible service products, such as insurance, should be marketed with as much visibility as possible and this visibility should extend to brochures, the ambience of the premises in which insurance is purchased, the way the service is presented and many more aspects.

The product or service is what consumers perceive it to be and not how the company perceives it. It is the task of marketing management to determine what this image is through marketing research and then correct this image if it is a negative one through product or image redesign. Here, of course, other elements of the marketing mix will come into play, but the product or service is really the starting point for marketing strategy, for without it, there is nothing to market.

In 1957 Igor Ansoff suggested a number of strategies for the marketing of products and his matrix still holds good today. Such strategies involve products (new and existing) on the one hand and markets (new and existing) on the other. Existing products into existing markets is a conservative strategy, whereas new products into new markets might be regarded as being risky. Existing products into new markets represents diversification and new products into existing markets suggests that the company is seeking to diversify its product range.

In terms of how it relates to marketing, a number of issues arise in relation to the product or service.

Product management

This relates to issues concerning the number and types of product being offered as well as the managerial decisions that are made concerning their relative success in the market-place.

Product planning

Here product/market decisions, similar to those suggested by Ansoff, will be needed. In addition, for new products, marketing research will be needed prior to embarking on new product research and development programmes.

The physical product

The concern here relates to issues of design, quality and the image that the product seeks to portray. Packaging decisions are particularly relevant where the pack is an important part of the display of the product on the shelves of supermarkets.

PRICE

This is a very important element owing to its direct impact on both the company and its customers. The company is concerned with price in terms of being able to make a profit and the customer looks at it in terms of value for money compared to other competitive offerings. The price customers will pay affects the company's profitability and its competitive position.

If a company is able to differentiate its products or services on a non-price basis, then it has a distinct advantage over competitive offerings. If, however, a company fails to match the standards of its competitors, then the importance of price will decrease in importance as an element of product choice. Price seems easy to define, but in practice there are many difficulties. To think of it in simplistic terms of financial value is too restrictive, as value includes other elements of the marketing mix. The more complicated the product, the more difficult it will be for buyers to put a price on it and psychological factors relating to buyer behaviour, as discussed in Chapter 3, also enter the equation.

As we shall see in Chapter 11, there is a term 'psychological pricing'. All other things being equal, buyers will choose the cheapest and, for example, this is why the ubiquitous hamburger chains now tend to fight their battles on price, although attempts are made to differentiate product offerings, largely through imagery.

When a seller first establishes a price there is a close relationship with costs. This might be due to the uncertainty as to how the market will view the new product, but at least as long as costs are covered plus a percentage for profit, then the company should remain in existence. However, to price on a cost plus basis is a dereliction of the duty of marketing. What the marketing orientated company should do is to view price as a single input to the marketing decision alongside other marketing variables that comprise the four Ps. Price can then be viewed as a single element of the marketing mix and this is all part of the equation towards achieving marketing's goals.

Pricing can be a problem both internally and externally. Marketing might decide on a price that it believes is correct for the market-place, but this decision might not be approved of by finance. It could be that in order to enter a market, a decision is taken by marketing to sell at a low or zero profit margin initially, in the expectation that better profits will ensue in the longer term when procession has been made along the learning curve. Marketing channel members (eg retailers and wholesalers) might disagree with the company's pricing strategy and competitors might engage in a price war in order to put the company under competitive pressure.

If a company's price is too high, this could eradicate the potential of an otherwise good marketing mix policy, and the company could face problems due to insufficient sales revenue. If it is set too low, then the company may not be able to cope with the extra sales volume generated through this low price. This might suggest an increase in price in order to curb demand, which would be viewed negatively in the market-place, and the firm's image might suffer as a result.

The strategic implications of pricing make this element of the marketing mix a crucial one and must be treated prudently.

PLACE

The term 'place' is slightly confusing and it would perhaps have been better to call it 'placement'. This involves the act of moving goods from the buyer to the seller. More correctly, it should be called 'distribution' and this topic revolves around two separate elements:

■ Channels of distribution through which the goods or services are sold in order to make the product available to customers.
■ The logistical feat involved in transporting the goods from the buyer to the seller, and also the task of ensuring that appropriate levels of service are provided. This latter aspect is sometimes called logistics management or physical distribution management (PDM).

Channels of distribution

Many changes have taken place in retailing and manufacturing channels over the past 30 years and there is more of a trend nowadays to sell direct, cutting out the intermediary 'middleman' whose function was to 'break bulk'. However, many large retailing chains are now, in effect, carrying out their own wholesaling function, so the use of channel intermediaries still accounts for a significant amount of business. Manufacturers are also part of this channel process, because as well as supplying their own customers, they are also customers for their own suppliers of raw material and components. Having a system of intermediaries has its advantages:

■ It reduces the volume of commercial dealings to be made, because middlemen assume the task of selling to small volume retailers and manufacturers.
■ Costs of storage, maintaining stock levels and transport are reduced, as these are shared by channel intermediaries.
■ Middlemen can generally remove some of the financial commitments, which the manufacturer would need to bear if marketing to the end customer.
■ Middlemen have an intimate knowledge of their local markets.
■ Middlemen market many related products, and have established local customers of their own (eg larger electrical wholesalers). They can promote the company's products to these customers and many also employ their own sales force.

Having a channel of distribution has advantages, but it also incurs costs in that the profit margins must be shared by others within the system and there is also a certain loss of control. The biggest disadvantage would seem to be that with a system of middlemen, a company is one stage removed from its final customers, so control has to be done voluntarily since these middlemen are not direct employees of the company. The channel should work to the advantage of all channel members, but there is always a propensity for disagreement. This is termed 'channel conflict', and it is dealt with in more detail in Chapter 12. In addition to this, there is also the notion of 'power' in channels of distribution in terms of who controls the channel (the 'channel captain'). Again, this detail is elaborated in Chapter 12.

Physical distribution management/logistics

This second aspect of distribution covers physical distribution management (PDM) or logistics and it relates to the transportation of finished goods to customers, as well as stock levels, warehouse management and order processing. In other words, it establishes the level of service that the customer receives in relation to delivery times and spare parts and accessories service.

The level of this support is a decision for marketing management. The system can be costly if the aim is to provide everything that the company produces ex-stock. As with promotion, PDM is a marketing cost to the company and the task of marketing management is to secure the optimum level of service that will satisfy the company's customers, at the same time making an acceptable profit for the company.

With the advent of 'just-in-time' or 'lean' manufacturing, the aim of the manufacturing company is to hold minimal stocks and the onus for stockholding is placed upon the supplier. The idea is that this principle of minimal stockholding should extend right back along the chain of supply (termed 'supply chain integration' (SCI)). The system has a lot to commend it, because stockholding is a waste of assets as goods do not normally appreciate in value while they are held in stock.

The costs associated with stockholding can be large when one considers the overheads of material control and the physical act of storing materials, coupled with the fact that valuable working capital is used to finance such stockholding. There is an increasing trend, started by automobile manufacturers, towards this system of manufacture through a realisation of the cost savings that such a system confers. The implications for PDM here are enormous, for in such manufacturing circumstances, supplies of materials are critical. If delivery deadlines are not met within a very tight window of time then it can literally mean a stoppage of the production line. The task of PDM is to strike a balance between minimum costs and maximum service and this is a decision for marketing management.

PROMOTION

Promotion, as one of the four Ps first described by McCarthy, covers advertising, sales promotion, personal selling and publicity. This is perhaps a misnomer, because advertising practitioners tend to regard the term 'promotion' as meaning sales promotion. More correctly, this function should be called 'communication' and the area of communication has now spawned its own mix called the 'communications mix'. The communications aspect of the overall marketing mix tends to emphasize different aspects in marketing practice. For instance, when marketing industrial products, selling is the prime element, whereas for fast moving consumer goods, advertising and sales promotion are probably more important.

The beneficial effects of communications expenditure are difficult to measure because of its lack of immediacy (eg people do not immediately buy a car because it is advertised on television) but procedures do exist for such measurement and these are examined in Chapter 8. Promotion is one aspect that impinges on buyer behaviour, alongside many other influences (see Chapter 3).

In order to be effective, a communications strategy must have a clear and well-defined set of objectives. Sometimes these are difficult to justify because of its lack of immediacy and unfortunately when economic conditions are difficult, and the company is looking for budget cuts, it is this promotional element that is the easiest target for such a cutback. The problem is that advertising in particular, and to a lesser extent sales promotion, tends to emphasise the long term, so although nothing might be felt immediately, it is the organisation's future that is being jeopardised as a result of such prunings of the communications budget.

Promotion is important to the company, as demand must be stimulated amongst buyers, be they consumers or organisational buyers. Throughout the purchasing process, as was seen in Chapter 3, it is important that different elements of promotion be adopted in order to progress the sale to the final decision stage. Even when the purchase has been made, it is important to emphasize to the customer that the decision was a good one in order to forestall cognitive dissonance and to encourage a positive image resulting in customer loyalty and repeat purchasing.

PERSONAL SELLING

Although personal selling has already been described in its context as a function of the communications/promotional mix, its importance is such that it is now considered as a separate province of marketing in its own right, for the end sale is the conclusion of all business activity.

The role of the modern salesperson generally includes more than face to face selling. Increasingly, the sales force is seen in the role of gathering information, particularly in relation to inputting into the company's marketing information system as discussed in Chapter 4. Public relations activity is increasingly included in this expanded role and this is examined in Chapter 9. However, this ancillary activity should not deflect from the primary task of selling. It is a fact though, that as relationship marketing becomes more firmly established in commercial practice, so the role of the salesperson will increasingly encompass these wider issues.

The task of selling is principally about communication by word of mouth. Purchasers normally need more than just advertisements and a view of the actual product when considering alternative offerings. The professional salesperson is a very flexible medium of communication and is able to establish purchasing motives through listening to the buyer. He or she should then emphasize appropriate aspects of the product or the company in terms of meeting and satisfying these motivational considerations. Modern selling skills now relate as much to listening as to talking and this is an important consideration when recruiting field sales personnel.

A company's image is personally delivered through the field sales force. This might be complemented by other communication variables such as advertising. The general perception of a company might be gathered from a variety of sources, such as the way telephones are answered, to company logotype, to the way staff are dressed and to their demeanour in general. There might exist what is termed a 'communication gap' in this perception, and misconceptions might predominate. It is often the task of selling to fill this communication gap by deliberately attempting to strengthen the company image in a message that can be individually tailored to the needs of different groups of customers.

The role of selling clearly involves the skill of persuasion, but this should be applied with care. As was demonstrated in Chapter 3, purchasers have needs and requirements corresponding to a scale of preferences which is connected in some way to a budget. When this range of preferences includes competitive as well as the salesperson's product or service, the task of selling demands that a competitive preference scale be adjusted and that price will not necessarily be the single deciding factor. Such persuasion means that the purchaser should be convinced of the unique advantages that the host company's product or service will supply.

MARKETING INFORMATION

Marketing information has already been discussed in some detail earlier in Chapter 4, because such information is the logical start of the marketing planning process and it is appropriate that it is considered before the marketing mix. It is not, therefore, our task here to describe the function of marketing information. As products and services are the fundamental requirements for a good company, it is important that information concerning these products is gathered in a scientific manner, through the utilization of appropriate marketing research techniques and that this information accurately reflects the needs of the market-place.

This information needs to be constant rather than ad hoc, as this allows it to be used interactively in the company's marketing information system. The principal need is to appraise the demands of the market-place and then take appropriate action. This underlies the need for adequate marketing information of the right quality in order to be able to make decisions that relate to products or services, and to ensure that the 'right' offerings can then be made to customers.

Marketing research is the most visible part of marketing information. Appropriate techniques have already been discussed in this respect, but these are the tools that tell us more specifically how our customers view our product offerings alongside those of our competitors. More importantly, the tools of marketing research can give a scientific indication as to the appropriateness and likely success of new product or service offerings. Marketing information through the MkIS cannot make decisions; it can only give scientific guidance to managers who make them.

SUMMARY

This chapter has described the marketing mix in addition to the information tools that are available to marketing, in order to be able to target its chosen market segments. This is achieved through the manipulation of the marketing mix. It is the skill of individual marketing management in orchestrating the elements of the mix into an appropriate sequence and in the correct manner that accounts for the success or otherwise of the company. This mix must link into a coherent marketing plan in order to give it a strategic emphasis, rather than merely producing a range of tactics. It is the business of senior marketing management to ensure that this planning process takes place and that it has the support of members of the department. Indeed, the whole organisation should be committed to this marketing planning process for this reflects the needs of the company's customers. Furthermore, this operation links into the overall corporate planning system, and as will be discussed later in the text, marketing planning is a functional component part of this process.

The next chapter now looks in detail at the first of these marketing tools – Personal Selling, which is still the most powerful tool in the marketing portfolio of commercial companies.

7

Personal Selling

PERSONAL SELLING AND MARKETING

As a part of the communications mix, selling is probably the most important component especially in organisational purchasing situations. The very fact that it is classed as part of promotion by McCarthy through his notion of the four Ps, or as part of the communications mix, tends to demean its value. Selling is concerned with direct contact with customers and this is the most flexible medium of communication that a company possesses. Messages can be altered immediately to suit individual purchasing situations and adapted as the sales process proceeds. More importantly, personal selling is the most likely medium through which an immediate sale can be realised.

In a competitive society, the way customers are handled is critical to business success and this has given rise to the new notion of 'customer care'. This is a raft of techniques that attempts to put customers on a pedestal and cater to their every need in a very ordered and competent manner. The objective in such situations is to keep customers loyal to the company, because it has been proved that customer retention is more economical in the long run that constantly having to seek out new customers. Thus the role of selling is increasingly being viewed as one of retaining existing customers and its importance can, therefore, be immediately recognised.

The role of selling differs in different purchasing situations. In the case of products and services which might only be sold rarely (eg a life insurance policy) selling will entail skills of prospecting and negotiation, whereas for regular repeat orders for a production line item, the task might be principally one of liaison and expediting the delivery of the materials and components that the customer has previously ordered. In this latter situation, purchasers will depend on the reliability of the salesperson to ensure that delivery promises are kept. Customer satisfaction is seen here to be of paramount importance. Personal selling is particularly important where complex negotiations form part of the commercial process. This is often the case where capital purchases are involved.

As an element of communications, personal selling is relatively expensive, because as well as the salesperson's salary and commission there are the on-costs of travel, entertainment and accommodation. An organisation must, therefore, manage its sales force effectively in order to ensure that it is productive in terms of how the company's portfolio of products and services is marketed to customers; this undoubtedly has a strong association with the prosperity of the enterprise.

SELLING'S WIDER REMIT

The role of selling has changed in line with developments in business practice. It now attracts a more professional type of person than it did less than 20 years ago and there has been a general move away from transactional selling towards relationship selling. Key account selling is now common practice in business where it is the sole responsibility of one senior salesperson to look after a single important account. Relationship selling is the tactical sales tool used to deliver the principles of relationship marketing with its long term customer implications, which were described in Chapter 1. Here salespeople with different qualities to the traditional view of the aggressive 'never take no for an answer' salesperson are needed. What is needed are salespeople with an eye for detail and the right kind of personality to keep in close contact with customers with a view to building up long-term relationships. In fact, this kind of salesperson is probably the very antithesis of the 'foot in the door' type.

'Team selling' is also the result of the fact that buyers are now more proactive in the commercial transaction than was the case only a few years ago when they generally adopted a passive stance in that sales representatives only met them in their offices. Now buyers actively scour the market-place with a view to sourcing appropriate suppliers who will deliver their requirements to the correct quality, in the right amounts and at the times requested. What they are looking for is reliability from their suppliers and this emphasises the long-term view. From the selling point of view, servicing key customers involves a team of personnel taken from sales as well as from other departments, such as research, production and finance. When non-sales problems arise, as they inevitably do, then advice is sought from other departments and may mean meeting directly with the customer. The important thing is that the entire team remains constant which implies consistency to the customer and helps to cement a long-term relationship.

SALES ROLES

Robert McMurry first recognised that many sales tasks were inherently different and proposed a distinct categorisation of roles for salespeople in 1961. These roles, plus more modern roles that reflect modern marketing practice, can be categorised as follows:

- The main task is concerned with delivery (eg milk to homes and bread to retailers). Little selling skill is needed here. The most important aspect is a pleasant manner. Remuneration is usually on the basis of a fixed salary plus some kind of bonus, although in the case of home deliveries, the income is determined by the size of the business.
- Similar to the above is the checkout operator where customers have already chosen their purchases and the checkout operator simply processes these through a till and collects payment. Again, an efficient manner and a pleasant personality are important qualities. Remuneration is normally on an hourly paid basis.
- Internal order taking where the task is a clerical routine such as processing orders or filling out order forms and when the opportunity to sell is limited. This is particularly prevalent in catalogue stores. By this stage customers have probably made their purchasing decision, so will only occasionally seek advice, but it is largely a matter of order processing. Remuneration, again, is normally on an hourly paid basis and the opportunity for commission is limited.
- An outside order taker is where the salesperson goes on a regular round of known customers (known as a 'sales journey

cycle'). Negotiation on price and quality has already been conducted by this stage at higher management levels and the salesperson's task amounts to servicing the account and ensuring that stock levels and deliveries are maintained. Sometimes merchandising and demonstration duties are included. Again, a pleasant manner is an important criterion and remuneration is usually a fixed amount plus expenses, but sometimes a bonus is linked to the salary package.

▦ Missionary selling normally involves 'one off' selling situations such as a life insurance policy. Here, salespeople must build up goodwill and ultimately influence the purchaser, rather than simply solicit orders. This type of task calls for creative selling skills. Commission tends to feature very highly in this type of sales situation.

▦ Technical selling comprises salespeople giving explanations of the function of a product or service to prospective customers. This task demands skilled applications knowledge by the sales-person, who is often technically qualified. This type of selling amounts to technical consultancy and demands an intimate product knowledge in order to canvass specifiers and designers. This type of job takes place in organisational purchasing situations, and selling arguments must be suitably tailored when canvassing individual component members of the decision making unit (DMU). Again, a creative approach is often called for. Remuneration tends to vary, and until relatively recently was based on a good basic salary plus some permutation of individual commission dependent on sales value or volume. However, modern marketing emphasises customer retention which is very much concerned with offering buyers the type of technical advice indicated above. This is non-selling time, but good relationships can be established and cemented as a result, ensuring the customer's long-term loyalty and repeat business. Therefore, to remunerate this type of sales-person more fairly, there is now a move away from personal to group commission-based structures, where members of the sales team share commissions and bonuses.

▦ Creative selling calls for a high degree of sales competence. Potential customers have to be 'educated' to understand that they need a particular product or service. The customer may not realise that there is a new product or service on offer which they might need. This is particularly relevant in the case of innovative products where customers do not perceive a need until they actually view the product or read about it. The creative salesperson communicates this need and the advantages of possession. For example, a faster and more powerful computer system with appropriate software and offered as a package for home use. This type of sales situation usually revolves around commission and the enthusiasm of the salespeople in many home computer retail outlets suggests that commission forms the major component of their remuneration package.

■ A final category relates to the 'sales engineer' which does not necessarily relate to engineering in the accepted sense. Designing sales territories is complicated in that some are easier to service than others. Some companies employ what are termed 'sales engineers' whose task it is to build sales territories and make adjustments by transferring sections from one territory to another as commercial situations change.

SALES QUALITIES

Listening skills are probably more important than talking skills. Listening is needed in order to recognise a person's reasons for wanting to possess, and this relates to either individual or organisational buyer behaviour. It is only by isolating purchasing motives that the professional salesperson can understand which points of the merchandise to emphasise as part of the sales routine. The task of selling then becomes simpler as inappropriate sales details can be discounted. Information 'overload' at an early stage of the purchasing cycle is one of the prime causes for not buying and a common phrase is: 'I will go away and think about it.' Listening can also help the salesperson to ascertain the level of technical competence that the prospective purchaser possesses, so that the sales discussion is pitched at the right level of sophistication.

It is the salesperson's persuasiveness that might ultimately win the order, but this persuasiveness must be woven into the sales presentation in an appropriate way to suit the purchasing situation. Otherwise the act of selling simply becomes one of a previously acquired routine and this negates the individuality that face-to-face sales contact seeks to encourage. It is widely recognised in selling that the salesperson should not seek to win arguments, even if he or she feels that the buyer is patently incorrect.

The purchaser's viewpoint should be recognised and then appropriate discussion and persuasion should be used to subtly alter that viewpoint and result in a sale.

The skill of listening is particularly highlighted because it is an ability that many would tend to discount in a salesperson. Other, more obvious skills are those of communication coupled with the right kind of temperament and personality to do the job required. Selling can be quite a lonely job, because by its very nature it is individualistic, so a good deal of self-discipline and motivation is required, coupled with determination.

Confidence is needed, but this does not mean over-confidence which might be a disadvantage if the buyer feels that they are being overpowered. Empathy is probably a more important attribute in this respect and empathic behaviour can also encompass such matters as the way the salesperson dresses to meet prospective purchasers, bearing in mind the fact that it is the purchaser who should be impressed by the salesperson and not the other way around.

Technical ability in terms of product knowledge will tend to vary, depending upon the complexity of the product or service being offered. The salesperson will need to have a good educational background and previous experience in addition to general intelligence and aptitude. When offering advice to a prospective purchaser who may be less technically competent, integrity is needed on the part of the modern salesperson, because if the purchaser is misled into purchasing an inappropriate piece of equipment then this could rebound on the salesperson's company.

The ability to anticipate and then act upon an opportunity is an important part of a salesperson's overall business sense. Adaptability is important here in terms of being able to anticipate and recognise the possibility of a business association that might eventually turn into a trading relationship.

SALES SEQUENCE

This is the universal description of the steps that are taken during a sales presentation from the seller to the buyer. It generally relates to more complex merchandise and does not concern the checkout operator or the inside order taker, for example, as this sales routine is too complicated and refined. It applies more to organisational purchasing where creative and technical selling skills are needed.

Adaptability is important in applying this sequence, otherwise it becomes a pre-learned routine (or 'canned selling') and the individuality of personal selling is negated. Here again, listening skills are important, for this is the only way that the salesperson can assess the buyer's purchasing motives and adjust the sales routine accordingly.

The sales sequence is described in Figure 7.1 followed by an explanation of the composition of each of the stages:

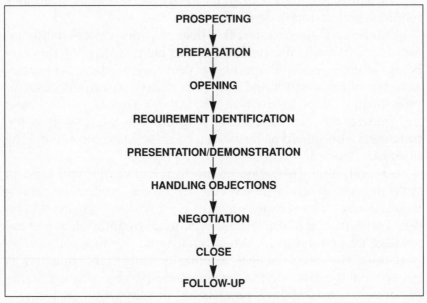

Figure 7.1 *The sales sequence*

Prospecting

Prior to the sales interview the potential purchasers ('prospects') should be identified and it should be determined whether or not they have the power (or are 'qualified') to make purchasing decisions. Even if they do not the interview might be with a 'gatekeeper' or some other member of the DMU, who could potentially pass on any recommendations to the ultimate buyer, or pave the way for a subsequent presentation to the buyer.

Preparation

This stage takes place before the sales interview. Much of this is routine and will form part of the knowledge gained during the salesperson's training, in addition to general knowledge about the company, its competitors and their procedures.

Fundamental facts are needed regarding company policy on prices and payment terms and how to handle complaints and deal with goods that are returned for reasons of quality or the fact that the customer might have over-stocked. A good working knowledge of the market-place for the company's products and services and those of its competitors is needed, including all of their limitations. In modern selling it is also the salesperson's task to find out market information as part of market intelligence and this should be used in the marketing information system, as discussed in Chapter 4.

Knowledge of the company's customers is important in relation to their previous patterns of purchase. At a sales routine level, many companies use a customer record card to detail each sales visit directly after the sales interview. Other companies require a visit report to be filled in after each sales interview and this is sent to sales management. This provides a record for monitoring purposes, and gives an element of continuity in the event of the salesperson being replaced for any reason. Commercial details such as delivery times or price are recorded along with general company information, for example on future contracts. In addition, personal matters can be recorded relating to the buyer (eg is keen on golf and has a 12 handicap), which might be useful in long term relationship marketing situations, when building confidence and friendships are very important.

The general demeanour of the salesperson is important. The rule is to avoid extremes of dress and personal behaviour that might make the buyer feel uncomfortable or embarrassed. The salesperson is meeting the buyer on his or her own territory, so it is basic etiquette to conform to the buyer's house rules.

Sales aids include company literature and samples and a sales presentation might incorporate spreadsheets and other computer support. Additions of this type can be helpful as it adds to the variety and quality of the presentation and demonstration stage.

Sales must be planned, and journey planning might include routine calls to regular clients on what is termed a 'sales journey cycle'. This cycle might be organised on 'differential call frequency' where some regular customers are visited more frequently than others. The objective of this regular calling pattern might not be to sell specific items, but merely to keep personal lines of communication open, thus it is very much a feature of organisation purchasing situations. A sales journey cycle, therefore, includes calls to regular customers as well as to prospective customers. The sales routine that follows relates more to this latter category.

Opening

The opening is very important when meeting a prospective buyer for the first time, because it is during this introductory phase that first impressions are formed. The general advice when selling in a western cultural setting is to be the first to speak by introducing yourself by your first name and surname. It can then be quickly ascertained whether or not the buyer wishes to deal at a familiar or a formal level (depending upon whether he or she refers to you by your first name or surname). Establishing this initial rapport can also include a brief statement about being pleased to meet the buyer, followed by key questions about the buyer's needs, which leads into the next stage.

Requirement identification

Here, the salesperson is attempting to ascertain purchasing motives. For organisational buying, these motives will principally involve value for money measures, but there might be subsidiary considerations and it is here that the probing skill of the sales-person will be an asset. This is sometimes termed a 'needs analysis'. This knowledge will affect the course of the presentation and the salesperson will have a clearer focus as to the points that should be emphasised. It is here, of course, that listening skills are appropriate. Personal selling is a very adaptable medium of communication and it is attention to this kind of detail that makes it so flexible.

Demonstration/presentation

Having determined the needs analysis, this is the stage where unique sales proposition (USP) features can be emphasized. USPs are benefits which competitive products or services do not possess and they can include the physical product itself, the service package, testimony from satisfied customers, a competitive price and even the image that surrounds the product or service. These benefits should be presented in a logical sequence that has been rehearsed prior to the sales interview.

A demonstration should be included, as this provides concrete evidence of any claims that may be made during the presentation and ideally are carried out concurrently. Some products do not lend themselves easily to demonstration and here suitable brochures as well as video presentations can be a useful supplement.

It is during this presentation stage that the salesperson concentrates on those matters that the buyer sees as being important and this is an ideal opportunity for the creative salesperson to adapt the sales process to suit buyer behavioural motives. The main problem here is 'over-presentation' and the danger of overwhelming the buyer with too much detail, so 'buying signals' should be looked for in order to bring this phase to a close.

Handling objections

Objections should not necessarily be viewed negatively. In many cases they are expressions of interest and a desire for further information. The professional salesperson should anticipate objections and seek to predict them by deliberately introducing them as part of the presentation. Experienced salespeople can turn objections, be they actual or hidden ones, into categorical reasons for purchasing. The most common objection is that of price, but the positive salesperson can prepare for this by emphasising value for money in the presentation. This technique is termed 'forestalling the objection'.

There are many other techniques for handling objections, and training courses exist for salespeople for this aspect of selling alone. Another popular technique is termed 'agree and counter'. Here the buyer might say something that is at odds with what the salesperson is saying, but rather than refute the buyer and attempt to prove the buyer incorrect, the salesperson agrees that it might be a valid point and then goes on to demonstrate his or her viewpoint. More colloquially, this is sometimes called 'shaking hands with the objection'.

Negotiation

This is a very broad subject with universal application in many areas of life. In the selling context we usually think of negotiation in the context of price, but it can of course include such matters as credit terms, service agreements, procedures for the return of goods in the case of inferior workmanship, penalty clauses if the contract is completed later than agreed and many more areas of commercial transactions. The ideal outcome is when both parties reach an agreement from which they derive mutual benefit.

Close

The principal purpose of selling is to reach a final agreement that will result in a purchase order. The reality is that many salespeople find this stage the most difficult one, perhaps because of having to ask for the order or not recognising closing signals from the buyer. A number of closing techniques exist such as negotiating and handling objections and it can form the entire theme of a sales training course.

The 'basic close' is the commonest and this simply consists of the seller completing the sales documentation. In the case of a major purchase it might even deter the buyer completely, as he or she really needs more time at this stage. The 'trail close' might be more appropriate as it seeks to test by asking questions such as: 'How would you want to pay?' Another method is 'alternative choice' and here the salesperson might ask questions like: 'Would you like to pay cash or use credit terms?' Yet another related method is the 'assumptive close' where the salesperson might ask: 'What is the address for delivery?'

There are many more techniques, but perhaps the one that sales professionals find most useful is the 'concession close'. In a particularly difficult negotiating situation, the salesperson might put forward one final concession which he or she hopes will finalise the sale which could be something like: 'If you place the order immediately, I could be persuaded to let you have it at a further 2 per cent discount.'

Follow-up

This is the final part of the sales process. In modern marketing the emphasis is on encouraging repeat custom, especially in the case of major purchases. It is this final follow-up that attempts to demonstrate to customers that they have been treated well. In many cases it might mean a simple telephone call or a personal letter to enquire whether or not the goods were to the purchaser's satisfaction. This type of follow-up, alongside other tactics, has witnessed the origin of the notion of 'customer care' which also includes such matters as the degree of service that is given to customers after the sale, all designed to build up long term goodwill.

Mild dissatisfaction is a common phenomenon after a major sale which relates to post-purchase conflict. Major purchases often involve a compromise decision, whereby other brands might in some respects be perceived as being better than the brand purchased. It is through such tactics as follow-up and a good subsequent customer care programme that the intensity and the incidence of dissatisfaction (or cognitive dissonance) can be reduced.

THE SALES MANAGEMENT PROCESS

The process of selling results in purchase orders without which a commercial company could not continue to operate. It is how well this process is managed that can determine the relative success of the concern. The process of sales management covers a number of areas of activity.

Recruitment

Sales force size is an important consideration here and this is determined by the 'coverage' the firm seeks to achieve. This is considered in detail in Chapter 12, 'Channels of Distribution', but coverage basically means whether the company wishes to sell its products direct to the maximum number of sales outlets (intensive distribution), or whether the product is bespoke and only a small number of outlets are covered (exclusive distribution), or whether there is some middle ground compromise (selective distribution). It is all a matter of examining the company's financial and production resources and its policy and then deciding which route to take.

The Personnel or Human Resource Management (HRM) function is responsible for recruitment, although this is done with the full collaboration and agreement of sales management. HRM will place the job advertisement in appropriate media. The job description, which is written by the sales department in conjunction with HRM, forms an important part of a potential salesperson's compendium which is sent out to prospective applicants, and it forms the blueprint for the job that is advertised. It typically contains the following elements:

▓ a job title and to whom responsible;

▓ the responsibilities and duties to be performed including frequencies of visits and after sales activities;
▓ product knowledge and specific sales abilities;
▓ the customers and locations to be covered;
▓ the degree and method of reporting sales activities to sales management.

SELECTION

HRM checks application forms against the job description and shortlists likely candidates for interview by sales management. Interviews can range from aptitude tests and an informal interview to 'stress' interviews (where the candidate is deliberately goaded into a position of stating why they are good enough to have the job). This latter method might be appropriate to some sales situations, where perseverance and never taking 'No' for an answer might be an asset.

References from previous employers might also form part of the selection process. The kind of information that should be elicited as general background, most of which can be gathered from the application form, includes:

▓ health;
▓ geographical location in which the candidate is willing to work;
▓ experience of selling and product knowledge;
▓ domestic situation;
▓ intellectual ability and outside interests;
▓ general traits deemed important to selling like interpersonal and presentation skills.

Motivation

Selling is an individualistic type of profession, often involving long periods away from home and sometimes having little to show for a lot of hard prospecting work. It can, therefore, be a very demotivating occupation and calls for a very distinct type of personality. This is why it is important for sales management to recognise this in terms of encouraging teamwork amongst members of the sales force.

It is one of the prime reasons for sales conferences, at both national and local levels, because apart from tackling issues that concern the company and its sales force, it is also an opportunity to get together with sales management and with colleagues in similar situations. It can also be an opportunity for sales management to impart confidence and motivate the sales force through 'positive stroking'.

Training

Sales training can be expensive not only in the cost of trainers, but in terms of the fact that training time means that the salesperson is not selling. Experienced salespeople need refresher programmes and new salespeople may need more basic elements to be included in their training package.

Sales training covers the following main areas:

■ the policies and organisation of the company;
■ the products and services;
■ competitors and their products and services;
■ selling procedures and specific techniques and sub-elements of the sales process;
■ work organization;
■ report preparation and how to summarise matters of market intelligence and perhaps how to use information technology in its dissemination to the marketing information system.

Training programmes can be 'in house', conducted by sales management and these generally relate to product knowledge, competitors' products and themes such as work routines and presentation of reports. Programmes can also be conducted by external trainers, who might impart a more objective element to the training than internal trainers. Such externally provided training can include 'refresher' training for existing staff or deal with such specific matters as 'negotiation' or 'closing' which form part of the sales routine.

Supervision

Because of its individualistic nature and its geographically dispersed nature, selling is an area where there is little close super-vision, except in very large companies which might have a regional management and an area management sales structure. However, in smaller companies the rule is normally to have a single representative covering a relatively large area and then reporting to sales management at the head office.

Supervision is a matter of how the sales task is organised, company culture and the nature of the product or service being marketed. When remuneration is closely linked to sales effort supervision will perhaps be less important because salespeople will tend to strive to attain maximum financial benefit. However, the problem here is that a policy might well lead to sales orientation, in that salespeople will tend to go for sales volume at the expense of customer care. As has already been mentioned, customer retention rather than winning new customers is important in modern day selling, so servicing the account, even when there may be no sales to be made, is important for long-term relationships.

Although quantitative performance measures might be best at providing supervision, qualitative measures can also be applied. Sales presentations can be assessed by the field sales manager by accompanying the salesperson on a number of visits. The field sales manager should be able to receive indications from customers as to whether or not they are receiving a satisfactory service. Quantitative measures need not only relate to the volume of sales, but they can also include such matters as the amount of orders attained, new accounts opened, service calls made and market intelligence collected.

Remuneration

Traditionally this is linked to the volume or value a salesperson sells. Nowadays this is less simple. 'Team selling' is one of the tactics of relationship marketing and a permanent team is linked to one or more of the company's long term important customers. This group can include not only members of the sales force, but personnel from finance, production, design, etc. It becomes difficult to measure individual inputs to the overall process of customer care that is accorded to such important clients, so there is now a tendency to operate on a shared commission or bonus basis when such a team services these kind of accounts.

The basic kinds of remuneration structure are:

■ 'Salary only'. Suitable in relationship marketing situations where customer retention is important and much of the salesperson's work might relate to customer care. This system of payment means more security and sales personnel in this type of situation usually stay in post longer than other categories. Incentives can be introduced through the application of individual or group bonus systems that are linked to the success of the company.

▨ 'Commission only', where the sole incentive is to sell. This has the disadvantage of sales personnel only wishing to perform duties that directly relate to individual sales. Where variable commissions apply a similar problem arises in that they will tend to 'push' those products that offer the greatest commission potential. It is very much a sales orientated formula and this reflects the negative side of selling. Such personnel will be unwilling to spend time on training and essential sales administrative duties. If customer care forms part of company policy then this type of remuneration structure can negate its successful application. However, from a purely commercial standpoint it is efficient because it is a variable cost that only increases as sales increase. However, the contradictory view is that it tends to be applied in financially precarious organisations.

▨ 'Salary plus commission' (or 'combination plan'), which attempts to combine the advantages of each system. Here, remuneration is not totally dependent upon commission. It is attractive to resourceful salespeople who may want to consolidate security with better earnings through improved personal endeavour. In many organisations this system involves what is termed an 'escalator' whereby commission increases at predetermined sales levels. The 'sales quota' or 'sales target' system is very popular and it operates on the basis that commission is only earned after an agreed target or quota has been reached during a specific period. This period is usually relatively short in order to 'reincentivise' salespeople who might not have done so well during a particular period and are ready to put in extra endeavour when the new period commences. The quota or target is mutually agreed beforehand with the sales manager. The sales that are agreed and which must be achieved, are sometimes termed the sales budget. This does not refer to a budgeted expenditure level, but it is in fact the sales target or quota by a different name.

Evaluation

By measuring actual performance against sales objectives deviations can be noted and appropriate action taken. Evaluation relates to supervision and control and this is the very essence of sales management. Both qualitative and quantitative performance measures have already been examined, and it is against these that sales performance can be evaluated. In order for evaluation to work successfully it is vital that the sales force understands its purpose, because if they view it as a policing system it will negate its purpose and can lead to dissatisfaction and a demotivated sales force.

SUMMARY

Personal selling along with product considerations are probably the most important elements within modern marketing. The subject of selling has been discussed here outside the context of the communications mix of which it forms a part. This is because its importance is such that to simply put it as a sub-component part of communications would demean its importance within modern business practice. Disparate market situations call for different types of selling arrangements and these have been discussed. Selling skills have also been examined in the context of the sales sequence.

Sales management provides the managerial and control processes and this covers the areas of recruitment, selection, motivation, training, supervision, remuneration and evaluation.

The next chapter considers another element of the communications mix, namely advertising or what is termed 'above the line' activity.

8

Above the Line Promotion

INTRODUCTION

The marketing communications mix consists of personal selling, a range of conventional advertising media and a range of non-media communication tools. The conventional media tools, which involve 'renting' space on television, newspapers, posters, radio, etc are referred to as 'above the line' promotional or communications techniques. Other marketing communications techniques, which do not necessitate the renting of time or space, such as sales promotion, sponsorship and exhibitions, are put into a separate category. Media that do not involve the commissioning of space or airtime in or on conventional media are referred to as 'below the line' techniques.

Marketing effectiveness relies crucially on communications effectiveness. The market is activated through information flows. The manner in which the potential buyer views the seller's market offering is significantly influenced by the amount and type of data he or she has about the product or service on offer from the marketing firm and his or her reaction to that information. Marketing, therefore, relies upon information flows between the seller and the prospective buyer as a way of achieving the desired buyer-seller interaction.

To the majority of lay people marketing communications, such as television advertising, sponsorship, telephone marketing, sales promotion, direct mail and poster advertising is marketing. This is because marketing communications is certainly the most highly visible aspect of marketing activity and it impacts on everyday life. Everyone comes into direct contact with some form of marketing communications every day and it is an intrinsic part of our everyday lives.

Marketing communications, whether above the line or below the line activity, is collectively just one of the four Ps of the marketing mix. However, it is a very important part, some would say the most important part. No matter how fantastic a firm's product or service offering is, the value and benefits to the consumer have to be communicated to prospective customers and communicated effectively in order to produce the desired results. Marketing communications, in the form of above the line and below the line promotion, lies at the very heart of any marketing plan.

The word 'promotion' here refers to everything to do with the promotion of an organisation, its products and/or services. In a sense all marketing communication activity is a type of promotion, that is trying to promote the brand, the product and/or the firm. What characterises above the line activity from below the line activity is somewhat arbitrary. There is no universally accepted definition of either. Below the line activity is usually classed as non-media advertising. If an advertisement is submitted to a publication and a commission is paid to the advertising agency to feature the piece then this is deemed to be above the line communication. If no commission has been paid to an agency for organising the work, for example in the case of a public relations press release, a trade exhibition or a sponsored sports event, this is referred to as below the line activity. Many authorities on the subject of 'promotion' accept this classification and it is the classification used in this chapter.

THE ROLE OF PROMOTION WITHIN THE MARKETING MIX

The four Ps, as we know, are made up of Product, Price, Place and Promotion. For services and products with a strong service component we use a seven P mix with the additions of People, Processes and Physical evidence. It is 'promotion' that is the most high profile and prominent 'P' in the four Ps. Promotion is a part of a firm's overall effort to communicate with consumers and others about its product or service 'offering'. The profit-making firm strives to improve or maintain profits and market share and gain a superior competitive position compared to its competitors. The consumer tries to reach his or her personal goals in as much as this can be achieved through the purchase of goods and services. The total product offering allows each party to move towards these goals, offering a 'bundle of satisfactions' which fulfil needs in both an instrumental and a psychological sense.

In the United Kingdom the phrase 'marketing communications' is generally preferred to the term 'promotion', which is usually reserved for a branch of communications called 'below the line sales promotion'. In the US the term 'promotion' is much more widely used and more generally applied and because many of the earlier marketing textbooks came from the US the term was used in those countries that had bought the textbooks. However, in the UK the term 'marketing communications' is thought to be a more accurate phrase to describe this particular group of marketing activities. We can really use the two terms 'promotion' and 'marketing communication' interchangeably.

All forms of marketing communication are purposeful communication, created to accomplish a specific commercially relevant effect. Some marketing communication activities are striving to bring about an actual sale. For example, an advertisement by a record company for a pop music album that cannot be purchased in the shops, where customers are invited to use their 'freephone' number to buy the product by credit card, is a form of direct marketing. It is an attempt to make a sale from anyone who sees the advertisement.

The majority of marketing communications, however, are not of this direct marketing type. The majority of marketing communications often have a more indirect role such as communicating certain product attributes to the consumer. They will be contributing to the final sale, but on their own they are merely making an intermediate contribution rather than having the specific objective of that activity resulting in a sale. That is, they are not really attempting to score a sale directly but are making a contribution to the communication process at the end of which a sale may take place. Whether the communication 'tool' being used is trade journal advertising, public relations, direct mail, telephone marketing, sponsorship or corporate advertising, all of these forms of communication, whether they are direct or not, are promoting either the product, service or firm. In this sense all forms of commercial marketing communications are a form of promotion.

From the livery painted onto articulated lorries delivering products to retail stores, to the labels on tins of grocery products and business cards held by salespeople working in the field, they all communicate something and combined they are referred to as the marketing communication mix.

Product and service attributes

The job of marketing communications is, as the name suggests, to communicate the benefits of the product, service or firm to potential consumers and other interested parties, such as shareholders. The same process is undertaken in 'not for profit' situations such as charitable organisations and political parties (the last 'New Labour' election campaign is a good example). The benefits that marketing communicators attempt to get across can be 'real' in the sense of the tangible attributes of the product, such as the speed of a car or the performance of a stereo system. Although many of the attributes are implied through association they are not tangible in the true meaning of the word.

Products and services have been described as a 'total bundle of attributes' which the consumer perceives in its entirety. In other words, consumers see the product or service offering as a unified whole, rather than a set of individual component parts such as its price, packaging, colour and so forth. A large number of products, especially in the fast moving consumer goods (FMCG) category, are very similar to other products in their class. For example, brands of packaged sugars are basically similar no matter which brand is selected and the same goes for many FMCG products, particularly packaged grocery products. In times of shortage, such as during the war years, goods were treated as homogenous commodities and basically soap was soap! In less developed countries the same is true today, as many basic products are viewed as commodities and there is less emphasis on packaging and branding.

The American psychologist Abraham Maslow hypothesised the various needs of people as being hierarchical in nature. In fact Maslow's model is known as the 'Hierarchy of Needs' model and is usually explained by referring to a pyramid.

▪ At the bottom of the pyramid physiological needs such as hunger and thirst are of primary importance to the individual, almost to the dismissal of anything else. Marketers can make use of this fact and it can be seen in advertising soft drinks such as 7 Up or fast food such as McDonald's. Only when these fundamental, but meaningful, physiological needs are satisfied will the individuals turn their mindfulness to the next level of need in the hierarchy.

■ Their next need is their safety and that of their family. In modern society these needs are manifest in goods and services such as burglar alarms, car locks and alarms, double glazing, external lighting, insurance, saving schemes etc. Marketers utilise the basic emotion of fear in order to market such products and services.

■ After these basic needs have been met, higher but less fundamentally important needs assume more significance. People need to feel that they are part of a group, valued by others and have the chance to both give and receive affection. Style items, perfume, supporting the same rock band or sports team, are all patterns of how marketing uses fundamental social needs to sell products and services. Esteem needs can be formed into products and services through the use of product and service design, pricing and of course marketing communications. Examples would include high status marque motor vehicles, 'designer' branded clothes or exotic health farms.

■ At the top of Maslow's pyramid of needs we eventually reach the higher order need of self-actualisation. Only in very rich countries is it possible to have large sections of the population put into this category. A good example here is probably in California, especially in cities such as San Francisco where people can indulge in a wide range of alternative lifestyles. Books by 'self-help' gurus, health supplements, exercise videos, some forms of alternative medicine especially 'psychological therapy' and plastic surgery are all examples of products and services aimed at the 'self-actualising' motive.

THE MARKETING COMMUNICATIONS MIX

Promotion refers to the communications activities of advertising, personal selling, sales promotion and publicity/public relations. Advertising is a non-personal form of mass communication, paid for by an identified sponsor. Personal selling involves a seller using personal contact to attempt to persuade a potential buyer to make a purchase. This method is very important in industrial and other business-to-business markets. Sales promotions encompass short-term activities such as giving coupons, free samples, extra product, price reductions, competitions, etc, which is supposed to encourage quick action by buyers, often acting on impulse to take advantage of the promotion.

The company has control over these variables, but has less control over the communication variable, publicity/public relations. This is another non-personal communication method that reaches a large number of people, but it is not paid for by the company and is usually in the form of news or editorial comment regarding a company's product or service. Put together, these promotional activities make up the promotional or communications mix, with a different importance attached to each element in relation to:

▓ the type of product or service;
▓ structure of the market;
▓ stage of the product life cycle;
▓ rate of market growth;
▓ degree of competition;
▓ characteristics of consumers;
▓ company resources.

Company size, competitive strengths and weaknesses and style of management all influence the choice and composition of communications mix. Other important factors with which promotion must be co-ordinated are the product itself, price and distribution channels. Product communication, including brand name, design of packaging and trademark are all product cues which communicate a specific message about the total product or service offering.

Price can communicate different things under varying circumstances, for instance conveying 'prestige appeal' for those buyers who perceive that a high price is equal to quality and prestige through the price–quality relationship. Price is also a very important promotional tool in the form of price reductions, especially within the packaged grocery market.

The place in which a product is distributed may also have an important communications dimension. Retail stores have 'personalities' or store images which consumers often associate with the quality or fashionability of the products they stock. Products receive a 'halo effect' from the retail outlets in which they can be found and two shops selling very similar products can project radically different product images. For example, a perfume sold through an upmarket store will have a much higher quality image than one sold through supermarkets. In fact some perfume manufacturers, such as Chanel, have done everything they can to prevent their products being sold through stores such as Superdrug and Kwiksave because of the fear that such stores might damage the carefully cultivated product image of their products.

THE MARKETING COMMUNICATIONS PROCESS

Effective communication is a prerequisite for effective marketing. If the marketing communications part of the overall marketing mix does not work, it does not really matter how well each of the other mix elements perform, the overall marketing effect is likely to be mediocre at best and at worst an outright failure.

Many products or services fail, not because there is anything wrong with the product or service itself or anything problematic with its distribution or price, but because of unimaginative and lacklustre marketing communications. Buyers' perceptions of market offerings are affected by the quantity and sort of information that travels to them and their reaction to that information. There must be a good flow of information between seller and buyer to allow for effective and informed decision-making which precedes an actual purchase. An effective marketing communications system also allows feedback from the consumer to the seller via the use of conventional marketing research techniques concentrating on communications research.

You can see from Figure 8.1 that the marketing communications process can be easily modelled using a simple schematic diagram. Starting from the left-hand side of the figure we have the sender of the message followed by the message, the media used and the receiver of the message. The message might be compromised by 'noise' or interference in the system. Finally there is a feedback loop in the form of communications research, to establish that the intended audience has received the message.

NEW PRODUCTS AND SERVICES

Some people have a psychological predisposition to buy products and services that are 'new' to the market. This predisposition can

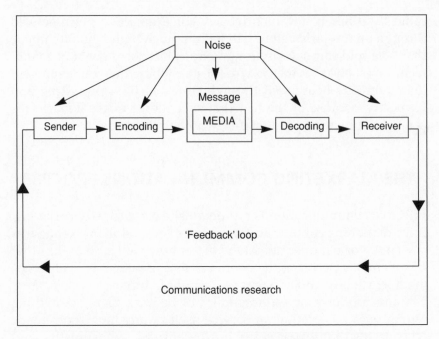

Figure 8.1 *The marketing communications process*

be modelled with the use of normal distribution. Some people derive a great deal of pleasure from acquiring new products and being first in the market. They have a low level of perceived risk and in fact they positively like the risk and excitement associated with the purchase of new, innovative products. These people are referred to as 'innovators' and according to Everett Rogers account for about 2.5 per cent of the population.

The next group of people display a tendency to buy new products and are known as 'early adopters', accounting for approximately 13.5 per cent of the market. These are still highly adventurous purchasers and the possession of innovative new products gives them a high present value. They still have a low level of perceived risk but are slightly more risk adverse than the 'innovator' category. The next two groups, 'early majority' and 'late majority' account for the bulk of the potential market, 64 per cent in all. Most people fall into one of these categories. Finally the 'laggards' are people who are not really interested in new product development and tend to purchase products only when their old product is worn out and stops working. This theme is returned to later under product issues.

A key question for the marketing communicator is: are the innovators and early adopters also opinion leaders? The majority of potential customers are too risk adverse or too disinterested to be 'first in the market' for an innovation. They are largely unaffected by the media communication about the innovation. Instead they are influenced by people who they regard as opinion leaders. Although some individuals may be innovators for many products and services, it is more likely that they will only be classified as such for a limited range of products. For example, a computer enthusiast may be regarded as an 'innovator' for new computer products. Similarly, someone who is interested in photography may be regarded as an opinion leader in relation to this product but not others.

A new brand of toothpaste containing baking soda is not really that new to people; after all, it is still just toothpaste. A vacuum cleaner for your garden is on the other hand quite a radical innovation. This product has recently come on to the market, although most people, even keen gardeners seem a little unsure as to whether they should buy one or not. If this product is any good, then the message will soon circulate by word of mouth and soon most households will own one, just as most own a lawn mower or a 'strimmer', which was considered to be a radical innovation only a few years ago.

MARKETING RELATED MESSAGES

Marketing communications can be defined as the process of:

1. presenting an integrated set of stimuli to a market target with the aim of raising a desired set of responses within that market target; and
2. setting up channels to receive, interpret and act on messages from the market to modify present company messages and identify new communications opportunities.

As both a sender and a receiver of market-related messages, a company can influence customers to buy its brands in order to make profits and, at the same time, stay in touch with its market so that it can adjust to changing market conditions and take advantage of new communications opportunities.

The source of the message

Receivers of a message are often greatly influenced by the nature of its source. If an audience perceives a communicator as credible, then they will be more likely to accept his or her views. If, on the other hand the audience believes that the communicator has underlying motives, particularly ones for personal gain, then he or she will be less persuasive than someone the audience perceives as being objective. Some advertisers use 'candid' television interviews with homemakers in order to enhance their credibility and eliminate intent to persuade, sometimes asking 'consumers' to explain why they buy a particular brand or asking them to trade their chosen brand for another.

Another method used by companies to increase credibility is to have the product endorsed by an expert who has appropriate education and knowledge on a given subject. This source will be more successful in changing audience opinions. Specialised sources of information are often perceived as expert sources and are successful due to the fact that messages are aimed at selected audiences, for example, the use of sports professionals as promoters for brands.

Its perceived status or prestige also affects the credibility of a source. The higher the perceived status, the more persuasive it will be. If a receiver likes a source, it will be more persuasive. It is clear that age, sex, dress, mannerisms, accent and voice inflection all affect source credibility and subtly influence the way an audience judges a communicator and his or her message.

A source high in credibility can change the opinion of receivers, but available evidence suggests that this influence disperses in a short time after the message is received. It has also been observed that where an audience initially receives a message from a low-credibility source, their opinions change over time in the direction promoted by the source. This is referred to as the 'sleeper effect'. Another aspect of this is when a high-credibility source is reinstated, for example by a repeat advertisement, it has been found that audience agreement with the source is higher after a period of time than if the source had not been reinstated. For a low-credibility source, reinstatement results in less agreement with the source than with no reinstatement and it is said that under these circumstances reinstatement negates the sleeper effect.

MEDIA ADVERTISING

Media advertising communicates information to a large number of recipients, paid for by a sponsor. It has three main aims:

1. To impart information.
2. To develop attitudes.
3. To induce action beneficial to the advertiser (generally the purchase of a product or service).

An advertisement for washing powder is paid for by the manufacturer to achieve greater sales; a party political broadcast aims to increase votes. It must be remembered that advertising is only one element of the communications mix, but it does perform certain parts of the communicating task faster and with greater economy and volume than other means.

How large a part advertising plays depends on the nature of the product and its frequency of purchase. It contributes the greatest part when:

1. buyer awareness of the product is low;
2. industry sales are rising rather than remaining stable or declining;
3. the product has features that are not obvious to the buyer;
4. the opportunities for product differentiation are strong;
5. discretionary incomes are high;
6. a new product or new service idea is being introduced.

ADVERTISING MODELS

These have been drawn from several sources, particularly psychology, and from advertising practitioners in order to explain how advertising works.

The stimulus/response formula

This was used at first very much as the psychologist Pavlov had postulated, but evolved over the years of being used by advertising researchers, with later models taking into consideration the environment in which the decision to buy is made. Daniel Starch said in 1925 'for an advertisement to be successful it must be seen, must be read, must be believed, must be remembered and must be acted upon'. This model assumed that the advertisement is the main influence on the state of mind of the consumer in respect of the product and makes no allowance for combined or multiple effects of advertisements.

The DAGMAR philosophy

Colley's DAGMAR model in 1961 (Defining Advertising Goals for Measured Advertising Results) allows for the cumulative impact of advertisements and also maps out the states of mind consumers pass through:

1. from unawareness to awareness;
2. to comprehension;
3. to conviction;
4. to action.

This is described as the marketing communications spectrum. Advertising, along with promotion, personal selling, publicity, price, packaging and distribution, moves the consumer through the various levels of the spectrum as follows:

Unawareness/awareness The advertisement tries to make potential customers aware of the product's existence.

Comprehension The customer recognises the brand name and trademark and also knows what the product is and what it does; knowledge gained from the advertisement or from an information search prompted by it.

Conviction The customer has a firm attitude, preferring a particular brand to all others. Preferences may have an emotional rather than rational basis.

Action Some move is made towards purchase, thus the advertisement has been acted upon.

This illustrates the concept that the purpose of advertising is to cause a change of mind leading toward purchase, but it is rare for a single advertisement to have the power to move a prospect from complete unawareness to action. Effectiveness is judged by how far an advertisement moves people along the spectrum.

The Lavidge and Steiner model

This consists of a hierarchical sequence of events on six levels:

1. awareness;
2. knowledge;
3. liking;
4. preference;
5. conviction;
6. purchase.

These steps divide behaviour into three dimensions: cognitive (the first two), affective (the second two) and motivational (the third two). Although this differs from the DAGMAR model in the number and nature of stages, there is agreement that purchase is the result of the persuasion elements, making the assumption between changes in knowledge and attitude towards a product and changes in buying behaviour so that there is a predictable outcome.

Dissonance theory, however, illustrates a two-way relationship, with behaviour influencing attitudes as well as attitudes influencing behaviour. After making a decision to purchase, the prospect will be involved in cognitive dissonance and will actively seek information to reinforce the decision, focusing on attractive features and 'filtering out' unfavourable data. The major implication of this is that advertising for existing brands in the repeat purchase market should be aimed at existing users to reassure them in the continuation of the buying habit at the expense of the competition.

The Unique Selling Proposition

This was developed by Rosser Reeves (1961), who reported the principles his agency had worked with for 30 years. This states that the consumer remembers one key element of an advertisement – a strong claim or concept. This proposition must be one that the competition does not offer, which will be recalled by the consumer and will result in purchase at the appropriate time.

The 'brand-image' school

This was led by advertising practitioner David Ogilvy who focused on non-verbal methods of communication to invest a brand with agreeable connotations, aside from its actual properties in use, such as prestige and quality.

It must be remembered that an advertisement is the channel through which the sponsor communicates its message. The encoded message reaches recipients, through advertising or sales-people, who then decode and absorb it either fully or partly. The quality of the transmission can be distorted by 'noise' occurring because the receiver does not interpret the message in the way that the source intended. This might be due to differences in the cultural backgrounds of the two parties or because of cognitive dissonance, which occurs when the message does not agree with what people previously believed.

Dissonance may cause a number of different reactions by the receiver:

1. rejecting the message;
2. ignoring the message;
3. altering the previous opinion;
4. searching for justifications.

The first two reactions are negative and the source may change the message or stop communicating altogether with a particular receiver who is not receptive to the source's ideas. It can, therefore, be seen that advertising does not always convert people into users of a particular product. It can have a positive effect in preventing loss of users and increasing their loyalty.

ADVERTISING BY OBJECTIVES

Advertising situations are so varied and unique that it is not possible to generalise about how advertising works. Any potential advertiser should therefore adopt an advertising-by-objectives approach that will make clear what they are trying to achieve, how they will achieve it and how they are going to measure its effects.

Few companies give any detailed scientific thought to exactly what they are trying to achieve through advertising. Clear objectives are needed to aid operational decisions, which include:

■ the amount to be spent on a particular campaign;
■ the content and presentation of the advertisement;
■ the most appropriate media;
■ the frequency of display of advertisements or campaigns;
■ any special geographical weighting of effort;
■ the best methods of evaluating the effects of the advertising.

Corkindale and Kennedy (1976) found that systematically setting and evaluating objectives provided the following benefits:

1. Marketing management has to consider and define in advance what each element in the programme is expected to accomplish.
2. An information system can be set up to monitor ongoing performance, with the nature of information required clearly defined.
3. Marketing management will learn about the system it is operating from accumulated experience of success (and failure) and can use this knowledge to improve future performance.

Majaro's (1970) major study on objective setting revealed that most managers saw increasing sales or market share as their main advertising objective. In fact this is a total marketing objective and it is unreasonable to expect to achieve this objective through advertising alone (unless it was the only element of the marketing mix used, as in direct mail and mail order businesses). Majaro's study also revealed that methods of evaluation used by most companies were not relevant and that clear, precise advertising objectives would rectify this situation. The following advantages of the advertising-by-objectives approach became clear:

1. It helps to integrate the advertising effort with other ingredients of the marketing mix, thus setting a consistent and logical marketing plan.
2. It facilitates the task of the advertising agency in preparing and evaluating creative work and recommending the most suitable media.
3. It assists in determining advertising budgets.
4. It enables marketing executives and top management to appraise the advertising plan realistically.
5. It permits meaningful measurement of advertising results.

When setting objectives, all personnel in a company who have an interest in, and influence on, advertising decisions have different ideas as to the purpose of advertising. The Chairperson may be concerned with corporate image, while the Advertising Manager may see it as an investment directly toward building a brand image and increasing market share. Marketing objectives have to be separated from advertising objectives. Overall marketing objectives should be defined and the next step is to determine the contribution that advertising can efficiently make to each of these. An advertising objective is one that advertising alone is expected to achieve.

Advertising objectives should be set with the following points in mind:

1. They should fit in with broader corporate objectives.
2. They should be realistic, taking into account internal resources and external opportunities, threats and constraints.
3. They should be universally known within the company, so that everyone can relate them to his or her own work and to the broader corporate objectives.
4. They need to be flexible, since all business decisions have to be made in conditions of partial ignorance.
5. They should be reviewed and adapted from time to time to take account of changing conditions.

Setting advertising objectives should not be undertaken until all relevant information on the product, the market and the consumer is available. Consumer behaviour and motivation must be thoroughly assessed, particularly that of the company's target group of customers. The statement of an advertising objective should then make clear what basic message is intended to be delivered, to what audience, with what intended effects and the specific criteria to be used to measure success.

Corkindale and Kennedy used five key words to summarise the elements of setting advertising objectives:

1. **WHAT**   What role is advertising expected to fulfil in the total marketing effort?
2. **WHY**   Why is it believed that advertising can achieve this role? (What evidence is there and what assumptions are necessary?)
3. **WHO**   Who should be involved in setting objectives; who should be responsible for agreeing the objectives, co-ordinating their implementation and subsequent evaluation? Who are the intended audience?
4. **HOW**   How are the advertising objectives to be put into practice?
5. **WHEN**   When are various parts of the programme to be implemented? When can response be expected to each stage of the programme?

Telephone marketing

Telemarketing can be defined as 'any measurable activity that creates and exploits a direct relationship between supplier and customer by the interactive use of the telephone'. The American Telephone and Telegraph Company defines it as 'the marketing of telecommunications technology and direct marketing techniques'.

Telephone marketing can take the forms of 'in-coming call' and 'out-going call'. In-coming call telephone marketing usually makes use of special numbers, which enables the caller to call 'free-phone' or at local call rates. Such campaigns are usually used in conjunction with other marketing communications 'tools'.

Direct mail and direct marketing

Direct mailing is the use of the postal service to distribute promotional material directly to a particular person, household or firm. It is often confused with the following related activities, which all fall under the general heading of 'direct marketing':

1. **Direct advertising**   One of the oldest methods of reaching the consumer, with printed matter being sent directly to the prospect by the advertiser, often by mail, but sometimes through the letter box by personal delivery, handed out to passers-by or left under the screen wiper of a car.
2. **Mail order**   Mail order advertising aims to persuade recipients to purchase a product or service by post, with deliveries being made through the mail or other carrier or through a local agent. Thus it is a special form of direct mail, seeking to complete the sale entirely by mail and being a complete plan in itself. Mail order is a type of direct mail, but not all direct mail is mail order.
3. **Direct response advertising**   This is a strategy of using specially designed advertisements, usually in magazines or newspapers, to invoke a direct response, such as the coupon-response press ad, which the reader uses to order the advertised product or request further information. Other variants offer money-off coupons and incentives to visit the retail outlet.

The usage and acceptance of direct mail is increasing rapidly and one reason for this is that the media has become increasingly fragmented, with many commercial TV channels and the rapid growth of 'freesheets' and special interest magazines. This means that advertisers have to either spend more money to reach their audience, or spread the same amount over a wider range of media. Improvements in the quality of large mailshots have attracted an increasing number of large advertisers. Direct mail, with increasing sophistication of computerisation, now enables advertisers to segment and target their markets with greater flexibility, selectivity and personal contact.

Direct mail can be used to sell a wide range of products or services, and its uses are also varied. To help define direct mail more fully, it is appropriate to deal with direct mail to consumers and businesses separately.

Consumer direct mail

Some of the most common uses of consumer-targeted direct mail are:

1. **Selling direct** Direct mail is a good medium for selling a product directly to the customer by a company that has a convincing sales message. It provides a facility for describing the product or service fully and for an order to be sent straight back, cutting out the 'middlemen'.
2. **Sales lead generation** Some products/services require a meeting between the customer and a specialised salesperson, and direct mail can be used to acquire 'qualified' leads. A mainsheet that has been well thought through can reveal the best prospects and rank other leads in terms of 'potential', enabling responses to be followed up by a salesperson. An invitation can be made for the customer to view the product in a retail outlet, showroom or exhibition. Such 'cordial-contact' mailings can create a receptive atmosphere for salespeople by building on the reputation of the company and creating a good impression, which can be converted into buying action later.
3. **Sales promotion** Promotional messages such as special offers will reach specific targets through direct mail and in the same way prospects can be encouraged to visit showrooms or exhibitions.
4. **Clubs** The most popular users of direct mail here are book clubs and companies marketing 'collectibles'.
5. **Mail order** Direct selling and recruitment of new customers and agents are possible through direct mail.
6. **Fundraising** It is easy through direct mail to communicate personally with an individual, and therefore it is an excellent

method of raising money for charitable organisations. Large amounts of information can be included to induce the recipient to make a donation.

7. **Dealer mailings**   Dealers or agents can use direct mail to reach the prospects in their own area.
8. **Follow-up mailings**   These help to keep the company's name before the customer following a sale, for example checking that the customer is satisfied with a purchase. New developments, products and services can also be communicated or invitations issued, thus maintaining contact and increasing repeat sales.

Business direct mail

For business, this is more effective than mass advertising for identifying different market sectors and communicating to each an appropriate message. Some of the more common uses are:

1. **Product launch**   Direct mail is able to target the small but significant number of people who influence buying decisions.
2. **Sales lead generation**   Direct mail provides qualified sales leads, as well as doing some initial selling.
3. **Dealer support**   Dealers, retail outlets, franchise holders, etc can be kept fully informed of marketing promotions and plans.
4. **Conferences**   Potential delegates in specific business sections can be issued with invitations through direct mail.
5. **Follow-up mailing using the customer base**   Mailing existing customers regularly encourages repeat sales.
6. **Market research/product testing**   Market research (especially amongst existing customers) can be very effective where it is possible to do this through direct mail, using questionnaires as part of a regular communication programme. Small-scale test mailings can give an accurate picture of market reaction, with low risk, and a successful product can later be mailed to the full list.

Direct mail as part of the promotional mix

When direct mail is added to, say, a television or press campaign, the effectiveness of the overall campaign can be significantly raised. The media reaches a broad audience and can raise general awareness of the company and its products, while the direct mail campaign is targeted specifically at the groups of people or companies most likely to buy. Mailing lists of respondents to couponed press advertisements or television or radio commercials with a 'phone-in' number can be used for direct mail approaches.

Packaging

Packaging is sometimes referred to as the 'silent salesperson'. Many products, especially fast moving consumer goods such as packaged groceries, are bought on a self-service basis and in a sense have to sell themselves. The packaging of the product is an intrinsic part of the product 'brand identity', in fact it is the very first part of the product that the customer actually sees. Many a poorly performing product has been turned around and made more successful simply by changing the pack. The pack often carries promotional messages as well as instructions and suggestions. Major brands are instantly recognisable by their packaging. Students of marketing communications often view packaging as an afterthought, when in fact the opposite should be true. Packaging, particularly for many consumer products, is at the very heart of the marketing communications mix.

SUMMARY

The word 'promotion' refers to everything to do with the promotion of an organisation, its products and/or services. In a sense all marketing communication activity is a type of promotion, that is trying to promote the brand and product and/or firm. In this marketing area there are two categories of promotional activity: the first is termed 'above the line' activity and the second is termed 'below the line'. What characterises above the line activity from below the line activity is somewhat arbitrary as there is no universally accepted definition of either.

Below the line activity is usually classed as non-media advertising. If an advertisement is submitted to a publication and a commission is paid to the advertising agency to feature the piece then this is deemed to be above the line communication. If no commission has been paid to an agency for organising the work, for example in the case of a public relations press release, a trade exhibition or a sponsored sports event, this is referred to as below the line activity. Many authorities on the subject of promotion accept this classification and it is the classification used in this chapter.

The marketing communications mix is made up of personal selling, a range of conventional advertising media and a range of non-media communication tools. The conventional media tools, which involve renting space on television, newspapers, posters, radio, etc are referred to as above the line promotional techniques. Other marketing communications techniques, such as sales promotion, sponsorship and exhibitions do not involve the commissioning of space or airtime in or on conventional media. These techniques are referred to as below the line techniques.

Marketing effectiveness depends significantly on communications effectiveness. The market is activated through information flows. The way a potential buyer perceives the seller's market offering is heavily influenced by the amount and kind of information he or she has about the product offering, and the reaction to that information. Marketing, therefore, relies heavily upon information flows between the seller and the prospective buyer.

To many people marketing communications, such as television advertising, direct mail and poster advertising is marketing. This is because marketing communications is certainly the most highly visible aspect of marketing activity and it impacts on everyday life. Marketing communications, whether above or below the line activity, is collectively just one of the four Ps of the marketing mix. However, it is a very important part. No matter how good a firm's product or service is, the benefits to the consumer need to be communicated effectively. Marketing communications, in the form of above and below the line promotion, lie at the very centre of any marketing plan.

9

Below the Line Promotion

INTRODUCTION

To most people not used to using the term the phrase 'below the line' seems rather odd and is often misinterpreted as having something to do with profit and related to the business jargon for profit, the bottom line. In actual fact it has nothing to do with this meaning. The phrase has been imported from the US, like so much established marketing speak, and like so many other pieces of marketing jargon, gives a veneer of technicality and sophistication to an otherwise very simple concept. Even after so many years of usage in marketing circles there is still no single, generally accepted definition of the term.

In general the term below the line promotion or communications, refers to forms of non-media communication, even non-media advertising. Examples of non-media promotions are exhibitions, sponsorship activities, public relations and sales promotions such as competitions, banded packs and price promotions. Below the line promotions are becoming more and more important within the communications mix of many firms, not only those concerned with fast moving consumer goods (FMCG products), but also for industrial goods and services. For example agent or distributor incentives, exhibitions and sponsorship activities are all increasing in use and importance. All types of non-media communications are a form of promotion if we use the word in a general sense. A specific form of below the line activity is known specifically as below the line sales promotion. This specific form of promotion is examined below.

BELOW THE LINE SALES PROMOTION

Below the line sales promotions are a specific kind of below the line activity which includes a range of marketing communications. Below the line sales promotions are short-term incentives, mainly targeted, as you would expect, at consumers, but also aimed at the trade, eg wholesalers, retailers, distributors, etc, along with company employees, usually the sales force. Over the past 25 years or so there has been increasing pressure on marketing budgets and a greater demand on marketing management to achieve marketing communications objectives more efficiently, particularly for less money.

Hence marketers have been looking for a more economic and efficient way to communicate with their target markets than conventional media advertising. A move to below the line promotion is one of the results of this search. There are many definitions of below the line sales promotions available. In fact every author of every standard text seems compelled to create his or her own and add to the existing very long list. The authors of this text have resisted the temptation and have used instead the definition of an expert in the field. A good definition of below the line sales promotion is given by Hugh Davidson, an acknowledged expert in the area, who describes it as:

> An immediate or delayed incentive to purchase, expressed in cash or
> in kind and having only a short term or temporary duration.

Hugh Davidson's definition highlights a salient characteristic of below the line sales promotions which is its short term time dimension. Most conventional above the line advertising campaigns are medium to long term in nature. Below the line sales promotions tend to be short term in nature. Rarely does a sales promotion last for more than six months and the majority last for much shorter periods, sometimes only a day, as with many store promotions, or a week or so.

All below the line sales promotions are variations of a few basic types. However, since the sales promotion is dynamic by nature, new types will be developed in the future. In fact many below the line sales promotions are repetitive and because they are used with such frequency they tend to diminish in impact. A competitive advantage can be secured by those firms that create unusual and innovative promotions with increased interest for the public and other target audiences.

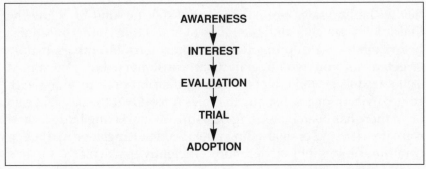

Figure 9.1 *Innovation-Adoption model (Rogers, 1962)*

SALES PROMOTION PLANNING

A full plan is needed to ensure that each stage of a promotion is reached:

1. Analyse the problem task.
2. Define objectives.
3. Consider and/or set the budget.
4. Examine the types of promotion likely to be of use.
5. Define the support activities (eg advertising, incentives, auxiliaries).
6. Testing (eg a limited store or panel test).
7. Decide measurements required.
8. Plan timetable.
9. Present details to sales force, retailers, etc.
10. Implement the promotion.
11. Evaluate the result.

ADVANTAGES AND DISADVANTAGES OF SALES PROMOTIONS

Advantages

■ direct involvement and support of those working in sales;

- versatility of operation;
- relatively efficient and fast in the achievement of objectives;
- the sales response is relatively straightforward to measure;
- cost effective;
- a high probability of having some form of sales effect;
- can be used for a wide range of different objectives;
- continuous innovation of new promotion formats;
- new technology gives the opportunity for more sophisticated promotions.

Disadvantages

- can cause problems with marketing intermediaries;
- generally only short term in their effects;
- price discounting can have an adverse effect on the image of the brand;
- customers expect promotions all the time, eg beer;
- many promotions have little effect;
- promotions bring about a competitive response leading to more promotional activity;
- some promotions go wrong, eg everyone wins. They need to be tested;
- wholesalers and retailers do not always deliver their promises when given incentives such as extra discounts.

PUBLIC RELATIONS

Public relations (PR) is a very versatile communications tool and is today used by just about every type of organisation whether it be a charity, a political party or a commercial firm. It is concerned with strategic management of information to ensure that specific communications goals are achieved by the firm. It is not always the case that positive publicity is the outcome of a formally administered PR programme, because it is often impossible to achieve a net positive outcome. Often PR is used to mitigate or reduce the effects of unfavourable publicity and it is an important and very flexible marketing communications element. It can be used both within and outside the organisation, although many feel that it is an external marketing tool, with the firm trying to communicate with a range of external publics in order to create a positive impression in people's minds. This view is very narrow and does not recognise its tremendous worth as an internal marketing communications tool.

The fact is we read and hear a lot about PR from an external point of view but little on the internal view. Effective internal marketing, ie creating the correct spirit within firms and persuading all staff to pull in the same direction in terms of marketing effort, is a vital prerequisite to successful external marketing. This is particularly important for marketing policies based on the concepts of long-term relationship marketing. PR has a key role in helping to bring about an effective internal marketing culture within the firm. In this sense there has been a realisation over more recent years of its importance as a strategic internal communication tool as well as an external tool.

PR has a particularly crucial role in the management of adverse publicity resulting from undesirable events or crisis management scenarios. Where a crisis has occurred, especially where people have been injured or lost their lives, it is often a case of damage limitation, putting a fair and balanced account of events forward to the general public and minimising the adverse effects of the crisis to the organisation involved or responsible.

A classic example is the case of Yorkshire Water plc, a newly privatised water company who actually managed to run out of water just after privatisation in 1994. This event coincided with the firm giving senior managers huge pay rises and declaring record profits and dividends to their shareholders. The public and the government found their behaviour distasteful and a number of senior Yorkshire Water managers responsible for the PR mess were asked to leave the firm. The firm then employed a new PR expert and tried to formulate a damage limitation public relations exercise to retrieve their lost reputation.

Communications and public relations

Because PR is not regarded by various publics as a paid-for type of communication, it tends to have greater source credibility than ordinary paid for advertising. That is because the write-ups in the press or business journal, television or radio programme, etc are regarded as emanating from an independent third party rather than a bought communications consultant. PR is not paid for in the direct sense of the term, unlike advertising, although the marketing firm will have to pay fees if it employs a PR firm or a salary if they have an internal PR expert.

It is often said that the mark of good PR is that the receiver of the message does not realise that it has been used; it is intended to be invisible. If it is clear to all that the message has been engineered then it loses much of its desired impact. Communications is central to PR and its role is to create a dyadic relationship or two-way communication, to help resolve conflicts of interest by seeking common ground or areas of mutual interest.

If we accept that this is the main role of PR, then we must also accept a further inference. It exists, whether implicitly or explicitly, whether an organisation likes it or not. Simply by carrying out its day to day business, an organisation communicates certain messages to those who, for whatever reason, interact with the company, who will then form a view about it and its business activities. The need for PR is to manage the conduct of the organisation and the communications that result from such conduct in order to create a favourable corporate image.

Defining public relations

The task of defining the precise nature of PR is difficult. A range of definitions are available in the textbooks and elsewhere, each focusing on a slightly different facet and each trying to produce a simple, to the point and accurate definition. The problem in deriving a single acceptable definition results from the complexity and diversity of the profession. The Institute of PR (IPR) in the UK states:

> PR practice is the deliberate, planned and sustained effort to establish and maintain mutual understanding between an organisation and its public.

The main aspects of this definition is that PR practice should be purposeful, planned and sustained. It should not be haphazard and mutual understanding is required in order to make sure that the communication between the organisation and its public is clear, ie the receiver perceives the same meaning as the sender intends. As we say there are more elaborate definitions but this one serves our purpose.

Publics

The idea of publics is central to the art of managed PR. The PR expert has to manage the publicity from events which concern every public with which the organisation has contact. This is because in order to exist, succeed and survive, an organisation depends on many individuals and groups of people. Even in the distribution of products for example, a manufacturer must communicate with salespeople, delivery staff, servicing staff, wholesalers, mail-order houses, agents, importers, exporters, overseas agents and many different kinds of retailer including chain stores, co-operatives, department stores, supermarkets and smaller independently owned shops.

There are many other people or groups that may impact on the success or failure of a firm. These include printers, packaging manufacturers, transport contractors, media owners and advertising agents. To these we can add others such as journalists who may write about the products or company, television producers of consumer affairs programmes and technical programmes. Business analysts, professional bodies, trade associations, government departments and other organisations are also important publics. PR includes all attempts by a firm to anticipate, track, review and possibly influence or control the type of publicity communicated, whether directly or indirectly, to various sections of the public. In doing this, the firm hopes to be able to create and sustain a positive corporate image. In fact the strategic management of publicity through the use of PR is often referred to as corporate communications. PR is concerned with communicating to an array of publics and not simply to the immediate customers.

Achieving a marketing orientation through public relations

In marketing literature there is a lot about how it is important for an organisation to become marketing orientated, customer focused and adopt the marketing concept. For a firm to be truly marketing oriented all the staff working for it have to be so. There is a saying adapted from Buddhist philosophy that states 'For a forest to be green each tree has to be green.' This principle also applies to the marketing orientation of the firm for it comes from within the minds of the people making up the organisation. But how does senior management achieve this change in attitude and bring about the right customer focused spirit within their organisation? Internal PR on its own cannot achieve this, but it can certainly make a significant contribution.

Corporate identity

The idea of corporate identity or personality or image is closely linked to PR, as activities must be conducted within the reference frame of a specific and agreed corporate image. This image or personality must be developed to reflect the style of the top management, since they control the firm's plans and business operations. A corporate personality is an asset if it is managed correctly and consistently, but it cannot be taken for granted that all managers will consider the role of corporate personality when they make decisions. Therefore, the PR expert needs to be positioned so that he or she is aware of all the issues, policies, attitudes and opinions that exist within the organisation that have an impact on how it is viewed by the public.

MEDIA USED IN PUBLIC RELATIONS

Printed communication includes the use of direct mail as a delivery mechanism which is a very versatile and flexible medium and suitable for a range of uses which include direct marketing, general advertising and PR. Direct mail can be used to send copies of press releases to targeted audiences and can be used to circulate house magazines or company newsletters to employees, customers, distributors, agents and other interested parties. This medium is also used to send details and invitations to sponsored events, exhibitions, conferences, demonstrations, film shows, etc. Invitations are a form of PR as are the events that the invitations relate to.

Literature can be usefully distributed to visitors, customers, dealers and members of the local community, while hand outs and press kits are used at conferences. PR activities of this kind can inspire confidence and trust in an enterprise. Printed literature delivered in the form of direct mail is often used to target printed messages to the required audience and can consist of leaflets, folders, booklets, books and other media including wall charts, diaries, postcards and pictures. PR literature is often educational in nature, it tends to be in the form of information that tells a story, rather than attempting to persuade or sell something.

The press release is often thought of as the most effective form of PR within the industry. Two salient aspects are timing and distribution, choosing the appropriate time to release news and ensuring that it reaches the appropriate audience. The role of press relations is to achieve maximum publication or broadcasting of PR information through newspapers, magazines, radio and television, in order to achieve specific PR goals with clearly defined target audiences. The common method of achieving this is a press release sent to appropriate journalists.

Visual communications includes photography which can have an affect and appeal that is not available in printed media such as magazines or newspapers. When an audience actually sees photographic evidence of an event it gives additional credibility to the PR report as it furnishes extra proof in the receivers' minds that what has been reported is genuine. Photographs are often used with a press release, the one form of PR backing up and augmenting the other. Television is a medium of high visual impact. Not only can PR messages be explained verbally on television programmes but products can also be shown on the programme. At times coverage of a firm's participation in a sponsored event or some other organised PR event is screened on television programmes.

The increase in sponsored events by commercial firms both in sport and in the arts has increased significantly over the past 25 years and it is now a routine type of programming when reporting events such as motor racing or football. There is an increasing demand for company personalities to appear on television programmes and also to give interviews on the radio, especially local radio. There has also been a significant growth in interest in all topics concerned with business, economics and management in general. This provides a chance for organisations to capitalise on the PR opportunities offered from this popular, highly visual and increasingly effective medium.

Personal forms of communication are perhaps the most effective and most persuasive method of delivering a message. The message is augmented by the strength and credibility of the personality and reputation of the communicator who can adapt both content and style of delivery to the reactions of his or her audience. A professional speaker can do a lot to improve the image of a firm, particularly at press conferences and on television and radio programmes. The role of the PR officer is not essentially to make an appearance on the programme him or herself, but to manage events so that an appropriate representative of the firm can communicate to the right audience and deliver the correct message.

PUBLIC RELATIONS AND INTERNAL MARKETING

The term internal marketing refers to the process of applying the general principles of marketing inside the firm. Marketing as a business philosophy is concerned with producing the appropriate internal company culture or internal spirit that will result in the firm becoming truly marketing orientated and customer focused. The process of internal marketing involves much more than simply the application of internal PR inside firms although, as we have discussed earlier, internal PR is of paramount importance here. Internal marketing takes place at the interface between marketing and human resource management and involves both of these management disciplines.

The application of internal PR has a salient role to play in the overall process of achieving an internal marketing culture because it too embraces both of these areas of management. The most common way of achieving internal PR objectives is through company communications. If these are to be of any real value, they must be more than paternalistic house journals and should provide a forum for open, two-way discussion on company issues. Whatever methods are employed, the important requirement is that they represent a genuine desire to communicate on behalf of both workers and management. This reinforces the point that PR can only reflect reality.

SPONSORSHIP

Like most below the line activity, this is growing in popularity. In some ways sponsorship achieves many of the functions of exhibitions, especially in terms of audience quality. We have already established that in business to business marketing environments, high status decision making unit members are notoriously difficult to contact on a personal basis. The firm sponsoring an event can invite important members of a prospective customer's DMU to the event thereby enabling personal contact to be made in a social setting.

Sponsorship has a strong PR component to it and firms can use it in a variety of ways. Being associated with the arts can give a strong sense of supporting and being part of the fabric of society. Important clients and other key individuals from other influential groups of publics can be invited to artistic events such as concerts, plays or opera. Afterwards they can mix with artists and directional staff so in this way key individuals who have been targeted for such promotion can be contacted, entertained and long-term relationships built and maintained.

Sponsorship of sport

Sponsorship of sporting events is of course big business and nearly everyone is familiar with some form of sponsored sports event, especially F1 motor racing, football, cricket, snooker and even bowls. Sponsorship of sport brings a high profile to the sponsoring organisation. There is also some entertainment value to the sponsorship of sport in terms of complementary tickets to key customers for a sponsored event, using it as a reward for sales staff who have achieved their targets and so on.

Corporate hospitality has become a very big part of the sports sponsorship industry. Hospitality tents are now common at all major sports events including Royal Ascot, the Royal Henley Regatta and the Wimbledon Tennis championships, to name but a few. Some of the main reasons for firms becoming involved in the commercial sponsorship of sport include the following. The list is not intended to be exhaustive but merely indicative:

■ building awareness of the company name;
■ achieving an association with a particular sporting activity such as formula one motor racing;
■ used to entertain important clients;
■ used to entertain staff;
■ to attempt to make an uninteresting product or service more interesting by association;
■ to relate the product to the success of a particular team;
■ to gain international recognition;
■ because the competition is involved;
■ the CEO is particularly interested in the sport in question.

Sponsorship of the arts

Most people can understand why firms get involved in the sponsorship of sport. It is less clear to many, however, why they get involved in the sponsorship of the arts. When we discuss the sponsorship of the arts we interpret the term arts very liberally. Basically the arts in this context is everything that is not sport. The reasons why commercial firms sponsor the arts include the following:

1. To obtain personal contact with high status visitors.
2. Firm seen as a benefactor of society.
3. Sponsor minority activities and education.
4. Seen to be putting something back into the community.

Sponsorship falls under the heading of below the line activity. Other below the line communication activities include exhibitions and PR, both of which are discussed in this chapter. The key concept is the integrated marketing communications mix where above the line and below the line activities are fully integrated, with the one class of activities supporting and augmenting the other.

EXHIBITIONS

In the UK there are hundreds of exhibitions of interest to companies and, if overseas opportunities are taken into account, the number extends to thousands. They vary considerably in scope, from a small show with perhaps 20 or 30 modest stands to vast international fairs with 1,000 or more exhibitors, covering the entire market for a particular product class or industry. Trade exhibitions appear to have a permanent place in the marketing communications mix of many firms and are another form of below the line promotional activity. As with many other below the line methods they are growing in use and popularity. There are three basic forms:

1. those aimed at the consumer;
2. those aimed solely at the trade;
3. those aimed at and open to both consumer and trader.

The third category has become the most common. Most exhibitions start off as trade exhibitions and then after the first week or so, when all the trade business has been seen to they are often opened to the general public. The public usually pays an entry fee which brings in extra cash for the exhibition organiser and helps to pay for the cost of putting on the show. The public may have an actual interest in the products and services being exhibited, for example clothes shows, motor shows and The Ideal Home Exhibition. At times the products and services are of little direct interest to the general public, that is they are highly unlikely to buy any of the products on show, but nevertheless attendance at the exhibition can be a good day out (eg an agricultural show or an air show).

An essential guide to forming a communications mix is deciding what the various elements of the mix are supposed to accomplish. Setting clear, operationally relevant communications objectives provides the basis for selecting how advertising, sponsorship, direct mail, exhibitions, personal selling and other communications tools will be used in the communications programme. An exhibition is just one medium by which a company may choose to communicate with its target markets. Generally exhibitions are used to complement other communications media. All the elements in the communications mix reinforce one another, producing a synergistic effect, with each element having its own part to play in the overall scheme of things. Exhibitions tend to draw a high quality group of visitors and company directors will frequently be present at an important trade exhibition.

Such trade exhibitions offer the marketing firm the chance to come into direct contact with high status decision making unit (DMU) members. There is a significant PR dimension to exhibitions. Many visitors to trade shows go to view the total industry range of products or services in an economic period of time and in one place. People visiting exhibitions seem to regard them as a viewing opportunity and a chance to obtain technical information. Often products are accessible for examination along with specially designed models of products. There can often be an important social aspect to trade shows with stands offering refreshments and a chance to socially interact for potential clients. Interacting and networking can be facilitated.

Purchasing agents and other executives involved in the buying process will often have their own preference for various information sources at different stages of the overall buying sequence. An understanding of the stages in the buying decision process is useful in selecting communications objectives and the appropriate communications tools to achieve them. In relation to new products the decision making process is described in the model quoted in Figure 3.8 (page 42).

Choice of target audience will usually include those people who either decide or can influence the buying decision. These individuals will be of varying status etc and will be situated at varying stages of the decision making process. It will be necessary to reach them through different communications channels. Communications tools differ in their cost effectiveness in accomplishing objectives. For example, although industrial marketers will generally spend far more on personal selling than on advertising, it would be inefficient to use the sales force for all communications purposes.

Exhibition evaluation

In order to evaluate the effectiveness of exhibitions and to plan for future exhibits, certain qualitative and quantitative data must be collected and analysed. As a first step it is necessary to decide what measures of cost effectiveness to use for evaluation, for example:

1. audience size;
2. audience quality;
3. media impact.

One of the more meaningful measures of the above is audience quality. This relates to the status of the visitors to the exhibition. Measurement of media impact requires some form of research to establish the effectiveness of the exhibition to both visitors and exhibitors. The most common measure used, simply because it is based very often on the only accurate data available, is audience size. This can be used as a measure of cost effectiveness when broken down into different categories as follows:

1. Cost per visitor = Total cost of exhibition/Total number of visitors.
This gives an indication of the potential audience size which might be exposed to the firm's promotional activities at the exhibition.

2. Cost per contact = Total cost of exhibition/Total number of visitors to stand.
This shows the ability of the firm to attract visitors to its stand. It reflects the extent of real interest and the contacts made with potential customers and is therefore related to one of the objectives of exhibiting.

3. Cost per enquiry = Total cost of exhibition/Total number of enquiries.
This gives an indication of the cost per number of enquiries.

When the cost-effectiveness of exhibitions is compared with other media, it would be unfair to argue that the contacts made with targets or publics by different communications media are of similar value. The difficulty in making a comparison indicates that the cost effectiveness of each activity needs to be made in the light of the objectives it is designed to achieve. Some objectives cost more to achieve than others and so this needs to be taken into consideration. Finally, it can be concluded that the role of the exhibition is a very important one, one that offers the marketing firm a unique opportunity in terms of personal contact, meeting high status visitors, following up on opportunities, creating databases for future marketing exercises to name but a few.

SUMMARY

To many not used to marketing terms the phrase 'below the line' seems strange and is often considered to be related to finance and profit and loss and as the business jargon for profit, the bottom line. In actual fact it has nothing to do with this meaning. The phrase has been imported from America like so much established marketing language, and like so many other pieces of marketing jargon, gives a thin layer of technicality and refinement to a very simple idea. Even after many years of usage in marketing circles, there is still no single, generally approved meaning of the term below the line. In general the terms below the line promotion or communications, refer to forms of non-media communication activity, even non-media advertising.

Examples of non-media promotions are exhibitions, sponsorship activities, PR and sales promotions such as competitions, banded packs and price promotions. Below the line promotions are more and more important within the communications mix of many firms, not only those involved with fast moving consumer goods (FMCG products), but also for industrial goods and services. For example agent or distributor incentives, exhibitions and sponsorship activities are all growing in importance. All types of non-media communications are a form of promotion if we use the word in an overall way. A particular kind of below the line activity is referred to as below the line sales promotion. Below the line sales promotions are a specific kind of below the line activity which includes a range of marketing communications. Below the line sales promotions are short term motivators, mainly targeted, as you would expect, at consumers, but also aimed at the trade eg wholesalers, retailers, distributors, etc, along with company employees, usually the sales force.

Over the past 25 years or so there has been increasing pressure on marketing budgets and an increased stress on management to achieve marketing communications objectives more efficiently and more economically. Hence marketers have been searching for a more economic and efficient way to communicate with their target markets than traditional media advertising. A shift in emphasis from the more traditional above the line methods of communications to below the line promotion is one of the results of this striving for greater efficiency by management.

An organisation is judged by its behaviour. PR is about goodwill and reputation. At its best, PR can be the discipline that really determines the content of the messages companies send to their customers and other target audiences. The process of achieving marketing orientation within organisations is a vital prerequisite to effective external marketing strategies, particularly those based on relationship marketing principles. PR has an important part to play and contribution to make to the achievement of an effective internal marketing spirit within a firm and to creating, fostering, nurturing and maintaining mutually beneficial long-term relationships with customers and other key groups of people.

In this respect PR has seen an increase in value as both a strategic internal and external marketing communications tool. PR can be utilised both within and outside the firm. PR is an important and versatile marketing communications tool. It forms an intrinsic part of the integrated marketing communications mix. There is a PR aspect to most marketing communications variables whether this is personal selling, sponsorship, exhibitions, direct mail or telephone marketing. The purpose of PR is to help foster a good relationship between a firm and its publics. This has the effect of improving and increasing the credibility and value of marketing messages from other elements in the communications mix by enhancing the image of the firm and its product and services.

Exhibitions tend to attract a high quality audience and company directors will often attend an important trade exhibition. Such trade exhibitions offer the marketing firm the opportunity to come into personal contact with high status decision making unit (DMU) members. Like most below the line activity, this is growing in popularity. In some ways sponsorship achieves many of the functions of exhibitions especially in terms of audience quality. We have already established that in business to business marketing environments, high status decision making unit members are notoriously difficult to contact on a personal basis. The firm sponsoring an event can invite important members of a prospective customer company's DMU to the event thereby enabling personal contact to be made in a social setting. Exhibitions can have a similar function.

Many high status decision makers attend exhibitions, especially very important international events. The cost per contact of exhibitions can be relatively high when it is compared to other media, but cost is relative to other factors, for example concepts such as audience quality should enter into the equation when evaluating the relative cost of exhibition participation. Most exhibitions start off as trade exhibitions and then after the first week or so when all of the trade business has been carried out they are usually opened to the public. This results in a wider audience and of course produces more revenue for the exhibition organisers. The public usually pays an entry fee which not only brings in revenue for the exhibition organiser but helps to pay for the costs of actually staging the exhibition. The public might have a genuine interest in the products and services being exhibited for example clothes shows, motor shows and The Ideal Home Exhibition. At times the products and services are of little direct interest to the general public, that is they are highly unlikely to buy any of the products on show, but nevertheless attendance at the exhibition can be a good day out (eg an agricultural show or an air show, for example most of the audience at an air show have no intention of placing an order for an aeroplane).

10

Product and Portfolio Analysis

The product or service is the most important element of the marketing mix for obvious reasons and will change between different products/services and business circumstances. It is the responsibility of marketing to manage this mix in an effective manner to establish the relative superiority that this mix holds over competitive offerings. It is this unique mix that will appeal to actual and potential customers and such a mix usually relates to products or services, but it also includes such matters as after sales service, spares availability and general customer care. It can also revolve around the reputation of the company or indeed the image that the product portrays through its promotion. In other words, what is looked for is some kind of USP that will set it apart from competitors, products or services.

In the product and service context our concern is with matters of design, function, appearance, durability and size or capacity to name but a few.

PRODUCT DEFINITIONS

Marketing terminology states that purchasers seek to obtain a 'bundle of satisfactions' which includes the product or service and the other features such as after sales service, extras, the 'image' of the product and much more. This is sometimes called the 'augmented service' and the tactics used to deliver this are called 'customer care' which has already been discussed earlier in this book.

For classification purposes we split goods and services into industrial and consumer categories and then into sub-categories.

Industrial goods

■ 'Raw materials' procurement in most industrial situations forms the principal acquisition necessity.

■ 'Components' used in the manufacturing process are also prime requirements and these are incorporated into products as part of the assembly programme.

■ 'Installations' are the plant and machinery needed as part of the company's manufacturing processes.

■ 'Accessories' are similar in nature to installations, but are less important and depreciate faster. This category includes items such as office fixtures and storage equipment.

■ 'Supplies' are everyday necessities such as maintenance items, stationery, oils and packaging.

Consumer goods

■ 'Staple products' are the everyday necessities of life such as bread and milk. Almost no planning goes into these routine purchases and in some cases delivery is direct to the home.

■ 'Convenience goods' are standard commodities with little thought given to their selection. Here companies advertise heavily to promote brand loyalty with the implication of regular repeat purchase.

■ 'Shopping goods' describe more simple durable products that are bought less regularly. Purchases here are more planned and a certain amount of consideration goes into their acquisition, so buyer behaviour is more elaborate than for convenience goods. Examples of such products are irons, kettles and cutlery.

■ 'Speciality purchases' are major items which are bought at infrequent periods. Here, a lot of thought is given to their purchase in terms of seeking out and evaluating alternative choices. In many cases the end result is a compromise between a number of rival purchasing motives and buyer behaviour is complex, often involving a family decision-making process. An example of such a purchase is a new house or a motor car.

■ 'Unsought goods' is the final category and here the buyer has not considered that they need the purchase. In such cases consumers have to be persuaded that they have such a requirement. Often these goods or services have a positive connotation and they provide a need that the consumer finds valuable (eg innovative labour-saving kitchen appliances). However, other products or services are sold using sales orientated methods for which the value to the consumer is very marginal. Sales approaches tend to be more direct through the telephone, direct mail and door-to-door, and 'hard sell' persuasion is often used in the case of this latter method.

THE MANAGEMENT OF PRODUCTS AND SERVICES

Many marketing orientated companies have what is called a 'product management' system. It is common practice in fast moving consumer goods (FMCG) companies, but many industrial companies also operate a similar system. Product management is in overall control of all company brands and then an individual 'brand manager' (usually in FMCG situations) or 'product manager' (usually in industrial situations) manages a single product or line of products. Their responsibility is to manage the marketing and overall image of the product and this involves close liaison with the advertising agency and marketing research. They have to work closely with the sales department, over whom they have no direct control, to ensure that the correct 'image' plus any promotional plans are communicated via field salespersons to the company's customers.

In 1957 Ansoff first introduced the concept of a matrix for managing products or services as described in Figure 10.1:

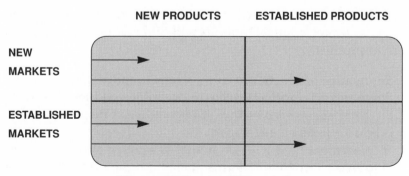

Figure 10.1 *Ansoff's matrix*

The descriptions he put forward in respect of each of the above strategies are:

■ new products into new markets: diversification;
■ new products into established markets: product extension/ development;
■ established products into new markets: market extension/ development;
■ established products into established markets: market penetration.

'Product line' and 'product mix' (or 'product assortment') are terms used to describe how products or services are associated. A product line is a collection of closely related product items (eg all the canned products made by an FMCG food producer). The width of this product line refers to all other similar products being produced (eg all canned vegetable products and all preservatives and, of course, all canned soups). The product mix relates to the number of individual products carried within a particular product line (eg soups such as tomato, carrot, mixed vegetable, mushroom, chicken, or leek and potato). The depth of this product mix refers to the range of items within each line (eg 24 different soups, 12 different preservatives, 20 different canned vegetables). 'Consistency' describes the closeness of the range of items in the total product line and how similarly their marketing characteristics relate to each other. Product management can thus look more impartially at its entire product mix in terms of deciding whether lines should be shortened or lengthened or cut.

NEW PRODUCTS AND SERVICES

Marketers divide new products and services into a number of categories, as strategic launch options will differ according to the category of product:

■ 'Innovative products' are entirely new to the market.
■ 'Re-launched' products relate to declining products, but where the company perceives there to be sufficient future sales if the product's image is revamped.
■ 'Replacement products' are similar to existing goods, but give a modified alternative in terms of, say, a more up to date design or improved facilities.

■ 'Imitative products', or 'me too' products, are when an innovative product is successful in the market-place and such a product is copied by other manufacturers.

When developing new products and services it is important that the procedure is well managed. There are a number of organisational alternatives possible:

■ 'New product managers' have the sole responsibility for new product development. In smaller organisations this task tends to form part of the task of the brand or product manager.
■ 'New product committees' obtain ideas from research and development, marketing or research and other appropriate sources. Their task is to evaluate these in terms of their likelihood for commercial exploitation.
■ 'New product departments' are organised so that their work extends across departmental boundaries. Sometimes a 'product (or project) champion' is appointed to supervise the entire scheme from inception to market launch. In other cases the project is passed on from one specialist to another during this development process.
■ 'Venture teams', comprising members from different departments, are gathered on a sporadic basis in order to debate and report different views on possible new products. Their deliberations are considered when deciding whether or not to pursue certain lines of progress.

Booz, Allen and Hamilton put forward the idea that when new products or services are developed this goes through a number of distinct stages from idea generation to launch. Figure 10.2 describes this process followed by the description of each category:

The 'idea generation' phase comes before the description given in Figure 10.2. Ideas can come from new product or brand managers, new product committees or departments, research and development, marketing research, venture teams, members of the field sales force or from a variety of sources including members of the workforce. The important thing is that there should be an organisational culture to encourage such initiatives. Brainstorming is a technique that can be used as long as the session is competently chaired and the group consists of people with good ideas.

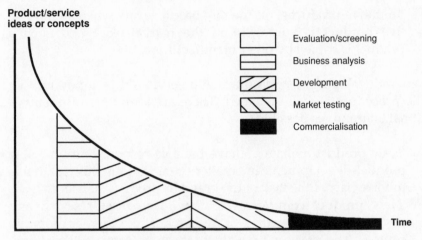

Figure 10.2 *Decay curve of new product ideas*

■ The first stage of eliminating unsuitable ideas is 'evaluation/ screening'. At this point 'Go' or 'Drop' decisions are made. The objective here is to decide whether or not such ideas would fit into the product range and whether its ultimate development might be conceivably worthwhile.

■ 'Business analysis' assesses its financial feasibility. It is after this commercial consideration that only suitable contenders ought to remain, because the next phase can be very costly.

■ 'Product development' relates to the research, design and development stage and by this time marketing research should be working in close liaison in terms of appraising and testing ideas, concepts and prototypes. Modifications and refinements should result from such feedback.

■ 'Test marketing' is where the product has been developed. For many FMCGs this might involve a test market in a specific town or area as described in Chapter 4. For more durable products, customer placement tests might be more appropriate. Again, modifications can be made after such a test marketing procedure.

■ Commercialization is the final stage where the launch takes place.

Even after this scientific filtration process success is not guaranteed, but at least its likelihood is more assured.

In 1980 McKinsey & Co examined a number of large organisations. They found that certain factors encouraged a culture of new product/service development which were:

Simple line and team staff organisation; a bias towards action; productivity improvement via people; continued contact with customers; operational autonomy and the encouragement of entrepreneurship (called 'empowerment'); simultaneous loose and tight controls; stress on a single key business value; an emphasis on sticking to what it knows best.

PRODUCT DIFFUSION AND ADOPTION

This topic is the logical follow on from new product development. Everett Rogers first suggested the notion of 'diffusion' relating to the speed of market progress and 'adoption' as the extent of initial market take-up by specific purchaser categories. The curve depicted in Figure 10.3 does not represent all of the population, because some people will never adopt a particular product or service.

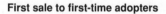

First sale to first-time adopters

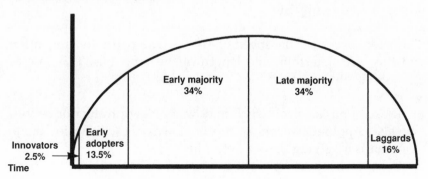

Figure 10.3 *Diffusion of innovations*

The first 2.5 per cent of the total market represents the 'innovator' category who are keen to try out new innovative products and are probably from higher social backgrounds with wide networks of friends and colleagues. Alternatively, they could be people whose interests lie specifically in the type of product being introduced to the market (eg a new computer software package will attract those with a keen interest in computing).

The next 13.5 per cent represent the 'early adopters' who are more cautious than the previous group. They tend to belong more to local groups than innovators, but still purchase early. Their role as opinion leaders who influence later adopter categories is important to marketers.

The next 34 per cent group represent the 'early majority' whose composition tends to be largely the middle and lower middle classes. Now that the product has become more widely accepted and consolidated in the market they feel more complacent about making a purchase and rely largely upon manufacturers' promotional material before they purchase.

The following 34 per cent is the 'late majority' who generally belong to working class groups and are more cautious about purchasing, principally because of financial constraints. They are, however, subject to social demands and this frequently motivates their first time purchase.

The last 16 per cent makes up the 'laggards' who are very careful, generally older and usually from the lower social groups.

A final category is the 'non adopter' group who do not appear in the above categories. A good case in point might be televisions which a small number of families will not purchase because of its intrusion into family life.

'Diffusion' describes the speed of market take-up of the innovation and this will determine the length of the time axis. This rate of adoption is governed by:

■ 'Relative advantage' which is how the new product or service feels to potential users in terms of what it will do for them, perhaps by giving them a better lifestyle.
■ 'Compatibility' is how the new product accords with current products in the market.
■ 'Complexity' relates to how complicated the product is. The more complex, the slower will be the rate of diffusion.
■ 'Divisibility' means how the new product can be tested prior to the act of purchasing. This is also linked to 'trialability' which concerns the ease of demonstration.
■ 'Communicability' is also linked to the above and it means the ease at which the new product can be promoted through communication mix activities to potential customers.

In Chapter 3 we discussed the buyer behavioural implications of the adoption process and Figure 3.5 described its operation. It is perhaps worthwhile referring to this model again as it relates to the practical implications of the stages through which purchasers proceed when making major purchases.

PRODUCT LIFE CYCLE

This early marketing concept shows that products pass through a number of stages from initial development to decline. As a planning tool it has a lot to commend it, but it is not without its critics. They contend that if it is taken too literally then many good products may be killed off prematurely in the belief that the decline stage has been reached, whereas the dip in sales might only be temporary.

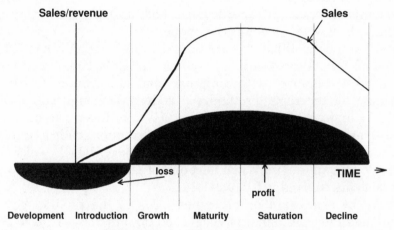

Figure 10.4 *The product life cycle*

Figure 10.4 shows this curve onto which is superimposed a revenue curve showing the product recovering its costs of development and launch before moving into profitability. Each of these stages is now discussed in terms of its marketing implications:

■ *Development* is when the product is going through the pre-launch stages, as described in Figure 10.2, so costs will reach their cumulative maximum before the product is introduced to the market-place when revenues start to flow. At this stage marketing research should be involved, in terms of placement tests and testing the product or service notion through techniques such as focus groups. A test market might be the final culmination of this activity and the trade will be informed prior to its launch.

▪ *Introduction* (or launch) is when the product comes on the market. Promotion tends to be informative, competitors are few or non-existent, and acceptance might be slow. Even after the filtration sequence described in Figure 10.2 a number of products still fail at this early stage. As the product is new it can usually sustain a high initial price (called 'skimming' and dealt with in the next chapter) and this can be justified in terms of recovering the high costs of development. Buyers tend to be 'innovators' which is examined later in this chapter and distribution is often 'exclusive', the implications of which are dealt with in Chapter 12.

▪ *Growth* (or exponential) is where the product takes off and competition appears with 'me too' products. In some cases manufacturers might have been researching along similar lines, but are slower to enter the market-place. High prices can normally be justified, but being first in the market carries the risk of competitors learning from what might be your expensive mistakes, because as the original innovator you have been taking all the risks. Promotional activity, although still relatively high, changes from creating new product awareness to seeking to establish a brand image. Distribution tends to move from exclusive to selective or even intensive, which seeks to exploit maximum impact at the point of sale, the implications of which are covered in Chapter 12.

▪ *Maturity and saturation* are when sales of the product have reached their peak and have levelled off. Purchases tend to be of a repeat nature and attempts are made by manufacturers to differentiate their products from those of their competitors. These product modifications are sometimes realised through superior features or better quality or they can be implied through promotional images. Sales during maturity and saturation tend to be at their maximum, but maturity represents a generally less competitive period when sales are peaking, whereas 'saturation' (with a similar sales level to maturity), sees increased competition and price cutting. The consequences are lower profit margins in order for a company to remain in business. The maturity phase can last for a season or for years, depending upon the nature of the product. During this phase, there is often a move from a 'pull' promotional strategy during the early maturity phase towards a 'push' strategy as the product reaches saturation.

▪ *Decline* is the final phase where sales fall and decisions to exit the market-place are made. This is often done owing to the simple fact that, as Figure 10.4 indicates, profits cease because of the declining sales and revenues. This is a difficult time for company management who might genuinely believe that their products are timeless, even though marketing research might have indicated otherwise. The phase is characterised by price cutting, but a few companies do remain in order to pick up residual demand and perhaps to provide after sales functions such as maintenance and spare parts provision.

■ The notion of the product life cycle can be extended to include a number of distinct shapes to suggest different marketing circumstances. Figure 10.5 describes the effects of different product and marketing situations:

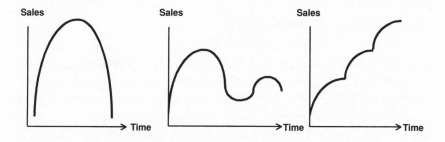

Figure 10.5 *Different configurations of the product life cycle*

■ The first figure above is for a 'fad' product that enters the market quickly and then quickly exits.

■ The second figure has been termed cycle/recycle where the first time a product comes around it behaves like a fad product and it is later regenerated for a second cycle. It can also represent products whose sales are cyclical in nature.

■ The third figure shows a scalloped pattern representing a number of mini life cycles. Here the product manager introduces a new version or a product update at a strategic point in time, which means that the product does not reach full maturity and runs the risk of becoming outdated. New modifications are introduced before the product reaches its peak and the idea is to build even further on the success of the original product. It should also be recognized that the shape of the curve can also be changed because of the actions of competitors.

The life cycle itself can relate to sales for an entire industry (product category life cycles) or for a type of product (product form life cycles) or even for an individual manufacturer's brands of products (brand life cycles), so application of the concept is very broad.

PRODUCT PORTFOLIO MODELS

Product portfolio models are particularly useful when engaging in strategic marketing planning and a full account is given in the logical follow-on text in the Kogan Page series called: *Strategic Marketing, Planning and Evaluation* by Geoff Lancaster and Lester Massingham (1996).

'Boston box' or the BCG matrix

This was developed by the Boston Consulting Group. It is a clear and easy to apply concept and it is now used extensively by strategic marketing planners. The solid circles in Figure 10.6 represent individual products or SBUs. Annual market growth year on year is calculated in percentage terms with 0–10 per cent being classed as low and 10–20 per cent (and above) being classed as high and this is a measure of market attractiveness. Relative market share is placed on a logarithmic scale and this is a measure of the SBUs strength in the market-place. Four types of SBU are indicated in the four box matrix:

▓ A 'star' has a high market share in a fast growth industry. It is likely that it is at an early stage in its life cycle, so profits might be good but promotional costs will probably be high.
▓ A 'cash cow' has a high market share but is probably in the maturity stage of its product life cycle with little market growth. In well-managed companies, customers will be loyal and there is much repeat business. Initial costs of research and development will have been recovered and these SBUs are safe 'bread and butter' investments that keep the company on a sound financial footing.
▓ The 'question mark' SBU has an interchangeable name of 'problem child' and 'wildcat'. They are problem SBUs in that they are in a high growth market, yet only have a small market share and marketing action should be taken to turn them into a

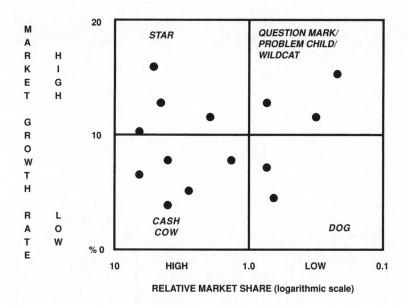

Figure 10.6 *BCG matrix*

star, otherwise the probability is that they will degenerate into a costly 'dog' SBU.

▓ A 'dog' SBU gained this name as it was initially referred to as a 'pet', with the correct imputation that they were products that management kept, but did not want to delete from the product range for a number of illogical reasons. It is distinguished by low market share and low growth with little profit and more likely loss making. These SBUs should be deleted from the product range unless they are vital to the company in the interests of keeping a balanced portfolio of products. However, they are a costly luxury and a company cannot afford to keep many in its portfolio.

The GE/McKinsey business screen

McKinsey & Co produced this nine box matrix for General Electric (USA) which is shown in Figure 10.7. It attempted to provide greater sophistication than the BCG matrix by using a wider range of market and company factors. 'Industry attractiveness' on the vertical axis and 'business strength' on the horizontal axis are its measures. It considers factors such as market share, growth, profits, sales effectiveness and market knowledge as 'industry attractiveness' factors. For 'business strength' an index is used rather than a simple measure of relative market share. It incorporates matters like the size of the SBU, price competitiveness, product quality, its comparative position in the market-place and research capabilities.

Strategies are suggested for each of the boxes into which an SBU falls. The size of the circle represents the relative size of the industry in which they compete and the slices in each circle represent the market share of each SBU.

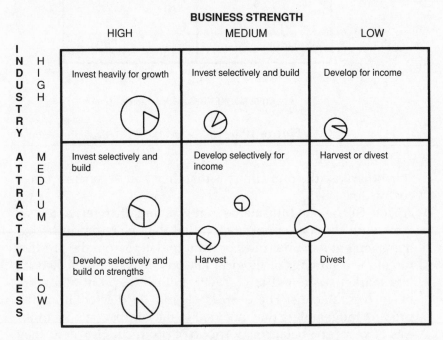

Figure 10.7   *General Electric (GE) matrix*

Shell directional policy matrix

Shell Chemicals needed a matrix that would be resilient and actionable in the ever-changing market in which they operated. It was important that each strategy should be evaluated against possible future contingencies.

In Figure 10.8 each axis looks at the measures of market growth, market quality, the industry situation and environmental considerations. Sector profitability on the horizontal axis looks at these from an industry point of view and company competitive

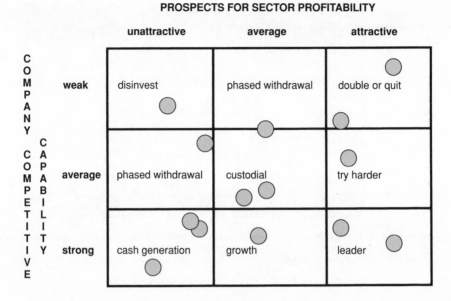

PROSPECTS FOR SECTOR PROFITABILITY

		unattractive	average	attractive
COMPANY	weak	disinvest	phased withdrawal	double or quit
COMPETITIVE CAPABILITY	average	phased withdrawal	custodial	try harder
	strong	cash generation	growth	leader

Figure 10.8 *Shell directional policy matrix*

capability on the vertical axis looks at each from a company viewpoint. Each SBU is given from one to five stars and this is quantified.

Industry/market evolution model

Michael Porter first recognised the generic strategies for success in a competitive market in 1980 as shown in Figure 10.9 where it can be seen that a high market share is not necessarily a major financial success criterion:

■ 'Cost leadership' simply means reducing prices to be lowest in the market;
■ 'Differentiation' is the establishment of some unique feature or USP, be it a product or image-related characteristic, which competitors cannot match;
■ 'Focus' is where the company consolidates its efforts on a small product range in a singular market niche.

'Stuck in the middle' is the term used by Porter to describe those companies at the bottom of the curve.

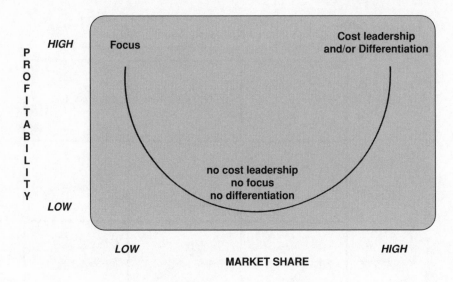

Figure 10.9 *Porter's generic strategies*

Porter produced a more sophisticated model in 1985 which was based on a number of evolutionary stages which were examined in terms of whether the company was a leader or a follower. These are illustrated in Figure 10.10:

■ 'Growth' is exemplified in an emerging industry by purchasing conservatism over the attributes of new products and the potential for them becoming quickly dated in the style or functional senses.

■ 'Transition to maturity' usually means diminished profit margins as more competitors enter the market and there is a slowing down of sales. Purchasing confidence is higher through product familiarity, and the emphasis is upon features and non-price factors like image. Focus is important in terms of attempting to serve individual market segment needs.

■ 'Decline' suggests that the market-place has become saturated and that products are uninteresting. Alternate products start to appear and this stage is when companies should seek to exit the market-place and look for alternative markets and products.

		GROWTH (emerging industry)	MATURITY (and transition to maturity)	DECLINE
S **T** **R** **A** **T** **E** **G** **I** **C** **P** **O** **S** **I** **T** **I** **O** **N**	**L** **E** **A** **D** **E** **R**	*keep ahead of the field*	*cost leadership; raise barriers to entry; deter competitors*	*redefine scope; divest peripheral activities; encourage departures*
	F **O** **L** **L** **O** **W** **E** **R**	*imitation at lower cost; joint ventures*	*differentiation; focus*	*differentiation; look for new opportunities*

Figure 10.10   *Strategic position in industry life cycle*

Industry maturity/competitive position matrix

This was proposed by the consultants Arthur D Little. The vertical axis cites a number of criteria from 'dominant' to 'weak' and the SBU is then entered into the appropriate box along the horizontal axis, depending upon the life-cycle stage the overall industry has reached. It is perhaps a slightly subjective set of measures, but at least it does give the analyst an immediate point of reference, and its utility is perhaps more one of comparing one company or SBU against another, rather than a practical marketing planning tool. It is depicted in Figure 10.11.

BCG/product life cycle matrix

This model was developed by Barksdale and Harris on the grounds that the BCG matrix ignores the position of the industry. Their matrix attempts to resolve this difficulty as indicated in Fig 10.12:

■ 'Infants' are seen at the pioneering (introduction) stage. Research and development costs are being recouped and promotional costs are high because most communication effort is being directed towards informing the market-place.

	Embryonic	Growth	Maturity	Ageing
Dominant				
Strong				
Favourable				
Tentative				
Weak				

COMPANY'S COMPETITIVE POSITION

Figure 10.11 *Industry maturity/competitive position matrix*

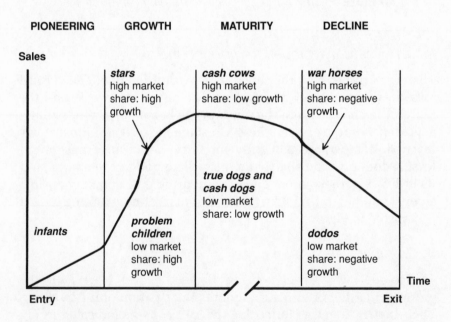

Figure 10.12 *BCG/product life cycle combined portfolio*

▧ 'Stars' are costly in terms of communication costs at this growth stage, but this SBU has good potential for the future once the product becomes accepted and the SBU moves into the 'cash cow' category.

■ 'Problem children' being in a low market share but high growth situation are costly to maintain and to become successful marketing action must be taken to move them to star or ultimately to cash cow status.
■ 'Cash cows' provide a steady revenue flow as they simply make money having a high market share, albeit in a low growth market.
■ 'True dogs' have a low market share in a saturated market and provide a flat or even negative cash flow. 'Cash dogs' have a low market share in a saturated market, but produce a small positive cash flow.
■ 'War horses' are seen in a declining market but are still supportable because of their high market share which contributes to a positive cash flow. The likelihood, too, is that competitors are leaving the market, so handing their market share back to the market-place.
■ 'Dodos' are precarious SBUs in that they are in a declining market and have a low market share and the likelihood is that their cash flow is negative. They should be deleted, but are probably still there because management clings to the belief that they might witness a revival.

SUMMARY

The product or service has been examined in the light of its importance to companies, for without it there would be no commercial activity. Product categorisations have first been examined followed by new product issues and then the notion of the product life cycle. The chapter has been concluded by an examination of some of the more strategic issues that are suggested through the more contemporary notions of matrix analysis.

11

Price

INTRODUCTION

The ultimate objective in commercial organisations is to make a profit, and prices charged must reflect total costs plus an element for profit. This marketing concept (which includes pricing issues) is also relevant in what are termed 'not for profit' organisations such as the police, fire services and various departments within public authorities, where budgeting within predetermined cost limits is important.

The significance of pricing as an element of the marketing mix varies according to conditions in the market-place and is a function of supply and demand that will be examined later. However, there are other factors that constitute a product offering, referred to as the 'augmented service', which relate to servicing arrangements, extra guarantees over and above the standard one and the general level of after-sales customer care that makes up a product. Pricing these 'extras' is less tangible than pricing a simple product, as it is all part of customers' perceptions. This is one of the reasons that makes pricing more interesting as an element of marketing, otherwise it would be a mechanistic matter of adding together all costs plus a percentage for profit.

In a capitalist, or market driven economy, it is competition between companies offering similar goods and services that tends to drive prices down, as buyers search for best value. Competitors who are unable to match these value criteria will soon go out of business. The inputs to pricing decisions are: costs, customers, competitors and company judgement:

■ *Costs* include labour, materials and overheads. In a competitive market-place, goods might be manufactured on a marginal cost basis – where overheads might have been recovered elsewhere. So cost here will include only elements of labour and materials and directly attributable overheads plus a profit margin.

■ *Customers* are influenced by prices in the market-place, but they also consider the other intangibles described earlier.

■ *Competitors* relates to how they behave in the market-place and also how well the market is serviced in terms of the volume of competitors. The nature of their aggressiveness will relate to the state of market conditions.

■ *Company* considerations relate to its policy in relation to whether it wishes to be a market leader or a follower, much of which will be determined by its financial resources. Factors such as legislation (eg VAT, sales tax, import tariffs and corporation tax) can also affect the end price. Government legislation might also affect price in terms of the possibility of a manufacturer becoming too powerful through a takeover or merger. In the UK the Monopolies and Mergers Commission looks at these cases, or action might be taken under the Restrictive Trade Practices Act.

NOTIONS OF PRICE

Three approaches to pricing are suggested in standard marketing texts: the economist's approach; the accountant's approach and the marketer's approach.

Economics is more of a theoretical notion, but is fundamental to an intellectual understanding of matters such as value and utility. Value quantifies utility as represented by the monetary unit, whereas utility is that aspect of a product or service which makes it capable of satisfying a specific need.

Accounting is more practical and it holds that demand, costs and competition are the main elements in pricing decisions. The final price should, however, be able to recover fixed costs eg rent, rates and heating plus variable costs, eg direct labour, materials and expenses.

The view of marketing is that price shall be set at what the market will bear. This statement encompasses a number of considerations such as competition in the market-place, customer goodwill and other longer term considerations. It might even mean sustaining an unprofitable SBU in the short term in anticipation of a market turnaround.

ECONOMIST'S APPROACH

This proposes that price is the medium through which supply and demand are brought into equilibrium and that profit will be maximized through this relationship between demand and price. Supply and demand are shown as demand and supply curves in Figures 11.1(a) and 11.1(b).

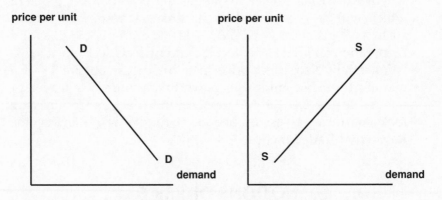

Figure 11.1(a) *Demand curve*   **Figure 11.1(b)** *Supply curve*

Figure 11.1(a) shows that the lower the price the higher the demand; the higher the price, the lower the demand. Figure 11.1(b) shows the supply curve and here the lower the price, the lower the amount that will be produced and the higher the price then producers will be prepared to supply more.

In Figure 11.2 the curves are combined and the market price will be where they bisect. At price P, the demand will be quantity Q.

'Elasticity' and 'inelasticity' are used to describe the nature of products or commodities and how this affects levels of demand. Elasticity is sometimes termed 'responsiveness'. 'Inelastic demand' is less receptive to price changes, whereas 'elastic demand' is very open to price shifts. The notion is shown in Figure 11.3(a) and (b). Figure 11.3(a) demonstrates that a big price reduction from P to P1 will barely affect demand which moves from Q to Q1 and is

price per unit

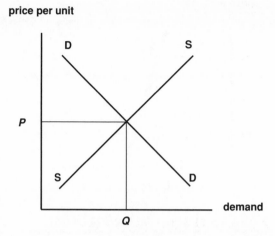

Figure 11.2 *Supply and demand curves*

termed 'inelasticity of demand'. Figure 11.3(b) shows that a small price reduction from P to P1 will affect demand considerably, moving it from Q to Q1. Product examples of the former are staple products like bread whereas the latter refers to postponable purchases such as a lounge suite. These measures of elasticity will tend to affect pricing decisions.

Products and services are marketed within a continuum from 'monopoly' to 'perfect competition'. Both extremes are theoretical notions and monopoly is where there is one single producer for which there are no substitutes. Perfect competition is where there are numerous buyers and sellers of similar products and no barriers of entry to or exit from the system.

An economic theory that has pertinence for marketers is 'oligopoly' which is between the parameters of perfect competition and monopoly. The market here is dominated by a few sellers, where each must consider the effects of its policies on the responses of its competitors. It contends that such sellers are inter-dependent and the goods or services they produce are similar (homogeneous). Here, companies are sensitive to price changes between each other as goods are similar and buyers will tend to go for the lowest price. Price as a competitive device will not be as effective as competition founded on non-price factors such as branding and the general 'image' of the product or firm. Manufacturers usually begin production at a level below their full

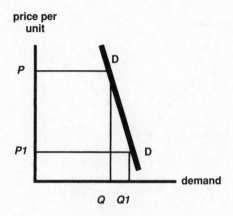

Figure 11.3(a) *Inelastic demand*

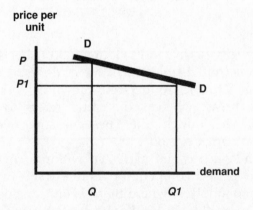

Figure 11.3(b) *Elastic demand*

capacity and entry as a first time manufacturer can be difficult, owing to the high cost of establishing non-price factors such as a strong brand and the right image. Initial set-up costs are high because of heavy capital investment in plant and machinery. In an oligopolistic situation, each participant tends to leave the price and running of the industry as it is and competition is based on non-price factors as described above. 'Oligopoly' is explained in Figure 11.4.

At price P demand states that quantity Q will be demanded. When price is reduced to P1, Q1 will be the amount demanded, and Q–Q1 represents the additional demand. In an oligopolistic

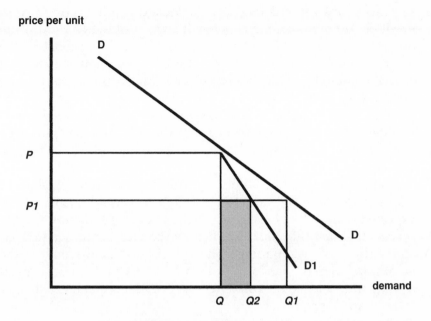

Figure 11.4 *Oligopoly*

situation where price competition is less effective, the demand curve will 'kink' to D1 and the area covered by Q–Q2 will be the additional quantity required. Price competition is less effective as purchasers will be loyal to their favourite brands through non-price competition elements such as strong promotion and branding.

ACCOUNTANT'S APPROACH

The objective here is to recover costs and make a profit. This proposal underlies the significance of distinguishing and categorising these costs. The approach tends to neglect size of demand and prevalent business conditions as it seeks to realise a targeted rate of return on investment for a specific level of sales. Once all costs have been calculated, the profit margin is determined. This is called 'cost plus' pricing and in retailing it is termed 'mark-up' pricing.

In the market-place, profit is the outcome of a number of pricing procedures applied to the company's portfolio of products or services in answer to competitive actions. Cost plus is thus a very negation of the marketing concept; it is more akin to a production orientated approach. However, in many engineering construction situations, where prices must be estimated from anticipated costs so that competitive tenders can be submitted, it might be the only logical way of attempting to set prices. How does one apply psychological pricing to the construction of a hospital? It is maintained that the oblivious application of a singular 'plus' in a cost plus scenario is the very negation of marketing's power of negotiation.

A solution is to agree with finance that 'target pricing' shall be adopted whereby the target rate of return should equate to the expected overall 'plus' as agreed with finance. Marketing has the power to adjust the 'plus' up or down to suit market conditions and individual negotiations. The rule is that at the end of the accounting period, plus (or profit) should be what has been agreed beforehand, and some customers will end up paying a bigger 'plus' than others.

Cash flow is important to accountants and in a new product situation there is often an impetus to recover development costs as soon as possible. This is where marketing and finance can be in accord and an approach known as 'skimming' is dealt with later as a marketing approach. Finance must maintain a balance between conflicting resource demands within the company such as staffing levels, capital requirements for production, research and development, training and promotional expenditure. A reconciliation is needed and a compromise solution will inevitably be the result.

In manufacturing situations there are fixed costs such as plant and equipment, rent and rates and much more, that a company incurs no matter how much it produces. To this must be added variable costs which increase with the level of manufacture and these include materials, labour and expenses incurred in the manufacturing process. Total costs are fixed costs plus variable costs, as illustrated in Figure 11.5.

Variable costs are shown to increase in proportion to the volume; the sum of variable costs and fixed costs is total costs. At a certain level of output a 'step' cost might be required (eg the introduction of a new production line or factory). This will represent a quantum rise in fixed costs and is shown as a step cost. Break-even is where the number of items sold produces enough revenue to cover total costs and this is shown as the break-even point. Total revenue is

COST AND REVENUE

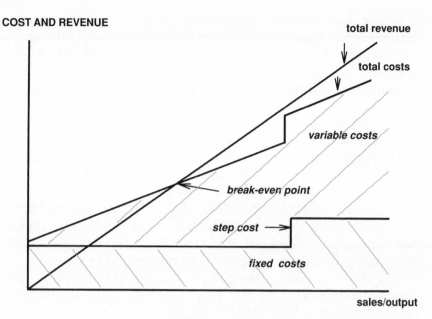

Figure 11.5 *Break-even*

what the company receives from its customers and increases with output. The market reality is that as output increases the company might have to trim its margins and, as a result, total revenue then starts to tail off, but the break-even concept is nevertheless fundamental to an accounting approach to pricing. Break-even has its disadvantages, but it is effectual where costs and demand are constant.

Having considered the traditional economist's and accountant's approaches we are now in a position to look at the marketer's approach.

MARKET BASED PRICING

The marketer's approach stresses price as an element of the marketing mix that can be varied as can any other marketing tools. Its concern is how it can affect the company's position in the market-place. Value is included in this notion of price, and the underlying marketing theme is to set prices at 'what the market will bear'. Marketing places significance on all of the marketing mix elements as well as buyer behaviour in relation to the way it is viewed.

Small companies generally cannot affect market price levels and set their costs so that they are able to follow prices prevailing in the market-place and still make a profit. (This is called 'going rate' pricing.) Non-price competition can improve market share through, for example, company image, customer care programmes and excellent maintenance and delivery systems which can encourage repeat purchasing, even to the extent of customers being prepared to pay more for these services.

Although maximising profits is the anticipated marketing outcome, it is impractical to do this on all products or services among all customer groups. Companies can employ a raft of pricing tactics that might promote sales but reduce margins in the short term. While the general objective might be profit maximisation, the company's product mix should be examined as individual items and pricing tactics applied individually, rather than singular pricing decisions across the complete range. Prices then should adopt a customer focus, for they will determine whether the product is eventually bought or not.

These decisions require a number of standard steps to be taken:

■ Customer or market identification emphasizes the needs of the market-place to the marketer. It avoids price being viewed as the sole criterion and ensures that other mix variables are also considered.
■ Demand estimation (sales forecasting) shows how total sales revenue will impact on costs and profits. Prices charged will differ according to market conditions and segments to be targeted and indeed the intangible value that buyers place on products.
■ Assessing competitive reactions is a function of competitive activity and it can be summarised as follows:
  − 'Direct' or 'head-on' competition from identical products or services;
  − Substitutes that might perform an alternative, but still satisfactory, function;
  − Products that are unrelated, but which compete for the same budgets (eg birthday gifts);
  − 'Market share analysis' which looks at volume produced against market share, anticipated against size of the overall market. Pricing strategy is determined from this equation.

There are two frequently quoted marketing based pricing strategies, 'penetration' and 'skimming'. They refer to first time pricing decisions when a new product is about to be sold and its life cycle in the market is commencing.

Penetration

Figure 11.6 illustrates penetration pricing. It relies on a large volume of sales from the outset to allow for economies of scale and its price is sufficiently low to make it attractive to the mass market from the outset. Such a policy might deter competitors because in such situations setting up costs are usually high and initial development costs are recovered over a long period of time. The objective is to achieve high sales initially and then maintain this during the life cycle of the product.

A low initial 'penetration' price attracts a mass market at the outset. Demand takes off exponentially during introduction and the pattern shown by the typical product life cycle concept hardly applies. The notion is particularly appropriate for products with a strong demand elasticity where unit cost reductions can be achieved through mass production at the beginning. An abundant sales volume must be assured from the outset to keep production levels high, in order to continue to realise these economies of scale. Marketing's task is to ensure that interest is maintained during the life of the product and that the concept remains 'fresh' in the eyes of consumers. The most cited example by way of illustration is a new car designed for the mass market (eg the Ford 'Ka').

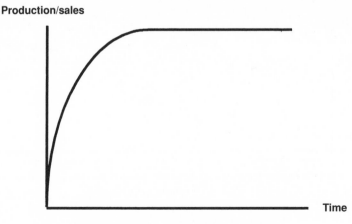

Figure 11.6 *Penetration pricing*

Skimming

This is a market based pricing policy which holds that companies will charge what the market will bear. When a new, innovative product is introduced to the market-place there will be initial purchasing interest from:

■ innovator categories (see Chapter 10);
■ higher social classes (see Chapter 2), who might feel that they want the product before anybody else and are prepared to pay a premium price;
■ special interest groups who wish to try it straight away (eg a new piece of computer software).

Promotion will tend to be informative and directed initially at a small potential segment.

Once the innovation has taken off, interest might begin to wane and in order to reach a wider spectrum of potential purchasers, prices are lowered at the first skim which brings in more innovator categories or different social groups. This process proceeds continuously until the final skim. Demand thereafter tends to reflect replacement demand. Figure 11.7 depicts this market skimming theory.

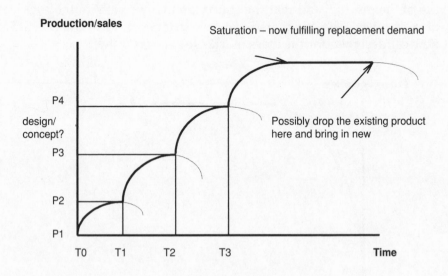

Figure 11.7 *Market skimming*

It can be seen that individual 'skims' have been taken at certain times (ie start at T0 with the initial price and then successively lowered at times T1, T2 and T3). The initial price is high (ie P1). This price is reduced at each of the time intervals (T1, T2 and T3) to the levels indicated (ie P2, P3 and P4 respectively). The point in time where each skim comes in, is a function of conditions in the market-place and competitive activity, but each skim generally reflects a significant reduction in price, often associated with some minor sophistication in design or features of the original product. The dotted line after each skim represents the theoretical downward market share that would have occurred had skimming not been introduced to revitalise demand in the market and bring in the next layer of purchasers.

In this illustration, the final skim, P4, occurs at T3. Thereafter, demand is a reflection of replacement demand, which is steady as the market has reached maturity. Towards the end of this maturity phase the product begins to tail off into its decline stage, there being no more skims possible as the product has now reached its final skim. It is suggested here that consideration might be given to dropping the product or bringing in a radically different alternative product and starting the cycle again.

Market skimming should also be accompanied by the manipulation of other marketing elements at each skim, in order to attempt to differentiate the product from other offerings in the marketplace. The principal benefit for manufacturers is that research and development costs can be recovered over a shorter time span than with penetration pricing and it is the manufacturers who were the first to do the basic research and development who stand to gain most from these early skims. 'Me too' products will appear later when the product has reached maturity. Products such as microwave ovens, miniature 'credit card' type calculators and personal computers are examples of products that best fit this theory.

TACTICAL ISSUES AND PROBLEMS OF PRICING

Prestige pricing

As a purchasing motivation, 'prestige' is rarely openly admitted. Many buyers do not realise that this might be their prime motivation for wanting to possess a particular item. At best, they might see the motive as the desire to possess something that is exclusive

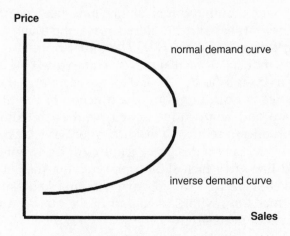

Figure 11.8   *Prestige pricing*

and such exclusivity is often associated with a high price. This is associated with what we term 'psychological pricing'. 'Prestige pricing' suggests a demand curve that is illustrated in Figure 11.8.

The top curve represents the normal demand curve and here the higher the price charged the lower will be the demand and, conversely, the lower the price charged the higher will be the amount required. However, for certain prestige products (exclusive brands of perfume being the most cited example) a reduction in price might harm the image of the brand and purchasers will feel that it has been 'cheapened', and associate it with inferior quality, so price reductions actually work against market demand. What we then see is an inverse demand curve which works in the opposite way to the normal demand curve. Here, price reductions below certain levels decrease demand.

Psychological aspects of pricing

It is now acknowledged that there are psychological price brackets for certain categories of products (ladies clothes are a particularly good illustration) in which price increases or reductions have little effect. When prices are reduced or raised to the next psychological price band, then demand will increase or decrease in a step-like manner. Closely linked to this is the notion of 'odd/even pricing' where a price of £9.95 means that there is a little change from £10.00. Anything over £10.00 is in the next psychological band which consumers perceive as being much more expensive than it actually is. 'Price lining' is also linked to psychological pricing and here retailers sell all of their products in a limited number of price bands of £29.95, £39.95 and £49.95.

Value based pricing

This is where a producer bases prices on the perceived value that the customer has of the product or service. It uses purchasers' price perceptions rather than costs as the principal measure. The marketing mix is manipulated so that non-price variables are accentuated and price perception is implanted in the minds of buyers. Price is then set to match the perceived value of the product or service. Cost-based price is accounting constrained using costs and the ultimate product as the basis for the pricing decision. Value based pricing is where the company establishes a target price, based on customer perceptions of the value that the product holds for them. If this turns out to be too high, the company must then reduce price and settle for a lower profit margin.

Price discrimination

Different prices are sometimes charged to certain categories of customers and this is termed 'price discrimination'. Discount structures operate in many industrial companies and 'trade discounts' apply for bona fide members of certain skilled professions. Volume discounts are also a feature in such circumstances and discounts are frequently offered as a promotional tool to encourage larger individual orders. Discounts are often used as an inducement to pay by a stipulated time or to bolster sales of slow moving lines.

Quite often price discrimination is applied to attract certain market segments that the company wishes to target. A current example is cheap initial loan rates, for a short period, offered by banks and building societies to attract first time home buyers in the expectation that they will remain loyal to the lender.

SUMMARY

Although there is increased emphasis nowadays on non-price factors, pricing decisions are still important and, in the final analysis, this is frequently the critical stage of any negotiating scenario. The company's general marketing strategy defines pricing policy, for example, whether or not the company sees itself as a 'price leader' (lowest price), or as a market leader or as a technological leader. It is thus a dynamic part of marketing strategy to be flexible enough to have a thorough understanding of market conditions and adjust its pricing policies accordingly. Such policies should be considered alongside other constituents of the marketing mix.

A number of external factors affect pricing decisions, including the general competitive nature of the market-place in terms of both suppliers and customers. Elasticity of demand is also an important consideration as in such situations there is little room to manoeuvre and it is here that the skill and judgement of the individual marketing manager is most important. Behavioural criteria are important in price setting, as customer and competitor reactions must be considered and then applied in conjunction with more logically based solutions.

12

Channels of Distribution

INTRODUCTION

The overall subject area of what we might call 'distribution' or 'place' in terms of the marketing mix's four Ps classification, can really be divided into two distinct areas. They are distinct in that they address different aspects of business activity that are nonetheless very closely related. They are both concerned with distribution and in the provision of what might be called 'time and place utility'. The first half of the 'distribution equation', channels of distribution, will be covered in this chapter. The second half of the distribution equation, business logistics, will be the subject of Chapter 13.

The area of distribution has been studied in depth by Professor Peter Drucker, who referred to it as the 'economy's Dark Continent'. What Professor Drucker intended to convey was that out of all the areas of the marketing mix, the subject of distribution is perhaps researched and studied less and has consequently developed less theoretically and conceptually than other marketing areas. It is sometimes referred to as the 'poor relation' of modern marketing. This is a very odd state of affairs when you realise that distribution is a key part of any business enterprise's marketing mix and has a strategic role within the mix of absolutely crucial salience. Many firms are excellent in terms of what they produce but often neglect the distribution side of things, relegating it to secondary importance. Other firms, often with inferior product or service offerings, are able to steal a competitive advantage over them because they have a more imaginative and effective distribution system.

THE RELATIONSHIP BETWEEN MARKETING AND CHANNEL MANAGEMENT

Marketing channels are often organised and serviced by companies or individuals that are independent from the manufacturing firm or service provider eg savings bonds for personal investment are often sold through independent financial advisors. These companies or individual agents act as channels for a product or service in order to make a profit. Hence the manufacturing firm relies on the expertise of the channel member to successfully market its products or services 'down stream' ie to the next stage of the distribution chain which might be the end user or another marketing intermediary. The marketing firm is trying to achieve business objectives such as market share, return on capital, growth and profit margins through third parties ie channel members. If their channel members are unsuccessful then they too will be unsuccessful. As separate, independent firms with their own set of business goals and objectives, they have needs and wants of their own which the marketing firm needs to fill in order to cement a long-term mutually beneficial relationship. Therefore the marketing process of addressing the satisfaction of specific needs and wants is not simply confined to the end users of the product but must also be applied to all intermediaries in the distribution chain. They too are customers of the original marketing firm.

One of the central concepts or principles of marketing is that business enterprises need to really understand their customers. In situations where a manufacturer delivers goods on site direct to the user, the definition of the customer is usually obvious. However, where a complicated, often 'multi-layered' distribution network is employed it is not so clear or so simple. There can be a 'tree' of customers at different levels in the distribution chain. More commonly the immediate customers are a group of marketing intermediaries. Hence, being 'customer directed' also applies to focusing the marketing effort on the firm's immediate customers, who might be other businesses in the channel chain, in what Professor Philip Kotler of North-Western University calls the 'task environment'. This includes another very important group of customers who are suppliers, as well as their marketing channel members. Suppliers are vital members of the marketing firm's task environment. Firms, especially those involved with manufacturing, rely on the quality of component parts, delivery reliability, stock availability and a keen market price from their suppliers in order to ensure that their own business is successful. Suppliers are independent businesses who have needs and wants just the same as any other individual or group of customers. The marketing firm must ensure that a good relationship with suppliers is created and maintained through the use of effective 'relationship marketing' programmes.

Two related aspects of distribution

The topic of distribution comprises two component parts, channels and physical distribution (often referred to as business logistics). It is the significant topic of channels of distribution that is discussed in this chapter. The term 'distribution system' refers to that network of agents, wholesalers and retailers through which manufacturers move products (and services, for example financial services such as pension products or savings plans) to the final customers or consumers. Marketing channels usually consist of independent firms or individual and independent entrepreneurs who are themselves in business to make a profit. These are known as marketing intermediaries or, to use the rather antiquated term still used today, 'middlemen'. Marketing channels may also include a combination of owned and independent outlets or arrangements such as business format franchising. Along with physical distribution, which is part of the total business logistics function, channels of distribution contribute to what economists often refer to as 'time and place utility'. This is a more esoteric way of explaining that to have real value many goods and services need to be available in a certain place and at a certain time. Goods and services may be manufactured or provided but to be of any real economic value they need to be made available for consumption in a certain place, eg a pub in the case of beer and at a certain time, eg immediately. In the UK fireworks are really only of interest to people on the 5th of November which is Guy Fawkes Night. Very few people purchase fireworks after the 5th of November even though shops try to sell their excess fireworks at dramatically reduced prices, often almost giving them away.

The correct choice of channels can add significant real and perceived value to the product or service offering and consequently is a very important area of the marketing mix. In fact the 'P' designating 'place' in McCarthy's categorisation of the four Ps actually refers to channels of distribution and physical distribution combined.

THE NATURE OF DISTRIBUTION

The nature of channels of distribution is dynamic rather than static and changing constantly, although slowly, and may be barely noticeable by the majority of people. At least this has been true in the past. There is evidence that the rate of change is accelerating over time and becoming more noticeable even to the casual observer. New channels for products and services are being developed all the time as firms try to find new and innovative ways to market their products and services before their competitors.

Think for a moment on the dramatic expansion in the range of goods and services made available for sale in petrol stations. Consider also the growth in availability and importance of television channel shopping, particularly in the United States, where it now forms the major marketing channel for some goods and services. This type of marketing channel was virtually unheard of even 20 years ago, but is now worth billions of dollars.

Because of the changing nature of channel types and design over time and the creation and introduction of completely new formats, often due to technological innovations, marketing management must continually monitor the external marketing environment and try to forecast possible changes and developments. They then need to use their research in a pro-active manner in order to have a chance of staying ahead of the competition. A further important factor to consider is the likely dramatic expansion of shopping on the Internet over the next 25 years, as more and more households get 'wired up' to use the new information technology.

The justification for selecting a channel system design is its potential superior effectiveness in achieving the effective distribution of product or service from the producer to the final customer. Marketing management tends to model this process in terms of the concept of 'flow'. Product 'flows' through the distribution 'pipeline' rather as fluid might flow through a pipeline plumbing system. As with the water system, products can face obstacles and other problems that may adversely affect the free flow of goods and services in the distribution system.

A firm does not alter its channel policy every five minutes. Quite the contrary, distribution arrangements generally are a long-term set up. Setting up a distribution arrangement, particularly if the arrangement is selective or exclusive, requires extensive discussion, negotiation and legal agreements. Because distribution arrangements are often relatively long term in nature, they are classed as strategic rather than tactical or operational decisions, for the following reasons:

■ Marketing channel decisions have a direct impact on the rest of the firm's marketing activities. For example, the selection of target markets and segmentation policy is influenced by and in turn affects, channel design and choice.
■ Once established, the channel system may be difficult to alter, at least in the short term. Because the most effective channel arrangements for a particular product or service are likely to change over time, albeit relatively slowly, marketers need to continually monitor the distributive environment and re-evaluate their existing channel arrangements and policies with a view to exploiting and capitalising on any changes.

The English word 'channel' is based on the Norman word for canal. In marketing terms this can be interpreted as the journey taken by products and/or services as they flow from their point of creation to points of intermediate and final use or consumption. Marketing is the key factor in an on-going cycle that starts and finishes with the satisfaction of the needs and wants of specific target consumers. Marketing firms must establish the needs and wants of potential consumers and then utilise the organisation's resources to create goods and services that meet or exceed the requirements and expectations of their customers.

When the manufacturing processes are finished, the completed product is moved through a system of marketing intermediaries and eventually on to the final purchaser. Marketing channels provide a system that enables the product or service to be made available to the final consumer and this availability produces value in the form of time and place utility. A product or service has to be made available to those customers who wish to purchase it at the right place and at the right time and in a condition acceptable to the customer. This process adds value to the product or service and it is this added value that is produced by efficient marketing channels.

CHANNEL SELECTION

The correct selection of marketing channels is of very great importance to the success of any firm. Often strategic and competitive advantage can be achieved by using innovative and imaginative channels of distribution. In fact as we shall see later in the chapter, new channels of distribution are being developed by businesses all the time in their search for a competitive lead.

For example in the UK the home magazines *Living* and *Family Circle* are distributed almost entirely in supermarkets and hypermarkets and, what is more interesting, unlike the majority of other magazines on sale in the supermarket, these two are retailed on the shop side of the checkout till, whereas most other newspapers and periodicals are on sale in areas available after you have paid for your main shopping. There are a number of other publications which have imitated the model of these two magazines, but for many years these two highly innovative publications had managed to carve out a strategic competitive advantage almost entirely by their choice of distribution channel.

When examining the flow of goods and/or services through a distribution channel, it is helpful to use an analogy and think of the system as a pipeline with main pipes, subsidiary branches, free flows and blockages. In fact marketing communicators working in the field of sales promotions think of distribution channels as a kind of plumbing system or 'pipeline' network, similar in nature to a drainage system and just as complicated. For example, they often model consumer promotions along the lines of 'out of the pipeline' or 'pull' promotions whereas promotions targeted at company employees or marketing intermediaries are referred to as 'into the pipeline' or 'push' promotions. In this context they are referring to products or services either being pulled through the distribution pipeline by consumer demand or pushed in to the distribution pipeline by the efforts of the salesperson or encouraged by dealer incentive schemes.

STRATEGIC ELEMENTS OF CHANNEL CHOICE

The amount of market exposure required by the firm influences the direction of channel policy and also how many marketing intermediaries are to be employed. Decisions regarding channel strategy will depend on a range of things including the type of the product or service, the technical complexity of the product and/or its servicing requirements and the perceived image the marketing firm wishes to achieve in the minds of consumers. Three basic distribution strategies can be categorised.

Exclusive distribution

Using only known official distributors will increase the standing of a product and evolve a high quality brand image. Exclusive distribution, a policy of conceding dealers' exclusive rights to market the product or service in a certain geographical area, is often used in association with a policy of exclusive trading, where the manufacturer requires the dealer not to carry rival lines, as in computer or motor cycle dealerships. By conceding exclusive distribution, the marketing firm gains more control over intermediaries in relation to price, credit and promotion policies, enhanced loyalty and a more offensive general marketing effort.

Selective distribution

As the name suggests, selective distribution involves the careful choosing of a limited range of channels. Such channels are usually selected on the basis of some criterion or criteria deemed necessary in the channel for the successful marketing of the product or service in question. For example the channel member may need some specialised skill for giving advice or after sales service such as repair facilities etc. The marketing firm may require channel members to have special storage facilities for their products such as refrigeration facilities.

Rather than spreading its marketing effort over a wide range of different channels, some of which might not be entirely suitable for the kind of reasons above, the marketing firm focuses on the most suitable outlets only. Selective distribution is therefore used where the facilities, resources or image of the outlet can have a direct impact on the buying public's overall attitude towards the product or service, as in the case of expensive brands of perfume for example. Distribution in 'discount chain' stores may adversely affect the brand image of such products.

Intensive distribution

This strategy is used when marketing firms want to achieve the widest possible distribution for their goods and services. It is used in conditions where there are no special criteria necessary to be a channel member, no special storage facilities required and where the type of outlet is unlikely to have any serious adverse impact on the perceived image of the product or service being marketed. For example, firms producing convenience goods and certain common raw materials aiming to stock their products in as many outlets as possible might use this strategy.

The important criteria in the marketing of such products are their place utility. Producers of pens, cigarettes and confectionery try to use every possible retail outlet, ranging from multiples to independent corner shops. With such products, every opportunity for the customer to see the product is an opportunity for them to buy and the perceived image of the channel used is not an important constituent in the buyer's attitude or overall impression of the product.

INDIRECT VERSUS DIRECT SYSTEMS

The selection of a distribution system will to some extent depend upon whether a marketing firm decides to distribute directly to customers, using a direct sales force, or to use channel members such as agents, wholesalers and retailers. Marketing channels in many industrial and business to business markets tend to be direct or at least more direct than in consumer markets. In industrial markets products are often a unique 'one off' made especially for the industrial customer from the customer's own plans, or are a standard product which has been modified in some way to meet the specific customer requirements.

For example, a standard fork-lift truck might be adapted for lifting rolls of carpet or sheets of glass. In such situations products are made or modified and then distributed direct to the client. In the case of products such as production equipment, eg drilling machines or power presses, they are usually installed and tested before being legally given over to the customer. It is not to say that channel intermediaries are never used in industrial and other business to business markets. Products such as electrical equipment are often sold to the trade through a type of wholesaler called a 'factor' in the United Kingdom, rather than being supplied straight from the manufacturer. Industrial vehicles and standard small machine tools such as drills and welding equipment and supplies are often distributed through agents or distributors, very often on an exclusive distribution agreement.

Marketing using direct distribution is generally used in consumer markets, especially in the case of fast moving consumer goods (FMCG) such as packaged grocery. There has been a shift in the direction of direct distribution within the consumer durable and consumer services markets. Direct distribution has also grown at an outstanding rate within the UK financial services sector. First Direct, now a subsidiary of the Bank of Scotland, was the first to offer consumers low cost insurance by telephone. This use of direct telephone marketing is now common throughout the financial services sector and it is now a straightforward process to order a pension, a mortgage or even open a conventional bank account by telephone directly with the supplier.

Direct distribution of goods has been developed and practised for a long time by such international companies as Avon Cosmetics who were innovators in the area of direct marketing. The expansion in what is often called 'Network' marketing or 'Multi-level' marketing (MLM) has also increased the use of direct distribution. A good example is the general household products firm Kleeneze which uses the MLM approach utilising a group of independent, self employed agents and distributors at various managerial levels within the MLM organisation. The decision to use direct or indirect distribution is often based on cost factors, taking into account factors such as:

1. costs allied with the operational aspects of the distributive operation, including transport, warehousing and stockholding;
2. the degree of market concentration;
3. the number of potential customers in the market;
4. the purchasing potential of customers in a given time period.

Marketing direct by using a company-employed sales team is often preferred by firms when there is a large enough potential sales volume. Industrial goods firms tend to utilise selling and direct delivery, although many use intermediaries such as factors (the same as wholesalers in consumer markets). Consumer goods companies tend to use a network of marketing intermediaries because of the geographical dispersion and large numbers of potential customers.

Manufacturers will sell to wholesalers who take legal possession, break bulk, mark up and sell on to retailers. It is common for manufacturers to sell direct to large multiples such as Asda, particularly in the packaged grocery market. Large multiples have significant market power and are big enough to act as their own wholesaler, usually with a central storage and distribution centre of their own. Whatever method of distribution is chosen by the marketing firm, the important point is that the manufacturer relies on intermediaries for ultimate marketing success, since they have the job of making the product available to the final customer.

CHANGING CHANNEL SYSTEMS

Single variation in channels may be tiny, but cumulative change can be very important. Like many other areas of our lives the velocity of change within many channel systems seems to be increasing. We mentioned earlier the immense growth in the use of direct marketing channels by firms such as Kleeneze. A period of nearly ten years, from the mid 1980s to the mid 1990s, saw what can be described as a sea change in the marketing of financial products and services using direct marketing, especially direct mail and telephone marketing.

The next transformation in distribution channel systems is already taking place, but at the present time only specialists and those studying distribution evolution over time, such as academic researchers, are fully cognisant of the change. The inherent enormity of this evolution is in the way that people will order and receive goods and services in the future. The technical developments bringing about this change are grounded on the fibre optic cable providing many thousands of communication channels that can be used simultaneously. The UK is presently engaged in the process of being 'wired up' with optical fibre cables being fed into every home, firm and other establishments such as hospitals and council offices. Most of us have seen the pavements in our town or city being dug up and often rather untidily replaced in order for the cable contractors to wire up a few more people in to the 21st century.

The Internet and World Wide Web (WWW) are a contemporary marketing phenomenon. In the United States cable television shopping channels are very popular and well established, more so than in Europe. Orders can be placed via a television hand set and the goods are sent to your home. You pay by typing your credit card number into a special hand-held mini computer or telephone, toll free, to order. Cable television and satellite television are allowing such 'shopping channels' to be established. Web site technology is going to be an even bigger marketing tool than cable and satellite television. All kinds of organisations, from universities advertising courses to banks advertising loans and investments are using the Web to create the direct marketing channel of the next century.

When devising long term channel strategy, firms need to observe these changes and attempt to anticipate future macro developments in the technological environment. It is no use waiting for things to alter and then be compelled to react to such changes in an effort to catch up with your competitors. To achieve a strategic competitive position an organisation must welcome change and it must be an intrinsic part of the company dynamics. The firm should be at the core of change, influencing what goes on and not be merely a quiescent observer, watching other firms propel themselves into a more competitive future.

Change happens at all levels, but it is possibly most conspicuous at retail level, where major changes in retail practice have happened, especially over the last decade. The 1980s and 1990s in particular witnessed a marked polarity in the turnover distribution of retail firms. At one end of the spectrum are the very large-scale operators: multiples such as Tesco, Asda and Sainsbury's and the large discount chains such as Kwiksave. At the other end there are still a plethora of small shops, some totally independent and others tied to wholesalers in the form of 'voluntary chains'. Generally speaking, the total number of shops has fallen with an increased concentration of market share going to a relatively small, but very powerful number of large multiple chains. This concentration is very obvious in the grocery sector. In general, the large multiples have expanded at the expense of independents, voluntary chains, co-operatives and small multiples.

The Monopolies and Mergers Commission (MMC) were so concerned about the dramatic increase of market and bargaining power vested in the large retail chains that they published a rather critical MMC report entitled *Discounts to Retailers* in 1981 (available from HMSO). The essence of the recommendations made by the MMC panel in the report was that the large multiples needed to practice responsible self restraint otherwise the MMC would make recommendations to the Government that it might be in the public interest for such large chains to divest themselves of some of their outlets thus rendering them less powerful.

THE STRUCTURE OF INDUSTRIAL MARKETING CHANNELS

Marketing channels in industrial or business to business markets are more complicated than in consumer markets. These relatively complex structures have two basic components:

1. the placement of channel types in relation to each other;
2. the number of different levels or stages included in the overall distribution channel.

Within industrial marketing, firms tend to use a more direct distribution method. As discussed earlier many products in industrial markets are 'buyer specified' rather than 'supplier specified' and this has profound implications for choice of channel configuration. It also means that products are often made or at least altered to a particular client's specifications or plans and these products are usually delivered direct to the customer. Manufacturers of machine tools and industrial vehicles make use of distributors and agents whilst manufacturers of such goods as electrical equipment make use of wholesalers, often referred to as 'factors'. Basically, the same codes of channel management apply as in consumer markets. The main variance between the two sectors is that generally speaking consumer markets use more channel stages in the distribution system than is the case in industrial markets.

TYPES AND CLASSIFICATION OF CHANNEL

Marketing channels can be distinguished with reference to the number of channel levels in the system. The number of members or 'middlemen' involved in the channel operation determines on how many levels it operates. There are four main types of channel configuration existing in consumer markets as shown below.

The first three levels are quite uncomplicated. The three level channel is usually made up of three intermediaries, a merchant wholesaler or 'jobber' who mediates between the other two, the wholesaler and retailer. As mentioned in the previous section industrial channels are usually more direct.

Many consumer markets are becoming similar to industrial markets. The tendency in consumer markets seems to be a more direct form of marketing which often replaces the need for any kind of intermediary and allows the manufacturer or service provider to do business straight with the end users. This trend has been especially noticeable in the financial services sector. Conventionally, if a person required a financial product such as insurance, a mortgage or a pension plan they would have probably visited a bank manager, an insurance broker, an estate agent or an independent financial adviser. These days it is possible for the customer to do business directly with the firm offering the financial product often by telephone or the World Wide Web. There appears to be less need for an elaborate arrangement of 'middlemen' all sharing in the profits. This sort of distribution method has assisted the providers of these financial products to leverage their profit margins and at the same time cut the cost of such 'products' to customers and deliver a more user friendly and effective service.

DEVELOPMENTS AND CHANGES IN RETAIL STRUCTURE

Change is a fundamental characteristic of the external business environment that has an effect on all marketing channel members at all levels in the channel system. We have already considered the subject of 'Marketing and the macro-environment' in Chapter 2 and have discussed how changes in the external business environment are usually outside the control of the individual marketing firm. Obviously these changes have a direct impact on the marketing procedures and customs of the marketing enterprise. Elements in the external environment, whether political, social, legal, demographic, technological or economic all have an effect on the company's future marketing activities and policies.

These outside environmental factors are driven by manifold interconnected forces that can result in quite dramatic change. Often the consequent change is speedy and sensational, for example, the re-unification of Germany after the fall of the Iron Curtain. More often change takes place at a gradual rate, in fact so slow that it is almost unnoticeable and can only be realised in retrospect. Nothing represents this principle more than the transformations that have taken place within the retail industry over the last 20 years.

Scrambled merchandising

The demand for food products in an advanced industrialised economy is relatively 'income inelastic', in that customers do not necessarily buy more food when their income increases, although they may trade up to more elaborate and sophisticated types of food. The demand for food in advanced nations is related to population growth and increased demand in the UK has been either zero in some years or relatively small in others. Because of this the large UK food multiples can only grow either at the expense of each other's 'food spend' market share, or by diversifying into non-food products on which people on increasing incomes are likely to spend their money.

In the UK, multiples have diversified into non-food items to advance their turnover and profits. Many now sell clothing, electrical goods, plants and flowers and have spread out of their conventional range of food products. However, a number have recently returned to their core business of food retailing because so much diversification has diminished their image in the minds of the general public.

'One-stop' shopping

Access to a motor vehicle is one of the main reasons for the fact that people tend to shop less frequently now than they used to 20 years ago, with once a week or longer between shopping trips becoming quite normal. Shopping is also developing into more of a family affair, particularly amongst the middle classes. This has accounted, at least in part, for the growth of 'out of town' shopping centres such as Meadow Hall near Sheffield, where most of a family's needs can be purchased within the same shopping mall.

It is not unusual to see that the national multiples are set up in certain centres with a number of satellite shops supplying goods that they do not sell themselves. For example Asda in Wakefield has a shoe shop, a travel agency, an optician and a building society situated within its concourse and trading as separate businesses under a concession from Asda. Such stores tend to be hypermarkets or megastores and the main reason why this trend might slow down is because of planning regulations and a recognition by planners that such out of town centres lead to the demise of traditional town shopping centres.

As well as increased mobility, many people own freezers which enables them to transport and store large quantities of frozen food. Increased microwave cooker ownership has also increased sales of 'instant' meals, many of which are cooked from frozen. A final point connected to the growth of 'one stop shopping' is the change in population from urban to suburban centres. Congestion in towns demoralises car drivers who elect to shop in big out-of-town complexes where parking is plentiful and usually at no charge.

Business format franchising

The business format franchise was evolved in the United States, but it has increased in importance in the UK since the early 1960s. It is basically a contract between a franchiser (the person or firm with a proven business idea) and each separately owned company of the franchisee (the person or group of people who want to make use of the proven business idea in exchange for an on-going commission). The franchiser's brand and standing is used for marketing a product or service and the support received by the franchisee from the franchiser will depend on the contract. The contract is usually written so as to minimise the risks in opening a business. That is why many entrepreneurs thinking of going into business for themselves choose this method of doing so. What attracts new franchisees is that others have successfully followed the 'blueprint' so why not them? The larger franchiser supplies the franchisee with a 'business package' or 'format', a trade name and specific products or services for sale. A complete set of operating manuals and a business plan, which the franchisee must adhere to, are also included.

Business format franchising is a system of selling and distribution organised through a contract between a principal seller (franchiser) and distributive outlets (owned by franchisees). Such a system depends on the franchiser having an idea, a name, a 'secret process' or specialised equipment or goodwill that will be commercially interesting to prospective franchisees. If this is the case, then the franchiser will grant the franchisee the legal right, for some kind of commercial compensation, for the franchisee to exploit that name, idea or product. Such an agreement might include rules for operating the business and details as to how the franchiser is to be compensated, which might be a royalty, an initial fee, a share of profits, the obligation to make bulk purchases from the franchiser, to abide by certain 'rules' of hygiene and presentation possibly involving training and many other things depending on the type of product or service being franchised. All business format franchise agreements are similar but no two are exactly the same. A franchise agreement for a Holiday Inn hotel is likely to be different to one for a Dyno-rod franchise. This is partly because of the differing nature of the product or service but also because of the amount of franchisee investment required and other commercial and financial considerations.

Expansion of multiple chains

As has been explained, multiples have been capable of eliminating wholesalers from commercial transactions through the use of central buying direct from the manufacturers, in effect acting as their own wholesalers. Bulk purchases have meant beneficial prices from producers, while independent shops have still to purchase through wholesalers, so there are tremendous difficulties for small retailers in terms of price competitiveness.

Some groups of wholesalers endeavoured to equalise this growing competition from multiples by setting up their own chains, called 'voluntary groups'. Retailers were requested to associate and display the group's logo and embrace the 'rules' of the group. Notably, Spar is still a flourishing voluntary group operator today, but many groups have now ceased to trade in the light of rivalry from the larger and more powerful multiple chains.

The 1970s saw the introduction of 'economy' lines by multiples in the UK. These were 'no frills' products which conveyed no advertising messages or sales promotion schemes and were packaged in simple functional containers. In fact, this intensified the 'pile it high and sell it cheap' image of the multiples and affected consumers' perception of a quality range of merchandise. However, during the early 1980s retailing saw the introduction of 'own label' products which were brands commissioned especially by particular multiple chains from manufacturers, often manufacturers of well known, major brands and bearing the chain's own logo. Specifications on such products meant that they had to be perceived as being amongst the best of traditional branded lines, not to be associated with economy line products of the 1970s.

The first multiple in the UK to do this was Sainsbury's, with others hastily following. In the UK, the result has been that power in retailing has passed to some extent from manufacturers' brands to retailers' own label brands. The dilemma for manufacturers was that they would in essence become the manufacturing arm of the multiples with little power in the market-place in terms of heavily branded goods. Many producers warded off this move to 'own label' by refusing to supply the multiples. However, such was the buying power of multiples that very few manufacturers still refuse to supply them, with some exceptions being Lever, Procter and Gamble, Kellogg's and Nestlé. These manufacturers make a commercial morality of not supplying 'own label' by clearly stating in their labelling and advertising that they do not manufacture products for other firms. However, despite these exceptions, in the UK (unlike many other countries) power within retailing has moved from manufacturers to retailers. This shift in power has come to the attention of the Monopolies and Mergers Commission who are concerned that such an imbalance of power might be against the public good.

The retail life cycle

This concept is similar to the 'product life cycle' concept and basically refers to evolutionary changes in retailing. So as not to be confused with the product life cycle concept it is sometimes referred to as the 'wheel of retailing'. The 'wheel' seems to be turning with ever increasing speed with each retailing idea taking less time to achieve maturity than the previous one. It took around 50 years for department stores to reach maturity, supermarkets took around 25 years and hypermarkets and now megastores only 10 years. This concept can be contrasted to Charles Darwin's theory of evolution which states that a changing environment leads to adaptation and hence evolution, in this sense retail evolution. Environmental changes that have happened which have contributed to this evolution can be summarised as follows:

■ Resale Price Maintenance (RPM) was abolished in the UK in 1964 by the Resale Prices Act. RPM meant that retailers had to sell at manufacturer determined prices with the threat of having supplies withheld if they did not agree to adhere to the terms. With the abolition of RPM and bigger stores going for price reductions as the main form of attraction, many smaller shops went out of business together with a number of the wholesalers who supplied such outlets. Multiples expanded into the 'freed up' market and used their purchasing power to compete on price and passing savings on to customers. Before the abolition of RPM retailers had competed on service, often providing a level of service which today would appear quite astonishing. Often the level of service was higher than customers actually wanted. Ordinary working people wanted cheaper prices not more service. This led to the self-explanatory phrase: 'Pile it high and sell it cheap.' Thus, multiples expanded at the expense of independents. It was Napoleon that called England a 'nation of shop keepers'. After this phase of retail history there were rather less shops in business within the UK and many people, particularly those who could not get around easily such as the old, or those who did not have access to cars or could not afford public transport, suffered as their local convenience store went out of business.

■ Selective employment tax (SET) was a tax on selected occupations which was introduced in the UK in 1966 under a Labour government. The Prime Minister of the day Harold Wilson, wanted a 'dash' for economic growth and foresaw the UK economy in the 'white heat' of a technological revolution. He wanted to force the workforce into what the government regarded as productive industries, making things, rather than service industries such as retailing. Retail shop workers were seen as being 'non-productive' so a tax of 7 per cent was levied on employers with a view to encouraging retail firms to automate any substitute capital for labour to save costs. As labour became more expensive, capital investment became relatively cheaper and many retailers were attracted to labour saving checkout systems that gave more stimulus to the introduction of self-service. These large capital investments meant that operators needed a faster turnover and the consequence was that the shelf life of consumer goods became shorter. Multiple chain retailers of FMCG produce were able to sell fresher merchandise that they exploited in their advertising, so this tax indirectly helped them to expand at the expense of independents.

■ Economic factors have obliged retailers to expand their scale of operation in order to achieve economies of scale in both size of establishments and buying power. This has resulted in retailing hypermarkets and megastores. Retailing has also become more concentrated with large multiples dominant in much of fast moving consumer goods (FMCG) trade. The general trend seems to be bigger and bigger stores, retail concessions within stores, a 'one stop shopping' concept and ever increasing retail power in the hands of the multiple chains.

Other significant developments

There has been an expansion in other types of retailing over the past 20 years including:

■ The World Wide Web (WWW) on the Internet is a marketing tool that actively persuades customers to search for the seller rather than the prospective seller contacting them. It is almost a complete role reversal. Researchers in this area often use the term 'virtual value chain' in relation to the use of the WWW and the 'market space' rather than the conventional term market-place. The WWW is still in its babyhood as a marketing tool, but it is increasing in importance, especially in the area of marketing communications where it is emerging as a new major medium. It will be interesting to see how this medium develops over the next decade; it is certainly a 'hot' topic in the journal literature at the moment.

■ Television shopping via on-line computer is still at an early stage, but it should become more accepted if companies invest enough in the innovation and evolution of appropriate software and hardware to make the search and ordering systems work more efficiently and to be more user friendly. This direct form of retailing is economical as orders are often placed straight with manufacturers cutting out the need for expensive 'middlemen' eating away at the profits. This shopping format is very popular in the United States. As with the Web, the developmental possibilities of this form of 'non shop shopping' are literally enormous and it will be very interesting to see how this form of retailing develops over the next ten years or so.

▓ Automatic vending has grown a lot since the 1960s and is now used for beverages, cigarettes, chocolate and many other goods. When you go to the swimming baths now you can buy swimming goggles, ear plugs, combs, soap, shampoo and a range of other related products out of a vending machine. Vending machines are placed in favourable locations like bus stations, colleges, public houses and factories, or as with the previous example, in the changing rooms at swimming baths. They have been used since the 1950s to provide entertainment through jukeboxes and more recently arcade games. Cash dispenser machines, another form of vending technology, only this time vending money, are comparatively new and in addition to dispensing cash they can answer balance inquiries, take requests for statements and cheque books and accept deposits. The Midland bank in particular seems almost 'human free' when you go in. Everything you need to do such as make a deposit, pay your mortgage or loan repayment etc can be done using one of their automatic teller machines.

▓ Door-to-door direct selling is relatively costly, but wholesaler and retailer margins are removed. As long as the salesperson can achieve a regular list of customers for relatively frequently purchased items then it can be successful. Avon Cosmetics and Betterware are two examples of companies who are thriving in this regard. Door to door selling faces the disadvantage of a bad image for a number of reasons. First there are many firms who try and solicit business by first of all sending callers around people's houses to screen out those who will not be interested and to try and identify serious prospects. Double glazing, other home improvement type products and services such as security systems and insurance products are all represented in the door to door selling repertoire. At times people get fed up with unsolicited calls, especially in the evening after they have had a hard day at work. Another related problem is the potential security risk. Some people simply will not open their doors to unsolicited callers no matter what.

▓ Party Plan is liked for goods such as cosmetics, kitchenware, jewellery and linen. A 'party' is arranged, usually in the home of a hostess who invites friends and then receives a 'consideration' in the form of cash or goods based upon what the people at the party buy. Party Plan schemes are a mixture of the commercial and social. People come to the party, not only to see the merchandise but also for an evening with friends. Guests at the 'party' feel obliged to purchase something even if it is only something small as a kind of token gesture.

■ Mail order marketing can be through catalogue or non-catalogue methods. The first relies on catalogues to obtain sales, sometimes using agents to deal with order collection and administration in return for a commission. Products can be purchased interest-free and extended credit terms are sometimes offered. There are some specialist mail order houses that deal with a limited range of lines that are difficult to access in ordinary retail outlets (eg clothes for very large people). Non-catalogue mail order depends on press and magazine advertising and is often used to sell a range of products. This range, which historically has always been quite limited, seems to be expanding all the time. In the Sunday papers you will find mail order advertisements or 'inserts' ie loose pieces of card with advertising messages on them which are inserted into the newspaper or magazine, for shirts, porcelain items, insurance, garden equipment and a plethora of other things.

■ Other direct marketing techniques include using direct mail, where a letter and instructions on ordering are sent through the post. Such methods are used by book and record clubs particularly. Television can also be used to convey the direct marketing commercial message, with orders often being placed by a telephone call to a free number with the requisition for the quotation of credit card details to an answering machine. Often the process of ordering is done entirely by machine with the use of a recorded message and the 'star' button on a 'touch type' telephone. Telephone ordering is often linked with press advertising, especially in colour supplements.

CHANNEL CONFLICT AND CO-OPERATION

Marketing channel members are frequently autonomous companies and often have clashing goals and aspirations. This often leads to tension, antagonism and inefficiency within the channel system. This can be detrimental business wise for all parties involved and not just for the original manufacturer. When the management of a manufacturing firm sets out to plan and design a distribution channel system for their products there are a number of factors they need to take into account. Channel strategy must be based on overall marketing strategy; it cannot be planned in isolation.

Because of the long term, strategic nature of channel decisions, channel arrangements are not generally altered with any frequency or in the short term. Hence it is crucial for the marketing firm to select marketing intermediaries with caution, as they are likely to have to live with their decision for a long time. In planning a distribution system, management tries to achieve an efficient running system where all channel members are working in collaboration towards a clearly defined common goal. If each member of the channel system is marching to his or her own tune then there is likely to be chaos and inefficiency within the system that will be detrimental to the marketing firm. All members of the channel 'team' at whatever level should see such associations in the system as being mutually advantageous. Unfortunately the reality is that channel systems are often full of conflict and rarely operate along the smooth lines desired by the planners of the system.

Co-ordination

Once marketing management has identified their target market, carried out market segmentation and established the marketing mix to yield the right kind of goods and services for these markets, they must then determine how and where these products and services can be made available for consumption. This needs to be done in a way that enables customers to access what they want in the most efficient way and in a way that fits in with the rest of the company's marketing strategy in terms of company and individual brand image.

As we said earlier channel members are often independent firms that have to make a profit to survive and hence have commercial needs and wants of their own which the marketing firm has to address. The long term objective of channel management is to achieve the maximum level of service for final customers in the most efficient way possible. At the same time this has to be achieved in such a way that individual channel members can obtain adequate levels of profit for themselves which are sufficient for them to remain in business and adequately compensates them for their contribution to the efficiency of the channel system as a whole. If they do a good job then they must be properly rewarded for their efforts

Lancaster and Massingham recommend four major steps in the co-ordination process. The first step in the process is to decide the level of service outputs required by the final users of the channel system. The second step is to ascertain the level of service outputs and which channel members have the capacity to perform the required functions. The third step in the co-ordination process is to ascertain and establish which strategies should be used to bring about the desired end results. It is crucial that marketing channels are organised and co-ordinated in an appropriate way. Without such co-ordination the activities within the overall channel system will not operate in an efficient manner causing commercial problems to the manufacturer and the channel members themselves.

Co-ordinative process

Channel members should try to co-ordinate their objectives, plans and activities with other intermediaries in such a way that the attainment of final customer satisfaction of the total distribution system of which they are an intrinsic part is enhanced. In reality such co-operation among channel members is rare; there seem to be two main reasons for this:

■ Channel members tend to only show any real interest and duty to those other members that impact directly on their business, for example, those intermediaries immediately above and below themselves in the channel system from whom they buy and to whom they sell. They tend not to take a more holistic view and rarely show any concern about members well 'up stream' or 'down stream' from them in the system or indeed how their problems might impact on their own business.
■ Channel members are usually entirely separate businesses that have to make a profit to survive. They are too busy looking after their own problems to pay attention or even to care about what goes on in other different levels of the channel system. They should do this but generally they do not.
■ The idea of a unified integrated channel system is more of an idealised model than a practical model of what actually goes on in the real world. Channel members do not on the whole function as constituents of a well ordered integrated distribution system. Quite the contrary in fact, they tend to behave as independent businesses and have little regard for other members of the channel system unless they have an immediate influence on their own businesses. A channel system as a whole should aim to add value by creating a 'synergistic dividend'. Synergism is a

phrase often used in strategic planning which refers to certain situations where the sum of all the parties acting together produces an effect greater than simply adding up the effects of each individual component part working in isolation. Ideally, channel members should attempt to plan their objectives together so that they are mutually beneficial, avoid damaging and possible unprofitable controversy and conflicts and work together as a harmonious integrated team.

CONFLICT

Conflict within distribution channels is a situation in which one member of a distribution channel system views another as an antagonist. As a result such a channel member might act towards the perceived 'enemy' in an unfriendly way and may even try to cause business problems. Such actions may upset the finally tuned distribution system and have damaging consequences for other members of the channel system; as we have said before, many of them are likely to be individually owned firms in their own right and the entrepreneurs that own them can ill afford any kind of commercial conflict. It might also have commercial consequences for the manufacturing firm that is relying on channel solidarity to achieve adequate distribution for their products or services. Conflicts in distribution channels may take different forms. The marketing channel writer Joseph Palamountain has identified three conflict types that are discussed below.

Intertype conflict

'Intertype conflict' refers to aggressive behaviour among different types of 'middleman' at the same level in the channel system. This sort of competition has increased in recent years principally because of the growing practice among intermediaries of 'scrambled' merchandising, a practice which involves intermediaries dealing with products that were previously outside their normal product range. Intertype conflict can be seen as a sort of Darwinian evolution taking place among different sorts of channel intermediary at the same level within the channel system eg 'cash and carry' wholesalers versus conventional wholesalers. It is a kind of 'survival of the fittest scenario' being played out on the channel 'battlefield'. Over time the most profitable, most efficient and most popular type of channel configuration will come forth and tower above the others until further configurations evolve and compete against the entrenched order of things and the whole cycle repeats itself.

Vertical conflict

This type of conflict is intrinsically more detrimental to the manufacturing firm as it can demolish the free flow of goods travelling along the channel 'pipeline' and result in a 'blockage' which can have serious outcomes for the business interests of the manufacturing firm and other channel members in all levels of the system. This type of conflict can be particularly damaging and very difficult to resolve because the channel members are situated within so many different layers within the channel system. Unlike 'horizontal conflict' which takes place among marketing intermediaries in the same level in the channel system, 'vertical conflict' takes place among marketing intermediaries at different levels or layers in the channel system. Communications becomes that much more difficult in such a situation and exacerbates the problem.

Horizontal conflict

A manufacturer who does not deal directly with customers is vicariously handing over the responsibility for business success to third parties (ie marketing intermediaries or independent firms). Each member of the marketing channel system should ideally be part of an integrated system. This is really what channel management is all about, creating a well organised, integrated system with all members working towards a common purpose. This common end should be profit through customer satisfaction. Horizontal conflict takes place between marketing intermediaries who are at the same level in the channel system and of the same type of 'middleman', for example two 'cash and carry' wholesalers working in the same area or two retail stores in the same area stocking a similar range of goods. The fact of the matter is that goals and objectives, far from being shared, are not always the same for every channel member and this can result in channel conflict. The overall channel system should be a set of interlocking and mutually dependent elements and it is in the interests of all the channel members for there to be a high degree of co-operation between each. Horizontal conflict is common and a major 'headache' for the marketing manager co-ordinating channel policy and management.

SUMMARY

The overall subject area of what we might call 'distribution' or 'place' in terms of the marketing mix's four Ps classification, can really be divided into two distinct areas. They are distinct in that they address different aspects of business activity that are nonetheless very closely related. They are both concerned with distribution and in the provision of what might be called 'time and place utility'. The topic of distribution is made up of two separate but connected parts, channels of distribution and logistics management. Business logistics, which forms part of the wider subject of the two, is covered next. In this chapter we have concentrated on channels of distribution, which are an often labyrinthine system of agents, wholesalers and retailers through which marketing firms move products and services to the final buyer. The right selection of channel is of paramount importance to the business performance of all firms. A strategic, competitive advantage can be secured from such choices. When modelling the flow of products or services through a distribution channel system it is often very helpful to use an analogy and think of the distribution system as a pipeline. The pipeline has the main pipes, subsidiary pipes, free flow and blockages. In consumer markets marketing channels can be made up of a complicated network of marketing 'middlemen'.

In certain marketing situations direct marketing is used which removes the 'middleman' from the channel system. In industrial marketing channels direct distribution is much more frequently employed particularly when the products being ordered by the customer are 'buyer specified' rather than 'supplier specified'. Wholesale type firms are used in industrial distribution channels although they are often called 'factors'. In a similar way to consumer markets, industrial marketing firms also make use of agents and distributors. The subject of channels is a key marketing subject and along with business logistics forms a major area of strategic marketing management. The correct choice of channels can add significant real and perceived value to the product or service offered and consequently is a very important area of the marketing mix – in fact the 'P' designating 'place' in McCarthy's categorisation of the four Ps actually refers to channels of distribution and physical distribution, usually referred to these days as marketing or business logistics, combined. It is to the second part of the 'distribution equation' that we turn in the next chapter, logistics.

13

Logistics Management

INTRODUCTION

Marketing logistics is a term that has developed from the military use of the term 'logistics'. From a military point of view logistics was a range of activities that made sure that supplies were in the right place at the right time in the right condition and delivered to the right people. In a marketing context the term has a very similar meaning except we are now using it in a commercial context rather than a military one. From a marketing standpoint the subject of distribution management is divided into two separate, but interrelated parts; these are channels of distribution and physical distribution management (logistics).

Channels of distribution were covered in the last chapter and are, as the name suggests, those channels of marketing 'middlemen' through which the product or service is made accessible to the final customer. A channel system may be made up of a number of independent firms such as agents, distributors, wholesalers, factors and of course retailers. Some manufacturers employ a direct system of distribution cutting out the so-called 'middleman'. Having carefully chosen a structure of intermediaries who will take over the administration of goods as they move along the channels of distribution, the enterprise next has to think about how these goods can be practically transferred from the manufacturer to the consumer.

PHYSICAL DISTRIBUTION

This part of the business falls within the area of management known as physical distribution management (PDM) which is an intrinsic area of marketing management. However, the term physical distribution management is somewhat outdated. Today the subject is often referred to as 'total business logistics' management. This holistic concept is concerned with much more than delivering finished products to customers in an economic and effective way. It is actually a total system which starts with sourcing and finishes with how transport for outward delivery is planned and executed. In fact logistics management is concerned with the totality of sourcing and securing materials from suppliers, storing, processing, retrieving and delivering them in the right condition and at the right time to the final customer.

NATURE OF LOGISTICS MANAGEMENT

Marketing has many definitions, one that relates to the process of getting the right goods to the right place at the right time. This is a simplistic definition, but it does encapsulate the importance of time and place. It has been said earlier that it is the mission of the marketing orientated firm to produce goods and/or services that satisfy the needs and wants of specifically defined target markets more efficiently and effectively than competitors.

Products can be perceived as a 'bundle of attributes', many of which are implied attributes created by branding, packaging and advertising. The core product or service is just a part of the total product offering. In order for the worth of goods and services to be fully realised by the user they need to be available to customers at the right place and at the right time. Some products have virtually no value at all unless they are in a certain place or available for consumption at a certain time.

At first glance the uninitiated might think that business logistics includes so many business areas that it is in fact the whole or at least most of business management. It is true that taken in its widest form 'total business logistics' management does indeed encompass or impact on many business activities and at all levels in the value chain. Logistics management embraces every stage of the physical distribution process:

- ordering and delivery of raw materials and component parts;
- materials handling and storage;
- stock control;
- sales prediction from which the predictions of individual parts, transport and storage requirements are derived;
- order processing;
- buying and replacement of stock;
- packing and delivery;
- achievement of set service levels;
- warehouse location;
- transport management and planning;

also, management and operation of a logistics information system which acts as a recording system, aids forecasting, scheduling and model building and produces the plethora of documentation needed for the effective administration of the logistics system.

In many business to business markets, factors such as stock availability and reliability of delivery are just as important, if not more important, than price. The efficiency with which a supplying organisation can process an order and deliver goods to the right place at the required time with the desired level of reliability over the long term may well be the deciding factor in issuing a contract, even if the supplying firm is less competitive on price. Different industrial sectors have differing service sensitivities or what the economist might refer to as the 'elasticities'. The level of service offered by the supplying firm is often the key marketing variable in obtaining business. You can see from this that logistics management is considerably more than just managing transport and distribution. It can help the company gain a long term strategic advantage and therefore must be recognised for what it really is, a long term strategic marketing tool.

TIME AND PLACE UTILITY

The importance of time and place will also depend on the character of the product or service and the situation in which they are used. For example if you walk into a pub or a café for a drink of beer, you expect the beer to be available more or less immediately. A Christmas present really only has maximum value on Christmas day, it is not quite the same if someone gives a child a delayed Christmas present say a week or so later. For any gift to children to have the desired 'magical' effect it must be there on the right day. If you order flowers by telephone to send to someone on Valentine's Day they are of little use if they are delivered the day after.

On the other hand, if you are ordering a new motor bike from a showroom you may be prepared to place an order and wait several weeks to get exactly the machine you want from the factory in terms of colour, engine size, trim and other specifications. In the case of the Valentine's Day flowers or the glass of beer, the time and the place of consumption form an intrinsic part of what the customer perceives to be the 'total product offering'. For other types of products and services time and place are less significant. Hence, for some product and service categories time and place produce a great deal of worth or utility to the consumer. Business logistics plays a key role in the creation and delivery of this notion of time and place utility and hence the creation of what customers regard as 'value'.

THE INTEGRATED NATURE OF LOGISTICS

In order to be truly effectual all of the functions within the logistics function must be fully integrated, which is what is at the heart of 'total business logistics'. Because the functions making up logistics management are often complex and highly specialised, they need to be managed by professional people. To illustrate this, the use of fork-lift trucks, cranes, gantries and lifts can be very dangerous business. Such equipment forms the tools of materials handling. The incorrect operation of such machinery can result in serious injury and damage or even death. Hence the personnel responsible for this kind of work must be fully qualified and experienced.

There is a plethora of professional bodies catering for people in the logistics business. The Chartered Institute of Purchasing and Supply and The Institute of Transport are two examples. There are other professional bodies in the field of warehousing, materials handling and administration. The growing importance of the business logistics function can be gauged by the fact that there are now undergraduate degree courses in logistics management run by such institutions as Huddersfield and Salford Universities. Cranfield University School of Management is one of the world leaders in the provision of advanced postgraduate courses in logistics and also in the provision of research facilities in the subject. Cranfield also has a Professor of Marketing and Logistics, Professor Martin Christopher, which illustrates very well the interlink between marketing and logistics. The general marketing philosophy taught at Cranfield University is based firmly on relationship marketing, that is the marketing firm forms long term, mutually beneficial relationships with customers, including immediate customers who might very well be agents, distributors, factors or some other type of marketing intermediary. In order to do this successfully every fact impacting on the marketing operation must be included. It is interesting to note that Cranfield, one of the UK's top business schools, not only has the only joint Professor of Marketing and Logistics, but acknowledges the very close relationship between marketing and the logistics function.

In the same way those administering the transport function must have technical knowledge. The proper loading of vehicles, the securing of loads, the correct weight distribution of loads, the management of hazardous and risky material all need expert knowledge. No one would expect a marketing manager or director, no matter how experienced, to be qualified in all of these specialist areas. Although it is becoming increasingly likely that senior marketing staff might have come from a physical distribution background, specialist staff will still be required. It is not intended that marketing should dictate the day to day management policy of the logistics function. This should be left to those people who are qualified to make the right management decisions. However, because logistics has such a salient long term strategic dimension within marketing strategy it is necessary for overall logistics policy to emanate from senior marketing staff. Overall logistics decisions must form part of the overall strategic marketing plan. Logistics management does not operate in a vacuum, but has an important, intrinsic role in the long term marketing strategy of the business enterprise.

EVOLUTION OF THE TOTAL LOGISTICS CONCEPT

Growing finesse of marketing analysis has resulted in more importance being placed on the costs of logistics. Firms must aim to provide customer satisfaction in order to make money and to achieve this, goods must be in the right place at the right time. There is an equilibrium that must be achieved between the costs of logistics and customer satisfaction. Greater levels of service usually mean higher costs and the balance is the task of logistics management.

The basic concept of logistics management is as old as military conflict itself and many of the principles of business logistics have emanated from its use in military strategy. Remaining for a moment with this military analogy, battles and wars have been lost, not because an army could not fight or because of lack of manpower or equipment, in fact many defeated armies have had plenty of both. Often defeat has been caused through lack of ammunition, food and drink or lack of blankets and warm clothing. It is said that armies 'march on their stomachs'; meaning that a well fed army has the strength and perseverance to fight. Without proper diet even the most remarkably trained army will eventually weaken. It is similarly useless having highly trained troops with sophisticated rifles if they are not given adequate ammunition or ammunition of the wrong type. It is often ostensibly tiny things that matter in the success of military operations.

As with war, so with business, which is a form of commercial warfare. Competitive firms are involved in the battle for the customer. A firm's strategic objective may not be the taking of a town from the enemy; its strategic concerns are the market share, turnover or profit margins. However, the principles are similar and the commercial battle for business is more likely to be won in the battlefield of the market-place with the aid of effective logistical back-up than without such support. Commercial firms can also come out on top by using business logistics more effectively than the competition and engineering a strategic advantage over them.

Armies that win battles usually have the ability to organise themselves. They manage to have a wide range of vital supplies in the right place at the right time and get supplies to where they are needed more effectively and efficiently than their enemies. In this sense logistical planning is just as much part of the war effort as any other kind of planning. They can thus seal a strategic, competitive advantage that may possibly decide, or at least influence the outcome of the battle. In the Second World War, the Korean war and Vietnam war, supplies officers were faced with the problem of moving a wide range of materials across much of the world. Marketing management has since seen that these skills could be applied to logistics in a commercial environment. Military planners had used the evolving mathematical and statistical science of operations research, often involving sophisticated techniques to work out logistical strategies. Operational researchers and production planners realised that war production could be made more effectual through scientific organisation which enabled the most efficient use of scarce wartime resources.

Such techniques have now allowed logistics managers to maximise the efficiency of operations in terms of time, materials cost and manpower and distribution can be analysed and organised in a more scientific way. The evolution of relatively cheap computer power and the greater availability of relevant computer software has helped the modern logistics planner immensely. In the war a whole team of 'boffins', usually university professors, would work for weeks to solve a logistical problem that needed large amounts of computation, often working with slide rules rather than computers which were still in their infancy at the time. Today the logistics planner can solve the same problem on an ordinary desktop computer in a matter of minutes.

Logistics has increased in significance as a marketing function because of the more demanding nature of the economic environment. In the past many firms carried large stocks of raw materials and components, but today stocks are generally kept to a minimum, with the role of carrying stock falling on the supplier of the products. This change has been driven partly by higher interest rates, in that carrying stock comes out of working capital which is largely financed through overdraft and also by the emphasis that management places on scientific treatment. This has had an impact right along the marketing channel, with each channel member compelled to provide a high service level to their immediate customers, ie the next individual or firm down stream in the channel system. The logistics function incorporates a wide range of activities and not just transport. Logistics involves the transit of goods from the receipt of an order to delivery to the customer, with close liaison between production planning, purchasing, order processing, material control and warehousing. These areas must work together in order that customers' needs are met and costs kept to a minimum.

Just-in-time management (JIT) has been extensively adopted by firms with large purchasing power who impose rigorous delivery conditions on their suppliers. This kind of system means that the buying firm only carries a very limited amount of raw materials and components which have to be replenished on a regular basis in order to keep up with production demands. Buying firms entering into such an agreement with suppliers insist on a very high level of service from suppliers. JIT (or, more correctly, 'lean manufacturing') has been widely adopted by the car industry where large firms need to operate to strict delivery plans. Such firms can make big economies in costs allied with keeping stocks when just in time management approaches are used.

DEFINITIONS

Modern management theory and practice takes a holistic approach to logistics management and today this managerial function is often referred to as 'total business logistics' with the emphasis on the word 'total'. It is intended to be a complete physical distribution system which employs a total cost approach. That is, each individual element of the total system is subordinate to the efficient running of the system as a whole. For example spare transport capacity might be needed in order to guarantee delivery times in cases of unusual demand. Likewise higher levels of stock may be needed to be carried so that order processing promises can be kept. It is the total cost of the system in delivering its final output of desired customer service that is important rather than the costs of individual components of the system viewed in isolation. The five main elements of total business logistics are:

1. service levels;
2. warehousing;
3. order processing;
4. transportation;
5. stock levels/inventory.

Business logistics management integrates these functions, making sure each element is used to best effect towards a single, well defined goal. This is known as the systems approach to logistics management.

A good grasp of the two main premises are important:

▓ The achievement of an effectual system is the outcome of hard work and dedication to purpose by all concerned. The overall service aim can be achieved, even though it may appear as if some individual elements of the system are not working to maximum efficiency. It is the total final output of the system that is important and the criterion by which the effectiveness of the system as a whole should be evaluated.

■ The best service cannot be provided at the lowest cost, since costs increase with the level of service offered. When this level has been decided, the company must then search for ways of keeping costs to a minimum without putting at risk the agreed service targets.

THE BUSINESS LOGISTICS PROCESS

This is started upon the receipt of an order by a supplier. The customer giving the order has no real interest in how the supplier's logistics system works, nor in any problems the supplier might have in distribution terms. All the customer is bothered about is that the logistics system is effective and results in the goods ordered being delivered in the right place, in the right condition and at the time agreed. The period of time between the placing of the order and delivery of goods is known as the lead time and this varies for different types of products and type of market and industry. Two extreme examples are in the shipbuilding industry, where lead time is measured in parts or multiples of years and the retail sector, where days or hours are more prevalent measures. The just-in-time approach to distribution removes any need for lead times.

The lead time quoted by the supplier is the base used by the customer when preparing for production. Customers nowadays expect the promised delivery time to be met otherwise it puts their whole production process in chaos.

Order processing

This is the first stage of the logistical process and an effective order processing department has a direct influence on lead times. Orders come from the sales team via the sales department, arriving only rarely on an ad hoc basis, most companies preferring to build up regular supply routes with an efficient supplier, which remain stable over a period of time. Contracts are frequently set up and regular repeat orders are made throughout the duration of the contract.

Fast and accurate order processing systems are essential so that other departments in the company are aware of the order and can pass on rapid confirmation to the customer, along with an exact delivery time. A company's image depends upon a high level of office efficiency and slow reaction to orders is an often overlooked route to ill-will and dissatisfaction. Effective order processing can make the difference when buyers are making decisions about their preferred suppliers.

Order processing has been made much more efficient by the use of computerised systems, which allow automatic updating of stock levels and delivery schedules, thus accurately illustrating the sales position. Such accuracy is essential in the order processing department, but this must be combined with speed of processing.

Inventory

This is a critical area of PDM, since customer satisfaction depends on the company not running out of stock and being able to deliver orders. An optimum stock level must be operated, whereby stock-out situations do not happen. However, stock levels should not be too high as this is costly to maintain. Techniques for ascertaining optimum stock levels are examined later.

Stocks mean cost – the 'opportunity cost' which exists through constant competition for the company's resources. If a high stock level has to be maintained, then the profit contribution must be larger than the costs associated with carrying extra stock. Some companies may have to carry high stock levels to meet short lead times in a particular market and these companies must look to reduce costs in other areas of the PDM mix.

Warehousing

Many firms dispatch goods direct to the customer from their own on-site warehouse. However, if a firm sells goods which are taken off regularly, but in small quantities, strategically located ware-houses around the country may be used. Large retail chains use this type of system, in which goods are transported in bulk from manufacturer to retail warehouse, where stocks are stored before being distributed to individual stores belonging to the retail chain. Levels of service and costs will increase with the number of ware-houses used and again, an optimum strategy should be laid down which enables operation at a desired level of service. What must be taken into consideration is location of customers, size of orders, frequency of deliveries and lead times.

Transportation

This is usually the greatest cost in distribution and is calculated according to numbers of units or weight. However, it must not be thought that management of the transportation function is easy, since costs must be carefully controlled and type of transport chosen, which must be kept under review. Many companies have dedicated transport managers, illustrating the importance of the PDM function:

■ Road transport, with its advantages of speed and door-to-door delivery, has become the most popular method of transportation. Its flexibility is essential for many companies operating on low stockholding and short lead times. Some firms purchase their own vehicles and others use sub-contractors; indeed, logistics experts have set up systems to manage the entire PDM requirements of large multiples.

■ Rail transport is often used when lead time is not of such paramount importance, or when attempting to bring down transport costs. Hazardous or very bulky goods are also often transported by rail, but it can also be suitable for light goods which must be delivered quickly and where the country has a good rail infrastructure. In the UK letter and parcel post use an integrated system of rail for transport over longer distances and then road for shorter distances.

■ Air transport is not widely used for distribution within the UK, although overseas long-distance routes can justify the cost. It is used for transporting goods which are highly perishable or valuable in relation to their weight. It also has the advantage of being less of a problem in terms of packaging as less substantial material is needed than for ocean transport, coupled with the fact that insurance premiums are less costly for air than for sea freight. Air freight is quite popular in the USA because of the great distances involved and its use in export markets can be very cost effective.

■ An alternative method of transportation in export markets is the roll-on roll-off (RORO) cargo ferries. These serve the European and near-European markets, but 'deep sea markets' such as Australia, the Pacific Rim and South America are served by traditional ocean-going freighters. This method of transportation has been made more effective with the development of containerisation.

Whatever mode of transportation is selected, goods should be protected during transit and this relates particularly to ocean transport where longer times and more robust handling methods mean that more protection is needed.

When the effects of the four elements of the logistics system are aggregated then the total output of the system can be ascertained. In the eyes of customers this relates to the level of service they receive. Customers are likely to view the products and services that they buy in their entirety; in fact Lancaster takes the position that customers view products and services as a 'total bundle of attributes'. Stock availability, the speed at which purchase orders are processed, the stock control, storage, materials handling procedures employed, location of warehouses and delivery reliability are rarely examined by customers individually, even in industrial markets.

The logistics component of the 'total bundle of product attributes' are seen as a particular level of service. Some customers or market segments are likely to attach varying levels of importance to the level of service they receive. Some will be more service sensitive or 'service elastic' than others. From this point of view, service sensitivity can be used by marketing management as a base for market segmentation.

BUSINESS LOGISTICS – A SYSTEMS APPROACH

It has already been emphasised that various marketing activities need to be combined to form a single marketing effort. Managers are now becoming more conscious of the potential of PDM and that logistical systems should be designed with the 'total' function in mind. A disconnected approach to PDM will result in a firm failing to provide satisfactory service and involve it in excessive costs. It should also be noted that within the PDM structure there will be possible conflict between individual managers aiming to achieve their personal goals to the detriment of the overall PDM objectives. For example, production managers will favour long production runs and standard products, while sales and marketing management will look towards high stock levels, special products and short production runs. At the same time, transport managers may want to lower costs by selecting a slower transportation method or waiting for a full load and financial managers will prefer reduced inventory and dislike extensive warehousing networks. Each department may appear efficient when they realise their individual goals, but marketing strategy might not be effectively served.

Companies aim to provide customers with an acceptable level of service at optimal cost and Burbridge (1987) has suggested how this might be achieved. Essentially senior management must ensure that overall distribution objectives are communicated and understood throughout the management structure, making it clear that company objectives should be considered before departmental objectives. If senior management fails to make objectives clear, this can cause organisational problems when implementing the systems approach. This should encircle production and production planning, purchasing and sales forecasting and involves the concept of total cost, where individual costs are held to be less important that the total cost. For example, the total cost of holding high stocks may look unacceptable, but if it enables the company to provide a service leading to higher sales and profits then the total cost of all the PDM activities will be justified.

PDM has now come to be recognised as a marketing tool in its own right. In a market where products are similar and price variations small, service counts as a major force in competition. It may even be possible to command a higher price for products that are always delivered on time. A salesperson in a company that provides a large spare parts and service facility for needy customers has an advantage in price discussions. It can therefore be seen that far from being merely an adjunct to marketing, distribution has a full place in the marketing mix and indeed is a fundamental part of marketing strategy. A well co-ordinated business logistics system can help to discover marketing opportunities and improve the overall marketing mix.

MONITORING AND CONTROL OF THE LOGISTICS FUNCTION

Getting the right goods to the right place at the right time for least cost is the objective of PDM. The basis of monitoring and control is to provide definite measures of operational effectiveness, giving management objectives which point to criteria which allow useful assessment of performance.

The output of a physical distribution system

The level of customer service is the key output from any system of physical distribution and this is a competitive benefit that can be offered to customers to keep existing business or to attract new business. The level of service offered should be at least comparable to that of major competitors. It is often perceived to be the time it takes to deliver a customer's order, or how many orders can be met from stock. Technical assistance, training and after-sales service is also involved.

The two most fundamental areas are reliability and frequency of delivery and the ability to meet orders quickly from stock. If a company sets a service policy of delivering a certain percentage of orders within a set number of days from the receipt of the order, this is a useful and specific objective which offers strict criteria for evaluation. From this, a simple delivery delay analysis, showing number of orders received, days late and relating this to the percentage of total orders can be prepared, making it clear to management whether such objectives are being reached or whether any adjustment of service level is needed. This analysis can be updated upon receipt of a copy of the dispatch note and will indicate any over- or under-provision of service.

Elasticity of service

The cost of providing service is measured in time and money, especially in industrial markets where service can often take precedence over price when potential customers are deciding on a supplier. Companies operating JIT manufacturing are particularly conscious of this fact. Marketing firms wishing to raise their service levels can face diminishing returns. For a company to offer 100 per cent service provision, every eventuality would have to be covered, which is costly. Maximum customer satisfaction and minimum distribution costs are not compatible and there has to be some compromise in other areas. This depends on the degree of service sensitivity or service elasticity in the particular market.

Two industries which use the same product from the same supplier may have differing criteria for choosing that supplier. As an example, both the oil exploration and the sugar processing industries use large high pressure on-line valves in their process. The oil industry is highly service sensitive because of the very high cost of operations and potential breakdowns. Therefore, price is not as important as service, whereas the sugar processing industry is more price sensitive. Much of the processing is done within two months and as long as service levels are adequate to avoid disruption during this period, they can be given a lower priority for the rest of the year. Service levels should be increased to the point where marginal marketing expense equals marginal marketing response.

Inventory management (stockholding)

Inventory gives cover against what may happen tomorrow and is kept to increase profitability with the support of manufacturing and marketing. Manufacturing support comes through two types of inventory; that of the materials for production and that of spare and repair parts for maintaining production equipment. Marketing support is provided through an inventory of the finished products and of spare and repair parts which support the products. Stocks are accumulated because supply and demand cannot be perfectly co-ordinated and because of the uncertainty of future demand and reliability of service. They ensure that raw materials, spare parts and finished goods are available when needed.

Inventories are kept because they act as a 'hedge' against such events as unexpected demand or machinery failure. They can assist production, transportation and purchasing economies. They also act as a 'hedge' against inflation, price or exchange rate fluctuations. In addition, inventories can enhance customer service levels by providing greater stock availability.

Different types of cost need to be balanced when planning inventories, weighing the cost of holding stock and procurement against the cost of running out of stock which could result in stopping production and loss of business and goodwill. Larger inventories reduce the possibility of this happening, but it means that more money is tied up in working capital. However, if quantity discounts are offered for large orders, then fewer orders being placed will reduce purchasing administrative costs.

The concept of economic order quantity (EOQ) assumes that total inventory costs are minimised at some definable purchase quantity. This method assumes that inventory costs are a function of the number of orders processed per unit of time and the costs of maintaining an inventory over and above the cost of items included in the inventory (eg warehousing). It takes no account of transportation costs (which may greatly increase for smaller shipments) or the effects of quantity discounts. These factors limit the usefulness of the EOQ concept in inventory management, but increasing use of business computing has allowed the operation of more sophisticated versions. Such models are beyond the limits of this discussion, but in order to give a general understanding of the principles there follows an example of the traditional EOQ method.

EOQ can be calculated using the following formula:

$$EOQ = \frac{2AS}{I}$$

where: A = annual usage (units)
S = ordering costs ($)
I = inventory carrying cost as a percentage of inventory value

eg for: Annual usage = 2,000 units
Ordering costs = $10
Inventory carrying cost = 15% (= 0.15)
Unit cost = $1.50

$$EOQ = \frac{2 \times 2,000 \times \$1.50 \times £10}{0.15}$$

$$= \frac{60,000}{0.15}$$

$$= 9,000$$

$$= \$94.87$$

The EOQ concept and its variations basically seek to define the most economical lot size, when considering the placement of an order. The order point method can be used to determine the ideal timing for placing an order. The relatively simple calculation uses the following equation:

$$OP = DL + SS$$

where: OP is the order point
D is the demand
L is the lead time
SS is the safety stock

eg for: Demand = 200 units per week
Lead time = 4 weeks
Safety stock = 400 units

$$OP = (200 \times 4) + 400$$
$$= 800 + 400$$
$$= 1,200 \text{ units}$$

A new order should be placed when inventory levels decrease to 1,200 units. The size of the order placed when stock reaches this level can be computed using the EOQ formula. This order point method assumes fixed lead times that can be evaluated accurately, which is not often the case. Despite certain limitations, EOQ and order point methods are basically valid and form the basis of the more meaningful computer-based inventory models.

SUMMARY

An understanding of business logistics is important to all those parties involved in whatever way in the 'value chain'. As well as a grasp of the logistics tasks facing the supplier, the purchasing department must also appreciate logistical techniques for stock control and the order cycle. Business logistics is therefore closely associated with purchasing, as well as with operations management. A logistical system should not be inflexible, but should have established routines for certain functions which will facilitate the distribution process.

Business logistics is related to all the marketing sub-functions and in this way a co-ordinated marketing effort is offered to the customer. The marketing manager should not necessarily have day to day hands on control of every element in the logistics system. Such expertise would most likely be beyond the scope of most marketing managers. The logistics function has many highly technical and specialised areas which require the use of specialist staff.

As we discussed earlier in this chapter logistics component areas such as purchasing and supply or transport management are professions in their own right. Likewise, materials handling, warehouse management and transport and distribution all have their own professional examinations and organisations. The logistics function plays a crucial role in delivering utility and satisfaction to customers. It is a long term strategic tool which can be used to gain a competitive advantage. It delivers a level of service and time and place utility to customers. Because of this, it must ultimately come under the influence of senior marketing staff. Specialist staff are needed to carry out the technical tasks that make up the logistics function, but strategy and policy formulation for logistics management must be part of the strategic marketing plan if logistics is to play its full part in achieving marketing orientation within the firm.

14

Macro Issues in Marketing

INTRODUCTION

Like most things in life the world of marketing is dynamic. Even over the last decade there have been many innovations within the subject. If you look at a standard marketing textbook from the 1970s and one from today and compare them, you will see many topics in today's version that were not even mentioned then. The fact is that marketing both as an academic and a practical functional management discipline is constantly evolving and redefining itself. The subject has expanded over more recent years to embrace many aspects of the economy, including areas not necessarily from the commercial side of our existence. For example over the last 20 years the environmental movement throughout the world has expanded dramatically. Most right thinking people today realise that if the human race does not take care of the world's environment there simply will not be a world worth living in for future generations.

Most people would agree that the capitalist system has produced material wealth for the vast majority of people that even 100 years ago would have been unimaginable. But capitalism has a price in terms of the use of scarce resources, environmental pollution and ethical standards of products, services and business methods. People still want economic growth and the material benefits that go with it but not at any price. They want a morally and ethically responsible capitalist system, which some critics say is a contradiction in terms.

The demand from consumers for firms to act more responsibly and ethically in their business practices and operations has been reflected in many of the products, services and corporate 'mission statements' of modern business. From a marketing point of view this relatively new way of thinking falls under the heading 'green marketing'. Related to this concept is the area of what might be called 'social marketing'. The process of marketing is no longer confined to the profit making enterprise. The same principles of marketing can be used for social causes such as drink driving campaigns, health programmes and so on. Socially oriented marketing is one of the fastest growing areas at the moment and is likely to become increasingly important in the future.

Finally, the world has seen an extraordinary expansion in international trade over the last 20 years and in particular over the last decade. Economists talk about the 'global market-place' and the 'globalisation' of markets including capital markets. This has had a profound effect on many firms and their marketing planning and strategy has had to reflect this 'new world order' of global markets. These concepts will be examined in more detail later in this final chapter.

RELATIONSHIP MARKETING

In 1954 Peter Drucker said: 'There is only one valid definition of business: to create customers. It is the customer who determines what the business is.' Therefore, customers are central to business and the underlying theme behind relationship marketing is in ensuring that such customers remain permanently loyal.

TQM as the starting point

In the 1970s W Edwards Deming, the renowned quality 'guru', drew up what is a now classic theory of quality based upon his intimate knowledge of Japanese manufacturing. This concerned 14 key quality points and changed many aspects of production management. His philosophy has been termed 'total quality management' (TQM) and this philosophy now permeates thinking throughout entire organisations.

Relationship marketing explained

Since the 1980s many organisations have acknowledged that the mechanism for business success is to mature from an emphasis on cost and price as key marketing elements to one of providing supreme service through personal interaction and the formation of relationships. There has thus been a change from a transactional focus in marketing towards a relationship approach and this is illustrated in Figure 14.1.

Figure 14.1 *The notion of reverse marketing*

The traditional role of the salesperson was seen as one of initiating commercial transactions by visiting buyers with the objective of securing orders or being considered for the next tendering round. However, with the advent of what is now termed lean manufacturing (formerly just-in-time manufacturing or JIT) where deliveries are very tightly scheduled and quality must presuppose 'zero defects', there has been a shift in this commercial emphasis. It is now common for buyers to actively source their suppliers with a view to establishing long term 'co-makership' partnerships. This is the notion of reverse marketing.

The implication for sellers is that they must build on these partnerships in the knowledge that sales will continue so long as they supply goods of the right quality, at the right time and at an agreed price. The term used for the techniques involved in this process is 'relationship marketing'. This has also led to the development of 'customer care', which involves a raft of techniques to ensure that customers are permanently satisfied in terms of meeting and exceeding their expectations. TQM driven by the market-place and total manufacturing quality (zero defects) are the realities of these partnership agreements. The tactics of relationship marketing mean that companies should sense changes in the market-place where the quality chain is based.

In a smoothly operating lean manufacturing system, demands from the customer are met and operating costs reduced through a reduction in stocks of raw materials and component parts. Holding stock is an unproductive resource that has to be financed, so lean manufacturing, through its practice of reducing stocks to an absolute minimum, is an efficient means of making cost savings. Close associations must be formed between customers and their suppliers and this normally means a reduction in the number of suppliers and long term relationships. The role of the transactional salesperson has changed to one of the relationship salesperson who spends more time acting in a trouble shooting capacity, keeping the flow of supplies secure and ensuring consistent quality and acting more in a liaison capacity.

The notion of relationship marketing means that marketing endeavours should be based on many customer contacts over time, rather than concentrating on singular transactions. It also involves the idea of 'team selling', where non marketing people, such as accountants and production personnel, all form part of this relationship team and they actively meet and associate with these major customers to nurture the relationship and ensure that the partnership (termed 'partnership sourcing') works.

THE PRACTICAL EFFECTS OF RELATIONSHIP MARKETING

There is now a tendency for many companies to bring marketing and new product development together at an earlier stage in the development process. Project teams are set up and include people from a number of departments, led by a project or product 'champion' to see through the entire development process of new products. This process begins when the idea is first being tested out through techniques such as brainstorming right through to the research and design stage and on to when the product is finally launched. This process means that there is a continuity of involvement by the project champion. An adaptation of this idea is termed 'best practice benchmarking' (BPB), where multifunctional personnel co-operate similarly to the process described above. The team's duty is to acquire data on products and companies in their industry that have higher performance and activity levels than their own company and use this to suggest ways in which improvements can be made. Because of the multi-functional nature of the team, it is acknowledged that the benefits that accrue from BPB exercises drive team members to establish better standards of performance.

SUPPLY CHAIN INTEGRATION (SCI)

In 1994 a study was undertaken in the UK by A T Kearney, consultants to investigate the supply chain from end of line manufacturers back to sources of raw materials. Its conclusions were that business improvements would be possible not just by simply viewing dealings between purchasers and sellers as isolated transactions each time, but by seeking to involve every-body down the supply chain and hence came the term: supply chain integration (SCI).

It was stated that different supply chain relationships should be possible, with some members merely being content to act as manu-facturers and fabricators and supplying to a specification (ie seeing their task as being good producers at the right quality and at the right time), but others might like to become more involved in end use applications and proffer suggestions for improvement, even though they may be towards the beginning of the supply chain. By considering the entire supply chain new opportunities would present themselves and would benefit everybody. This would improve overall effectiveness in the chain with regard to the elimi-nation of waste and suggesting better ways of doing things, thus reducing overall costs.

The result would be that by concentrating the complete supply chain in this direction it would be possible to drive service stan-dards for the customers up to superior levels through mutual co-operation, rather than weakening the attempts of individual elements of the chain through conflicting objectives. The outcome would be that it would be essential to develop closer relationships between suppliers and customers. The task would not be easy because of the problems of integration and the need to investigate the measures of sophistication that individual members of the supply chain wanted or expected.

A NEW PARADIGM

Following the discussions relating to relationship marketing and SCI it is appropriate to consider the view put forward by Christian Gronroos in 1990, who argued that traditional views of marketing are unsatisfactory in a modern business environment. He emphasised the shortcomings of McCarthy's four Ps and went on to say that more 'Ps' such as 'people' and 'planning' should be added as new marketing viewpoints. The basic concept of supplying customer needs and wants in target markets, he states, has always had relevance, but he contends that this still views the firm as supplying the solutions and not receiving its ideas from the market-place. He attempted to redefine marketing in a way that applies the principles of relationship marketing:

> Marketing is to establish, maintain and enhance long term customer relationships at a profit so that the objectives of the parties involved are met. This is done by a mutual exchange of promises.

INTERNAL MARKETING

We have discussed the concept of internal marketing elsewhere in this text, particularly in Chapter 9, when we examined the contribution of public relations to achieving good internal marketing. The subject of internal marketing is not strictly a 'macro issue' in marketing per se, but it does have an impact on the external policies and performance of the marketing firm.

Good internal marketing can be viewed as a prerequisite for good, effective external marketing policies. It would be difficult to have one without the other. In a very real sense the internal marketing is actually an intrinsic part of the relationship marketing process. However, the mass adoption of the internal marketing ethos by firms could be regarded as a 'macro' issue. The principles of internal marketing are being widely adopted by all kinds of firms as they strive to create a truly customer orientated culture within their organisations. More than ever before, good marketing is seen as much as an internal process as an external one.

Internal marketing and its widespread adoption by firms

Internal marketing takes place at the interface between marketing and human resource management and involves both of these management disciplines. The application of internal public relations has a salient role to play in the overall process of achieving an internal marketing 'culture' because it too, embraces both of these areas of management. Management are discovering that it is all very well to talk about their firm becoming more 'customer focused' or 'marketing oriented' but they need to know how to make it a reality. Whether the firm wishes to employ relationship marketing policies, engage in social marketing activities or practice 'green marketing' policies, those working for the organisation will still need the right spirit, ethos and internal culture.

More and more firms are embracing the notion of internal marketing and this widespread adoption of internal marketing is itself a form of 'macro' issue in marketing. The trend in marketing firms throughout the world is to pay much more attention to getting the 'spirit' or the 'culture' right before attempting to improve the external marketing performance of the organisation. 'Internal marketing' has now become an important and intrinsic part of conventional marketing 'wisdom' and refers to the process of applying the general principles of marketing inside the firm.

Marketing as a business philosophy is concerned with producing the appropriate internal company culture or 'internal spirit' that will result in the firm becoming truly marketing orientated and customer focused. The process of internal marketing involves much more than simply the application of internal public relations, although they are of paramount importance here.

SOCIAL MARKETING

Marketing was developed in the United States as a form of applied capitalist economics. In the conventional US universities students were taught that the US way was based on free market economics and the principle of competition. The system was viewed as a kind of economic 'Darwinism', whereby only those firms that were fit for the job of providing material wealth and a good standard of living to the US people would survive. Those firms that were inefficient and produced goods and services that were not demanded by the market-place in sufficient quantity or at a sufficient price to make an adequate profit would fail. This was the system, this was the US way, the way that had delivered the highest standard of living to any mass population in the world.

When material goods were in relatively short supply, as they were in the US and throughout Europe in the last century and there was much less competition, firms could get away with not listening closely to their customers. After all, it was a sellers market and the customer could take it or leave it. Today things are very different, the global economy has produced global competition. Firms in the US, for example, are no longer protected by political and economic policies of protectionism and isolationism an they have to compete for their right to exist in the global market-place.

Marketing focuses the minds of management on to the real needs and wants of their existing and potential customers. It is the pragmatic application of theoretical western capitalist economics and is the mechanism that makes free market economics and modern capitalism work. Marketing takes theoretical models of free market based economics out of the learned journal articles and university textbooks and, in a highly pragmatic and applied manner, makes the principles work in the white heat of competi-tion in the market-place. But can such a philosophy and process as marketing be applied to other areas of our lives and not just to profit making enterprises?

The wider application of marketing principles

As the concept of marketing proved successful in helping firms to stay in business and produce goods and services that people really wanted and were prepared to pay for, some people working in the field began to think of other applications for this very powerful business philosophy. If marketing could produce goods and services that encapsulated real value in the commercial market-place, why could not the same basic principles be put to use to provide consumer value in the social arena of our lives? Libraries, museums, public sector education and health care, local govern-ment and a host of other areas could all be transformed by the application of business oriented marketing principles.

In January 1969 two US professors, Kotler and Levy, wrote a seminal article in the prestigious *Journal of Marketing* (pp 10–15) in which they examined the social roles and dimension of marketing. Marketing had been viewed by most in the profession as some-thing only really applicable to profit making business firms. Kotler and Levy challenged this notion fundamentally. An extract from their article gives you the general direction of their thoughts which were regarded as rather revolutionary all of those years ago, although today they do not seem anything out of the ordinary:

> The term 'marketing' connotes to most people a function peculiar to business firms. Marketing is seen as the task of finding and stimulating buyers for the firm's output. It is the authors' contention that marketing is a pervasive societal activity that goes considerably beyond the selling of toothpaste, soap and steel. Political contests remind us that candidates are marketed as well as soap; student recruitment reminds us that higher education is marketed; and fund raising reminds us that 'causes' are marketed. The authors see a great opportunity for marketing people to expand their thinking and to apply their skills to an increasingly interesting range of *social* activity. The challenge depends on the attention given to marketing; marketing will either take on a broader *social* meaning or remain a narrowly defined business activity.

As predicted by Kotler and Levy, marketing has indeed taken on a much more expanded role, both within commercial firms in the form of internal marketing, relationship marketing and so forth, and in society as a whole. We are all familiar with the use of political marketing with the use of so called 'spin doctors', and targeting strategies to make sure party members stay 'on message'. But today marketing principles are being applied everywhere: to the Church of England, the Royal Family, the institution of marriage, charities, welfare groups and a whole host of other organisations which have a social impact on our everyday lives.

Marketing has indeed matured and moved out of the purely commercial environment where it originated and developed. It has evolved to become a very powerful force for social good but also, in some cases, for potential social evil. Marketing has come of age and its social dimension has only recently been discovered by many institutions and organisations within our modern society. It is envisaged by the authors of this book that the importance of marketing as a purposeful planning and strategic tool within a social context will continue to develop and expand dramatically as we move into the next century.

There is likely to become a time when marketing will become so widespread in its application that it will no longer be viewed as a fundamentally commercial tool. All purposeful organisations have objectives that they must achieve in order to justify staying in existence, to justify taxpayers' money, the charitable contribution of the public, the support and confidence of the local community and so on. The process that these organisations and institutions use to help them accomplish their aims may eventually be called by another name, but in essence the process will be a variant of commercial marketing, ie social marketing.

The fundamental right of consumers

Another important aspect of the social marketing area is the fact that the general public, politicians and other parties are demanding socially responsible behaviour from firms in the conduct of their business. As you will see in the next section, some organisations have responded to the demands from the public for socially responsible marketing by adopting 'green' marketing policies and marketing 'green' products. Hence the distinction between social marketing and green marketing is blurred, as there is so much overlap.

The consumer movement is well established and very powerful in the United States and growing in importance in Europe and other parts of the world. Consumer groups have lobbied the government in the USA and have devised a form of consumer charter in conjunction with politicians. It sets out the rights of consumers and what is expected of commercial enterprises in terms of their policies and operations in the largely free market and capitalist economy of America. A number of these basic, fundamental consumer rights emanated from the government of President John F Kennedy in 1963. These were as follows:

■ the consumer's right to be informed;
■ the right to safety;
■ the right to choose;
■ the right to be heard.

Since President Kennedy's time additional items have been added to this list, and these are:

■ the right to privacy (enshrined in the Data Protection Act in this country and similar legislation elsewhere including the USA);
■ the right to a clean and healthy environment.

Marketing firms need to take the above principles into account in all aspects of their business and consumers have a right to know about the product or service they are purchasing. This manifests itself in greater consumer education in advertising, in printed literature and even in the wording on product labels. Products that are sold should be safe for people to use and this point is particularly important when the goods in question are to be used by children. Consumers have a right to choice and therefore restrictive practices that limit competition and therefore choice are seen to be against the public interest.

Consumers have a right to be heard and they need their complaints to be listened to and acted upon by firms. Many firms now have a customer service department and attach high priority to dealing efficiently with customers' worries and complaints. Consumer programmes on television and radio as well as consumer magazines give consumers additional opportunities to voice their opinions about products and services and the actions of firms. People have the right to privacy and to know that the information given to firms in confidence is not used for other purposes or sold on to other organisations for mailing lists or other commercial reasons. And finally, they have a right to live in a clean and healthy environment.

People will no longer tolerate the destruction and desecration of the environment and will actively boycott the products of firms that do. They are demanding a higher standard of social responsibility and moral and ethical standards from firms if they are to secure the consumers' long term support. Marketing is about meeting the genuine needs and desires of consumers and in the context of this chapter this means delivering value to the consumer in a socially and ethically responsible manner.

GREEN MARKETING

The term 'green' marketing is in some ways similar to the concept of social marketing discussed above, in that they both have a 'social' dimension. We hear the term 'green' being applied in a number of situations these days. There are 'green' political parties both in the UK and Germany and elsewhere in the world. Recycling of waste materials is another manifestation of what has come to be referred to as 'green consciousness'. Firms have become more 'green' in their business methods, particularly production and other operational methods. They have also become more 'green' in terms of the packaging used on their products and in terms of the products and services themselves.

A firm that perhaps epitomises the 'green' marketing firm is The Body Shop which offers a range of environmentally friendly, not tested on animals, ethically, non-exploitatively produced cosmetic and related products. A marketing firm that is a good example of a 'green' firm in the service sector is the Co-operative Bank, which prides itself on only investing and lending to ethically run enterprises. For example it will not lend to any firm that exploits cheap labour overseas or pollutes the environment or tests products on animals.

Green marketing as a pro-active policy

If you look at the labelling of many everyday packaged grocery products the next time you are in the supermarket you will see some form of 'green' message on most of them. Many firms are now adopting a 'pro active' rather than reactive 'green' marketing strategy in an attempt to gain a competitive business environment. Marketing is all about the enterprise meeting the needs and delivering the wants of specifically defined target markets more effectively and efficiently than the competition. If the market wants, and is prepared to pay for, 'green' products and services, then marketing orientated firms are duty bound to find ways of offering such goods and services to their customers. They simply would not be doing their job if they did not and if they do not satisfy customers it will only be a matter of time before those customers find another marketing firm that does.

'Green' issues are no longer simply side issues and only practised by a few firms such as The Body Shop. Today green issues often have a key position in the long term corporate policy of many firms. Firms are seeking advice from a whole raft of 'environmental consultants' who claim to offer professional advice on all areas of environmental and green issues. In fact offering advice on green issues is today one of the growth areas of the business consultancy world. Most marketing courses taught at colleges and universities today usually have a 'green marketing' component to them. At the post graduate level at the major business schools 'green issues' are so important that they are given full module status and are woven into all aspects of marketing and business teaching.

INTERNATIONAL ASPECTS

The global economy

The main international 'macro' issue currently affecting marketing firms and that is likely to have increasing effect in the future, is what is known as the 'globalisation' of markets. Obviously this affects some marketing firms more than others. In general smaller firms operating within the service sector will be less affected, as it is difficult for more competitive countries, such as those with very low labour costs, to export services to the UK on a small scale. Larger providers of services, especially in areas such as financial services, are feeling the full competitive force of the global marketplace.

As the world economy becomes more and more interconnected, events thousands of miles away can affect businesses in this country, even the smaller enterprise. For example, the economic problems being faced by many of the far eastern countries such as Malaysia, Singapore and the Special Administrative Region of Hong Kong have meant that the supply of students entering the plethora of private colleges in London, Oxford and elsewhere in the UK has greatly diminished.

Trading blocks

The best example of an economic trading block and the one that is closest to 'home' so to speak, is the European Union (EU). The earlier title of the EU was the European Economic Community (EEC) with the emphasis on the word 'economic' as it was basically a single, unfettered free trade area. The name has now been changed to European Union because the economic dimension of the union of free states has become less important. The important issue driving the evolution of the union is full economic and political integration ie a United States of Europe in all but name.

Trading blocks are quite common in many parts of the world:

■ Canada, Mexico and the United States are all part of the North American Free Trade Area, which is similar to the European Union but without the ambition of political union and hence the need for a single currency.
■ The Association of Southeast Asian Nations (ASEAN) formed the ASEAN Free Trade Area (AFTA) in 1991, consisting of Brunei, Indonesia, Malaysia, Philippines, Singapore, Thailand

and since 1995, Vietnam. Completion of this free trade area will be completed in 2003.

■ Australia has put a proposal forward for the creation of an annual Asia Pacific Economic Co-operation (APEC) conference and has suggested that the original ASEAN members be joined by Australia, New Zealand, Japan, China, Hong Kong, Taiwan, South Korea, Canada and the United States. At present, APEC has 18 members with a combined GNP of over $16 trillion. The key objectives of APEC are to liberalise trade in the area by 2020. Marketing firms throughout the world are monitoring APEC related developments closely.

The major regional trade associations are as follows:

AFTA – ASEAN Free Trade Area
Brunei, Indonesia, Malaysia, Philippines, Singapore, Thailand, Vietnam

APEC – Asia Pacific Economic Co-operation
Australia, Brunei, Canada, Chile, China, Hong Kong, Indonesia, Japan, Malaysia, Mexico, New Zealand, Papua New guinea, Philippines, Singapore, South Korea, Taiwan, Thailand, United States

CACM – Central American Common Market
Costa Rica, El Salvador, Guatemala, Honduras, Nicaragua

CARICOM – Caribbean Community
Anguilla, Antigua, Bahamas, Barbados, Belize, Dominica, Grenada, Guyana, Jamaica, Montserrat, St. Kitts-Nevis, St. Lucia, St. Vincent and the Grenadines, Trinidad-Tobago

ECOWAS – Economic Community of West African States
Benin, Burkina Faso, Cape Verde, Gambia, Ghana, Guinea-Bissau, Ivory Coast, Liberia, Mali, Mauritania, Niger, Nigeria, Senegal, Sierra Leone, Togo

EFTA – European Free Trade Association
Iceland, Liechtenstein, Norway, Switzerland

EU – European Union
Austria, Belgium, Denmark, Finland, France, Germany, Greece, Ireland, Italy, Luxembourg, Netherlands, Portugal, Spain, Sweden, United Kingdom

GCC – Gulf Co-operation Council
Bahrain, Kuwait, Oman, Qatar, Saudi Arabia, United Arab Emirates

LAIA - Latin America Integration Associate
Argentina, Bolivia, Brazil, Chile, Colombia, Ecuador, Mexico, Paraguay, Peru, Uruguay, Venezuela

MERCOSUR – Southern Common Market
Argentina, Brazil, Paraguay, Uruguay

NAFTA – North American Free Trade Agreement
Canada, Mexico, United States

The creation of major trading blocks is an important factor that marketing firms will have to build into their future marketing policies and strategies and will have a serious impact on every facet of their international and domestic operations.

SUMMARY

This final chapter has covered a number of macro issues in marketing. As we said earlier in this chapter, like most things in this life the world of marketing is dynamic and constantly changing. Even over the last decade there have been many developments and innovations within the topic. If you examine marketing textbooks from 20 or 30 years ago and compare them with a modern one, you will see many topics in today's version that were not even mentioned then.

Marketing as an academic discipline and as a practical, functional management discipline is continually developing. The subject has enlarged, especially over more recent years, to comprise many aspects of the economy and even our day to day lives, areas not necessarily from the purely commercial side of our lives. For example over the last 20 years the environmental movement throughout the world has grown exponentially. The environmental movement has huge political and economic power and is a force to be listened to. Most right thinking people today realise that if the human race does not take care of the world now there will not be a world worth living in for future generations.

Most people would agree that free market economics and the capitalist system has produced material wealth for the vast majority of people, in a superior fashion to competing political and economic ideologies such as communism. But capitalism has a price in terms of the use of scarce resources, environmental pollution and ethical standards of products, services and the business practices employed by firms in their pursuit of profit. People still want economic growth and the material benefits that go with it but not at any price.

People are questioning the value system that pollutes the environment or allows cosmetics to be tested on animals or uses non replaceable or non sustainable sources of scarce raw materials such as hard woods from the tropical rainforests. Today people want morally and ethically responsible capitalism which some of the capitalist system's critics say is a contradiction in terms.

The demand from consumers for firms to be more responsible and ethical in their business methods has impacted on firms in many ways, not least many of the products, services and corporate 'mission statements' of modern business which today often have a social or 'green' component in them. From a marketing point of view this relatively new way of thinking falls under the heading of 'green marketing' and 'social' or societal marketing.

Finally, the world has seen an expansion in international trade over the last 20 years and in particular over the last 10 years. Economists talk about the 'global market-place' and the 'globalisation' of markets including capital markets. This has had a big effect on many firms and their marketing planning and strategy has had to reflect this new world order of global markets. The pace of global economic integration is continuing and is accelerating. Such a situation has never occurred before and even the economic experts are unsure of what the long term effects and impact of globalisation will be. Marketing firms are having to operate in an increasingly complex international business environment and this offers a big challenge to individual firms and to the future development of the subject of marketing itself.

References

Abell, D F (1980) *Defining The Business: The starting point of strategic planning*, Prentice-Hall, New Jersey

Ansoff, I (1957) Strategies for diversification, *Harvard Business Review*, Sept/Oct

Barksdale, H C and Harris, C E Jr (1982) Portfolio analysis and the product life cycle, *Journal of Long Range Planning*, **15**, (6)

Booz, Allen & Hamilton Consultants (1982) *New Products Management for the 1980s*, Booz, Allen & Hamilton, New York

'Boston box' or the BCG matrix (1992), developed by the Boston Consulting Group and reported in *Harvard Business Review*, March/April

Burbridge (1987) The implementation of a distribution plan, *International Journal of Physical Distribution & Logistics Management*, **17**, (1)

Colley, P H (1961 & 1983) 'DAGMAR' model, Association of National Advertisers, New York

Consolidated Analysis Centres Incorporated (CACI) (1993) 'ACORN' segmentation system developed by Richard Webber

Corkindale, D and Kennedy, S H (1978) *Process of Advertising*, MCB Publications, Bradford

Davidson, H (1997) *Even More Offensive Marketing*, Penguin Books, Middlesex

Drucker, P (1964) *Managing for Results*, Heinemann, London

Edwards Deming, W (1986) *Out of the Crisis*, Cambridge University Press, Cambridge

Gronroos, C (1990) Marketing redefined, *Management Decision*, **28**

Gummesson, E (1991) Marketing orientation revisited: the crucial role of the part-time marketer, *European Journal of Marketing*, **25**

Holt, C (1957) *Forecasting Seasonals by Exponentially Weighted Moving Averages*, Office of Naval Research memo (USA), **52**

Holt, C (1957) *Forecasting Seasonals and Trends by Exponentially Weighted Moving Averages*, Carnegie Institute of Technology, Pittsburgh, PA

Jerome McCarthy, E (1963) 'Organization for new product development' in *Product Management and Strategy*, Libery, T and Stuchman, A (eds), Holt, Rhinehart & Winston, New York

Kearney, A T (1994) *Partnership of Power Play*, A T Kearney Consultants, London

Kotler, P (1997) *Marketing Management: Analysis, planning, implementation and control*, Prentice-Hall, New Jersey

Lancaster, G and Massingham, L (1996) *Strategic Marketing, Planning and Evaluation*, Kogan Page, London

Lavidge, R T and Steiner, G A (1962) A model for predictive measurement of advertising effectiveness, *Journal of Marketing*, October

Ledbetter, W N and Cox, J F (1977) Operations research in production management, *Production & Inventory Management*, (18)

Little, A D *Concepts of Market/Industry Evolution*, Arthur D Little Consultants, USA

McGregor, D (1960) *The Human Side of Enterprise*, McGraw-Hill, New York/London

McMurry, R (1961) The mystique of supersalesmanship, *Harvard Business Review*, March/April

Majaro, S (1970) Advertising by objectives, *Management Today*, January

Maslow, A (1954) *Motivation and Personality*, Harper & Row, New York

Nevin, E C (1963) *Textbook of Economic Analysis*, 3rd edn, Macmillan, London

Nevin, E C (1983) 'Towards a hierarchy of needs for People's Republic of China' in *The Journal of Applied Behavioural Science*, pp 249–64

Ogilvy, D (1983) *Ogilvy on Advertising*, Pan, London

Palamountain, J C (1968) *The Politics of Distribution*, Greenwood Press, New York

Porter, M (1980 & 1985) *Competitive Advantage*, Free Press, New York

Reeves, R (1960) *Reality in Advertising*, Alfred Knopf, New York

Rogers, E (1983) *Diffusion of Innovations*, Free Press, New York

Shapiro, B P and Bonoma, T V (1984) How to segment industrial markets, *Harvard Business Review*, May/June

Shell Chemicals UK (1975) The Directional Policy Matrix: A new aid to corporate planning, *Journal of Long Range Planning*, June, pp 8–15

Starch, D (1925) *Principles of Advertising*, McGraw-Hill, New York

Wells, W D & Gubar, G (1988) in *Consumer Market Research Handbook*, Worcester, R and Downham, J (eds), McGraw-Hill, Maidenhead

Index

VISIT KOGAN PAGE
ON-LINE

http://www.kogan-page.co.uk

For comprehensive information on Kogan Page titles, visit our website.

Features include

- **complete catalogue listings, including book reviews and descriptions**

- **special monthly promotions**

- **information on NEW titles and BESTSELLING titles**

- **a secure shopping basket facility for on-line ordering**

PLUS everything you need to know about KOGAN PAGE